WILLIAM LAW
AND EIGHTEENTH CENTURY QUAKERISM

A LONDON QUAKER—FROM A PRINT OF 1711

WILLIAM LAW
AND EIGHTEENTH CENTURY QUAKERISM

INCLUDING

SOME UNPUBLISHED LETTERS AND FRAGMENTS

OF

WILLIAM LAW AND JOHN BYROM

BY

STEPHEN HOBHOUSE, M.A.

"Faith is not a fortress, but a camp on the march;
a camp, too, not of armed men, but of explorers."

HENRY NEWBOLT

BENJAMIN BLOM, INC.
Publishers New York 1972

First published London, 1927
Reissued 1971 by
Benjamin Blom, Inc.
New York, N.Y. 10025

Library of Congress
Catalog Card Number 77-175870

Printed in the
United States of America

CONTENTS

NOTES ON THE ILLUSTRATIONS

William Law carried his practice of humility so far as to refuse
ever to sit for his portrait; and we have accordingly to content
ourselves with specimens of his handwriting and with the remains
of his library. The page shown here is the first of a number
of sheets of double foolscap covered with Law's admirable
writing. Almost the only peculiarity which differentiates it
from a modern hand is the frequent (though not consistent) use
of abbreviations for *the, that, then, their,* etc. (Several examples
of the first two occur on the page reproduced here.) These
symbols are an interesting epistolary survival of one of the old
English forms of the letter *th* (called *thorn*), which was confused
with the letter *y*. But y^e, y^t, y^n were of course pronounced
as *the, that, then.*

The original from which this illustration is taken is a fine portrait in oils now in the possession of Mr. Esplin Stewart of
Nightingales, Chalfont St. Giles, Bucks. Both artist and date
are unknown, but it appears to represent the Scotch Quakeress at
an age of between forty and fifty, *i.e.* in about the year 1755.
Her costume is probably a survival of what was customary for
Quakeresses some twenty years earlier. (See page 162 below,
especially the second footnote.)

Pierce Tempest (1653–1717), printseller and publisher, has to
his credit a remarkable volume of engravings entitled " The
Cryes of the City of London, drawne after the Life," from
which is taken this figure of *John the Quaker,* engraved by
Savage. The book was published in the year 1711.

This is the only authentic likeness of William Law's disciple
and friend. It is copied from an engraving forming the frontis-
piece of the 1854 (Chetham Society) edition of Byrom's
Journal and Remains. The engraving had been made from
a miniature in the possession of his descendant, Miss Atherton.

Byrom is in full academic costume, including the wig and linen bands of the day. The characteristic boyishness of his face, which he probably retained to a great extent till late in life, makes him look some years younger than he actually is. Remarkably slim in build, he is reputed to have been one of the tallest men to be found in the England of his time.

The picture here reproduced appears to be the only contemporary representation of a Friends' Meeting during the eighteenth century which exists or is easily accessible. The original is an oil painting in the possession of Mr. Theodore Lucas of Wratten Cottage, Hitchin, who has inherited it from the original purchaser. It shows the Friends gathered in worship within their Meeting House in Gracechurch Street, London (since destroyed by fire), as it was in or about the year 1770. It will be noticed that by this date the poke bonnet, black or pale, has become customary for the woman Friends. The bent and aged figure in the centre of the picture is conspicuous for her green apron after the fashion of a quarter of a century before. (See page 162 below.) The artist, whose name is unknown, has introduced himself in the right-hand corner with his arm over the seat. The story is that he was in love with a Quaker maiden who is sitting among her fellow ministers and elders in the " gallery " : hence, in part at least, his frequent attendance at this Meeting.

The photographs of this picture and of May Drummond were secured with the kind assistance of the Librarians at Friends' House. A fuller description of the picture will be found in the Friends' Biographical Catalogue (1888), page 767. Enquiries have failed to discover the existence of any likeness of Fanny Henshaw.

It will be remarked that Byrom's habitual use of shorthand writing has done no manner of damage to the clearness of his long-hand. He is more modern than William Law, in so far as he has discarded the old symbol " y " for *th* (in a letter of Law's " y^r " would probably stand for *their* not *your* as in Byrom's writing), and has indicated by adding a small " 7 " after the date that a reform of the British calendar is overdue. (See page 239 *note* below.)

This letter and William Law's mentioned above have been photographed by kind permission of the Trustees of Dr. Williams' Library.

Among a number of buildings in the little village of King's Cliffe, near Peterborough, Northants, that are reminiscent of William Law, the one containing the remains of his extensive library easily holds the first place in interest. This is the building which William Law and his friend, Mrs. Hutcheson, caused to be constructed as a schoolmaster's house and a lending Library about the year 1753. It is now amalgamated with his almshouses for aged women, but the Library is still kept intact, with over 600 of the original volumes. One section of the Library contains, as provided by the original rules, a number of "Hebrew, Greek, and Latin Bibles, and a choice collection of the most spiritual Christian writers in the learned and foreign languages, for the use and benefit of the neighbouring clergy ". See further on pages 250–51 and 282 below.

The photograph was specially taken by Mr. A. J. Ball of Peterborough.

On this literary antagonist of William Law, afterwards successively Bishop of Bangor, Hereford, Salisbury, and Winchester, see pages 229–30 below. There is a later portrait of him in the National Portrait Gallery; but this early engraving has been chosen because it shows the ordinary clerical costume—black gown, linen bands, and wig—of the eighteenth century. Tradition has it that William Law's attire usually included "a clerical hat, with the loops let down, black coat, and grey wig ", and also, I presume, the clerical and academic " bands ".

PREFACE

IT was while engaged on a study of the literary remains of William Law, undertaken for quite another purpose, that I became aware of the manuscripts relating to Quakerism, which are published in the present volume. The only two really useful authorities for Law's life and correspondence are the Journal of Dr. John Byrom (1692–1763) and the so-called *Notes and Materials for an adequate Biography of William Law* by Christopher Walton (1809–1877). Considerable use of these authorities has been made in Overton's careful *Life* and in the article on William Law by Leslie Stephen in the *Dictionary of National Biography*. Byrom's Journal furnishes invaluable contemporary evidence, but of a quite incidental and unsystematic nature. Walton's rare and formidable volume consists of over seven hundred pages of minute print, full of long extracts from mystical and " theosophic " writings. But he has gathered together with enormous perseverance a large quantity of material relating to his hero, and this in a congested and unattractive form is given to us in his " mammoth footnote " to page 334, which extends as far as page 628 ! (To do the excellent Walton justice, he only printed these " materials " for the use of the " adequate biographer " of Law, whom he had himself failed to discover.)

Walton purchased from collateral descendants of William Law, who were still residing in his native village of Kingscliffe near Peterborough, a number of letters and other manuscripts of the saint, which had been inherited from Law's companion and legatee, Miss Hester Gibbon, aunt to the historian. Among these papers he secured " Five Letters in MS. addressed to a Serious Lady about quitting the Church of England to join the Quakers, 1736 : written at the special request of Dr. Byrom of Manchester ". (*Notes and Materials*, pp. 51–2 and 364.)

Walton had intended to publish these letters in a complete new edition of Law.

In the fifties of the last century the Rev. Dr. Parkinson of Manchester undertook on behalf of the Chetham Society the task of editing the Journal and correspondence of John Byrom. Having heard that Mr. Walton had in his possession some valuable letters of and connected with Byrom, he asked and secured the loan of them. Amongst them were sent (in 1855) Law's five letters on Quakerism mentioned above. In 1857 the fourth and last volume of *Byrom's Remains* was published by the Chetham Society. Walton tells us that it was not till April, 1858, that he received a copy of the volumes, and that then he found to his surprise that the five letters to the future Quakeress had not been inserted therein. (This was perhaps natural, as they do not form any part of Byrom's own correspondence, but only passed through his hands.) It further appears that, owing probably to some confusion caused by Parkinson's premature death, Walton had considerable difficulty in procuring the return of these and other manuscripts, which apparently only took place after May, 1859.[1] It is possible that to these circumstances may be due the loss of those portions of the Letters, to which a reference is made later on.

Christopher Walton had collected an immense and very heterogeneous mass of papers bearing upon mystical religion, and as he grew old he naturally looked around him for the most desirable place to deposit these treasures. His choice fell upon Dr. Williams' Library, and there accordingly they were all despatched, partly before and partly shortly after his death in 1877. The Letters on Quakerism went with the rest. The bare existence of these Letters is mentioned by Overton and Leslie Stephen in

---

[1] The above particulars are taken from a sixteen-page pamphlet (1859) addressed to "the Literary Public of the City of Manchester", in which Walton sets forth his complaint against the Chetham Society on various points connected with the loan of his manuscripts.

the accounts of Law they wrote shortly after this date :
but apparently solely on the evidence of the earlier reference to them in Walton's book. It is curious that they
should not have shown any sign of knowing that these
Letters and other Law manuscripts were in the Walton
Collection at Dr. Williams' Library.[1]

Being myself a Quaker, I was naturally interested in
the Letters, especially as I found in Byrom's fascinating
Journal a number of scattered but most entertaining
references to one Fanny Henshaw, who was evidently
Christopher Walton's " serious lady ". Moreover, I ascer-
tained that the same person had afterwards had a long and
active career as a member of the Quaker body. As it
happened, too, the indefatigable editor of the Friends'
Historical Society Journal had begun within the last two
years to investigate the facts relating to her life. Nothing,
however, was known, on the Quaker side, of her temporary
connection with Law and Byrom, just as, on the other
side, whatever interest there was in her, ceased when she
became a Quaker.

I soon discovered the existence of the Walton collection
at Dr. Williams' Library. The number of original manuscripts of Law (excluding his transcripts of other writings)
is not large, but is of great interest. Among them, to my
delight, I found the letters to Fanny Henshaw, which have
apparently received no literary attention since the day of
their arrival in the Library.

Unfortunately, however, of the five letters mentioned
by Walton, two are incomplete ; and there was probably
a sixth letter (the third in order), which is missing altogether.
To balance this, I found two most interesting letters of
Byrom bearing on the correspondence, about thirty sheets
of drafts in Law's handwriting relating to Quakerism, and

---

[1] As far as I can discover, no other collection of letters or manuscripts
of William Law is in existence. The British Museum and the Bodleian
Library have each only two letters of Law's, all but one of these having to
do with Law's position as a Nonjuror.

several other later letters to and from Law on the same subject. Of these the most valuable have never been published ; the others are imbedded in Walton's prodigious footnote and therefore as good as lost to the general reader.

Here surely, I thought, was sufficient excuse for a book. William Law is admittedly one of the greatest of our prose writers, and there is to-day a revival of interest in his mystical teachings. John Byrom is a delightful character, not without importance in eighteenth-century literary history, who has been too easily forgotten. (Would that some adventurous publisher would dare to reprint his Journal !) Moreover, the study of Law's gradual development in later years, towards the spirit of that Quakerism which he condemned so strongly in 1736, affords an opportunity of reprinting some of the most magnificent passages in his writings. The theological questions involved, especially those regarding the observance of the sacraments, are still living and practical issues in the Christian world ; and both Anglican and Quaker may be helped to get at the essentials through their restatement in eighteenth-century dress.

Finally, it seemed worth while to rescue from oblivion the character and career of Fanny Henshaw, matched as she was as a young and solitary woman against the most influential religious writer of her day (for so the author of the Serious Call was by almost universal admission at that date). I have therefore transcribed and arranged a considerable proportion of the records of her that are preserved in the Library of the Society of Friends.[1]

William Law disapproved strongly of critics. He wished his books to be read " more with the heart than with the head " ; and he warns us again and again against

[1] Those who know their Boswell will recall the somewhat parallel case of Jane Harry, who also left the established Church for the Quakers, greatly to the wrath of her friend, Dr. Johnson. See the record of his conversation with Mrs. Knowles on April 15, 1778, and also her touching life-story admirably told by Joseph J. Green in two articles on Jenny Harry [c. 1756–1784] in the Friends' Quarterly Examiner for 1913 and 1914.

" that learning, which, robbing us of the true fruits of the Tree of Life, leaves us nothing to feed upon but the dry dust of words." I have striven in the following pages to let the speaking be as far as possible done by him and his friends, and to be myself interpreter rather than critic. But I am aware that even thus I have been treading on dangerous ground. It is, alas, only too easy to write of those sacred and intimate realities which are involved in the conception of the sacraments of the Church, and to forget the constant attitude of love and trust which we owe as Christians to our Saviour and Lord. I pray that nothing written in this book may encourage the critical spirit at the expense of the spirit of prayer and of love, on the increase of which William Law's great heart was set.

It remains for me to acknowledge the generous assistance that I have received from various quarters in the preparation of this volume.

My first debt is to the Council of Woodbrooke Settlement (at Selly Oak, Birmingham), who by the award of a research fellowship have made it possible for me to spend my time on the study of William Law. To my friend Herbert G. Wood, the Director of Studies at Woodbrooke, I am also specially indebted.

The Trustees of Dr. Williams' Library, Gordon Square, W.C., gave permission for the making of copies of the unpublished manuscripts of William Law and John Byrom specified at the end of this Preface, but they are of course not responsible for the selection made. Similarly the manuscript letters relating to the career of Fanny Henshaw in Chapters II and IV of Part I were copied by permission of the Society of Friends in their Library at Friends House, Euston Road, N.W.

To the Librarians and the assistant staff of both these libraries, and especially to Mr. Stephen K. Jones and Dr. Norman Penney, I am deeply indebted for many courtesies and for much material assistance extended to me.

It is perhaps unnecessary to mention by name all the

B

other friends who have been kind enough to read the whole or parts of this book either in manuscript or proof : but I would especially acknowledge the helpful comments which I have received from my friends A. Neave Brayshaw and T. E. Harvey, as well as from two members of the communion to which Law himself belonged, the Rev. Dr. Edward Lyttelton and the Rev. E. R. Morgan of the College of the Ascension, Selly Oak.

The most accessible edition of the works of William Law is the excellent facsimile reprint published in nine volumes in 1893 by *G. Moreton* (*i.e.* G. B. Morgan). My references to *pages* are throughout to those of that edition : for a list of the volumes in which the particular works of Law in that edition occur, the reader should turn to Appendix II at the end of this book. As regards the manuscripts printed here for the first time, my general rule has been to retain the original spelling (except where it was obviously a slip), but to exercise discretion in amending and interpreting the punctuation, paragraphing, under-linings, and the use of capital letters, which are often employed by the writers in an utterly casual manner. (For instance, William Law will sometimes in the course of a single paragraph write " He " and " he " quite indis-criminately with reference to God and to an ordinary human being.)

The letters and manuscripts of William Law and John Byrom, which are here published for the first time, are printed on pages 26–72, 131–138, 205–226, 231 and 287. Other transcripts of William Law's letters which have not appeared in print, except in a comparatively inaccessible position in the footnotes to Christopher Walton's *Notes and Materials*, are on pages 248, 249, and 306–8.

STEPHEN HOBHOUSE

Stanford-le-Hope,
November, 1926

PART I

WILLIAM LAW, FANNY HENSHAW, AND JOHN BYROM

CHAPTER I

WILLIAM LAW'S LETTERS TO FANNY HENSHAW

INTRODUCTORY NOTE

THE circumstances under which the following letters were written will be found fully described in the portion of this book devoted to the narrative of Dr. John Byrom. It must suffice here to say that they were sent in November and December, 1736, to " Mrs. F. H.", otherwise *Miss* Fanny Henshaw, who was on the verge of leaving the Church of England to join the Society of Friends (usually known as the Quakers). All that William Law knew of the lady was her so-called " Case", to which I shall presently refer, together with some other information, probably of little value, sent him by Byrom.[1]

---

[1] At the risk of being scolded for inserting advice of this kind in a footnote (incidentally I must apologize for having had in this book to put so much of interest into footnotes!) I would suggest that anyone who is unacquainted with William Law and his writings may find it preferable to begin by reading the more biographical Chapter III, and then revert to the two earlier chapters.

For the benefit of any such readers I give here the few important facts of William Law's life—apart from his publications, which are strikingly impersonal in character. He was born in 1686, the son of a Northampton-shire village grocer. He took a degree at Cambridge and became a clergy-man and a Fellow of his College. But in 1716 his career in the University and the Established Church came to a sudden end, through his being forced, by extreme conscientiousness, into the position of a *Nonjuror* (see page 111 below). After eleven years in poverty and obscurity he secured a comfort-able place in the household of a rich London merchant, the grandfather of the historian Edward Gibbon. After the appearance of his fifth book, the famous *Serious Call*, in 1729, he became for a time probably the best known religious writer in England. On his patron's death, he retired (in 1740) to his native village of King's Cliffe, and there, till his death in 1761, he lived the life of a saint, engrossed in his mystical studies, his devotions, and his

Four of the five letters (one of these four being incomplete) bear on the reverse side of the final sheet (which served for an envelope) the address " For Dr. Byrom at Manchester in Lancashire", together with postmarks consisting of the date and, in two cases, the words " Penny Post paid." The remaining document is probably a draft of a letter never sent. They are all in Law's unmistakable, flowing, and easily legible handwriting ; and were probably written by him from Mr. Gibbon's house at Putney. Byrom was to forward them to Fanny Henshaw, who was then on a visit to an uncle in Doncaster.

We may infer from the Law–Byrom correspondence that Fanny only saw the first three of the six letters actually written by William Law. These she appears to have posted back to Byrom, who returned to Law all he had received, in the hope that Law might publish them, or at least something against Quakerism based in part upon them.

Law's first letter is headed " Observations upon a Paper of Mrs. F. H.", and begins with a considerable quotation from the paper in question. This document I propose for convenience' sake to call Fanny's *Case*, as was done by Law and Byrom in their correspondence. It is fortunately preserved for us among the manuscripts at the Library of the Society of Friends, and will be found printed in full on pages 87–91 below.

Law makes extensive quotations from this *Case* in letters 1, 2, and 5 that follow. In fact, these three letters are to a large extent a systematic commentary on and dissection of Fanny's record of her experiences. I have compared Law's quotations with the most authentic of the existing versions of the *Case*, and find that they are always substantially accurate. Fanny evidently made more than one copy

philanthropies, in company with two maiden ladies, who shared his aspirations.

Some brief characterizations of William Law's principal writings (as set out in Appendix II on page 341) will be found in the course of Part II of this book.

of her apologia, and the slight verbal variations that occur in Law's version are doubtless in part due to her and in part to Law. The first sentence quoted at the head of the first letter does not actually occur in any of the existing copies, but it was evidently present in another copy which had been sent to the clergyman to whom was addressed the letter on page 98 below. (See note *ad loc.* and compare Fanny's first sentence on page 79.)

I have placed within inverted commas the words or passages in the letters 1, 2, and 5 which are quotations from the *Case*. In Law's manuscript such quotations are indicated by underlinings, which in these letters hardly ever occur, except in the case of reported speech. (In the manuscripts of his treatises Law uses underlinings extremely freely, and, one is tempted to think, with a bewildering absence of discrimination.)

As was his constant and admirable custom, when dealing with controversial writings with which he disagreed, Law selects and uses his quotations from the *Case* quite fairly, allowing for his Anglican standpoint and his conviction that Fanny's experiences were in no way the result of divine guidance.

There is a group of letters among the published works of William Law, with which it would be natural to compare the letters to Fanny Henshaw. Only five to six years previously (in 1731 and 1732) Law had written three long " Letters to a Lady inclined to enter into the Communion of the Church of Rome." They were published after his death in 1779. To my mind they are far less interesting than the Henshaw letters, both intrinsically and because little or nothing is known of the lady to whom they were written—her very identity is uncertain—and we have no genial John Byrom as intermediary. Law's method of argument was here very different. He refrains almost entirely from attacking the errors of the Church of Rome. Indeed, he expresses the hope that " the means of Christian salvation are fully preserved both in the English and

Roman Communion, for all such as are disposed to make a right use of them ", and he takes the position that whereas each of these Churches (as well as all other divided parts of the Church) is in some degree guilty of schism, " if you are a private member of a Church that has the full means of salvation in it ", it is your duty to remain in that Church. By leaving the one communion for another, or on the other hand by indulging in party zeal or hatred, he thinks you bring upon yourself some of the guilt of the schism, from which you are free, if you simply live, within a schismatical communion, a life of Christian humility and devotion.

A great proportion of the forty-five pages covered by these earlier letters is occupied by largely irrelevant issues that seem to have been raised by Law's correspondent. The nearest parallel to his letters to Fanny is in his equally severe rebukes of this other young woman for giving way to her restless and emotional temperament. It appears that her deep distress over the falling away of a dearly loved brother from Christianity into Deism made her want to bury her sorrows and perplexities in the infallible repose of the Roman Church. It is interesting to see that in the last of the three letters Law sternly insists that it is " a restless, inquisitive, self-seeking temper ", which has been governing and distorting her piety and making her wrongfully dis-contented with the Church of her fathers, when " humility and resignation of heart to God " was all that she needed to secure peace of soul ; just as he tells Fanny that it is " meer nature " and the turbulence of youthful emotion that has diverted her God-given piety into a passion for joining the Quakers, whereas a similar resignation was alone required. We know nothing of the history of the lady inclined to Romanism, but we should hardly be surprised to learn that she also, like Fanny, had made a precipitate flight into the Church of her dreams not long after Law was writing to her. Law had not as yet the sympathetic touch in dealing with his correspondents to which he attained in later years when the spirit of love had got the upper hand in his soul.

Nevertheless there is, in these Henshaw Letters, not only much controversial skill, but much that is truly and beautifully put, many arguments indeed that will probably be found much more convincing to some who read them here than they are to myself as a Quaker. There is an entire avoidance, too, of the irrelevant and abusive style of controversy characteristic of nearly all the earlier writers against Quakerism. It is possible that the result of the letters would have been different, if they had been written at a somewhat earlier stage of the drama and if Fanny had had some personal contact with the writer.

The particular treatise of William Law with which the Henshaw Letters have most affinity is the one published less than three years later under the title of *The Grounds and Reasons of Christian Regeneration* ; more especially the later sections of this book, which deal with spiritual impressions and the marks of the new birth, with implicit reference to the experiences and teachings of the Methodists. I have quoted a number of parallel passages in the footnotes ; and other similarities might be pointed out.

It is an interesting problem to what extent the Letters show any trace of the influence upon William Law of the mystic Jacob Boehme, an influence which was just beginning to appear about this date. I have dealt with this briefly in Chapter VI of the second part of this book.

LETTER 1

Note.—The postmark is $\frac{30}{NO}$, *i.e.* November 30th (1736). The letter is undated. The " Mrs." in Law's heading is eighteenth-century style for " Miss ", being used for both unmarried and married women.

Observations upon a Paper of Mrs. F. H—.

" My manner of life from a child, none here are strangers to ; I shall therefore only give a faithfull account [of] what of late has befallen me. It is now about a year and [a] half since God was pleased to declare to me His will, which He condescended to do in the following manner. That if I would obey and be governed by His will, He would accept me and make me a disciple of His beloved Son. But to attain this desireable blessing, He required that I should entirely lay aside the vanities and foolish amusements of the world, etc." [1]

You should have told your manner of life,[2] which cannot be known, even by them that knew you ; viz., what kind and degree of religion you practised, what sort of books you read, what sort of devotion and prayer you sought after, whether you wanted or wished to know more of God and His will towards you, than is to be had in the ordinary way ; whether you had read or heard of persons that had been thus admonished by God, and hoped or desired to have the same favour. Did you at this time know nothing of the Quakers' pretences to this kind of communications with God ? Had you then no knowledge of their books

[1] See page 22 above.   [2] See note to page 29 below.

or of their opinions from any personal conversation with them ? You say, " God condescended to declare His will," etc. Do you only mean that such thoughts came forcibly into your mind, as when in other cases a person may say, the devil tempted or prompted him to do so or so ? Was it any thing more than certain thoughts in your mind ? Did you hear a voice speaking distinctly these words to you, as you hear other sounds ? If not, how can you say that " God condescended to declare," etc. ? If you heard such a voice, how did you know that it was God's, how comes it that you was not in some degree of astonishment and doubt about it ? Was it not plainly owing to this, because such things had been made familiar to you and perhaps desired by you, from what you had heard the Quakers speak of the frequency of such things amongst them and the mighty effects of them, and of God's declaring them to be His people by such manifestations of Himself unto them ? [1]

In reading the Scripture you say, " I seldom took up the book, but it opened in the fourth c. [chapter] of St. John ; which happening so many times, much affected me," etc.[2] This shews me that you are upon the watch for things extraordinary, and therefore it is no wonder that you often find them, and that a little proof will serve to convince you, that God is doing that for you, which we have no reason to believe that He ever did for any body else ; viz. that He opens your book for you whenever you are going to read.

[1] It was not uncommon among the Quakers, as among other adherents of a mystical creed, for spiritual guidance to come in the form of an audible voice. A fine example is that of Marmaduke Stevenson, the Boston martyr, who describes how, as he walked after the plough in Yorkshire, the love of God ravished his heart and made him stand still, and " the word of the Lord came to me in a still, small voice, which I did hear perfectly, saying to me in the secret of my heart and conscience, ' I have ordained thee a prophet unto the nations ' ". (Quoted in the First Part of the *Friends' Book of Discipline*, 1922, p. 32.)

Compare also the instance given by Rufus Jones in his Introduction to Braithwaite's *Beginnings of Quakerism*, p. xxxvi.

[2] The reason of course being that this chapter contains verse 24, " God is a spirit ", etc., which, as Law truly observed (see page 206 below), is the " foundation of Quakerism ".

This chapter, as I shall show you hereafter, is most evidently against the Quakers.[1]   Did the Quakers never discourse to you upon the doctrine of this chapter, did they never recommend it to your consideration, did you never read it by their direction ?   If anything of this is true, does not this sufficiently account for the ready opening of your book in that place ?

You say, " I happened at this time to see a person (a Quaker) from whose opinion the world imagined I conceived mine ; how far I did so, I will shew in as faithfull and true a manner as I am capable," etc.   Here you mention only one conversation, where, seeing you look troubled, he told you, that " you must apply to God and His holy word and submit your self entirely to Him."   Did neither this person, nor any other Quaker before this time, say anything to you in favour of their opinions ?   Was this all that had been done by any Quaker to recommend their doctrines, or to give you a distrust or dislike of the Church to which you belonged ?   Now if there had [been] anything of this kind by this or any other Quaker either by discourse or putting their books into your hands, then that which you call " a faithfull and true account " is very far from being so.   For you mention what he here said, to shew " faithfully how far " you had been influenced by him, that is by a Quaker ; but if he had before that time either said or done more, or any other Quaker had done so, then your only relating what he said at one particular time is by no means a true and faithfull account, how far you have been led into your present state by the Quakers.   How easie and natural was it for you to have said (if you could with truth have said it) that neither he nor any other Quaker had to that time made any attempt upon you, either as recommending their own tenents [2] to you, or discrediting those of the Church.

You go on, " But how great was my concern, when I found (not from him, who as I remember said no more to

---

[1] See Law's Second Letter.   [2] *i.e.* tenets.

me at that time) that to be a disciple of Christ I must make a thorough change in my life and manner, and become entirely a new creature, and be born again ; and this by a secret impulse, till that time unknown to me, was in a very plain manner revealed to my understanding."

And then you add these strange unaccountable words, viz. " Unwilling still to beleive, or entertain a thought in favour of the Quakers," etc. Is not this a demonstration that the Quakers had at that time made great attempts upon you, and that your difficulty was how to yeild to them ? For how could you say that you was " unwilling to beleive or entertain a thought " in favour of them, unless you had been pressed to it ? Or that you was still unwilling, unless the same application was still made to you ? To suppose that no application of this kind had been made to you, is to take all sense from your words ; [1] and to suppose that the Quakers had done anything of this kind with you, is to take away the fidelity of the above account of your self. I say not this to accuse you of unfaithfullness, but to shew you, that you mistake the state of your own case, and that what you take to be a miraculous, supernatural call of God to joyn your self to the Quakers, is only the *plain, natural* effect of what the Quakers and you have been jointly doing to prepare your mind not only to expect, but to want such calls. Though you have said nothing in your *Case* of your reading the Quakers' books, or of having had any conversation with the Quakers, yet I know it to be a fact and am as well assured of it, as if I had lived with you and seen it all with my own eyes.

And let me tell you this great truth, that if a priest of the Church of Rome had found you in the state that the Quakers first found you in, viz. young, of tender passions, capable of

---

[1] Fanny's own account of how far she had previously come into contact with Quakers will be found on pages 81–85 below. She had had some little acquaintance with them and their writings and had been to two of their meetings, when very young ; otherwise she mentions no other Quaker besides the one referred to on the last page, with whom she was rumoured to be in love.

any fire that should be put to them, piously disposed, loving the service of God, and perhaps anxious about the best way of pleasing Him, that a month or two of his conversation and instruction would have done all that for you with regard to the Church of Rome, which is now done for you with regard to the Quakers, only with this remarkable difference, that if the priest had had the care of you and brought you to a necessity of declaring for his Church, you would have appeared to others and seemed to your self to be free from any natural disorders, and to do what you then did, from great humility, self-denial, faith, and a full conviction of the necessity of being a member of that one, apostolical Church which Christ founded upon a rock and promised to be with to the end of the world. Whereas the frights, the sickness, the faintings and disorders of your body, the sudden starts and convulsions of your mind, the confusion of your passions, the light and darkness which alternately arise within you, the flashes of strange terrors and damnation, thoughts of evil spirits, and fears of being possessed by them (for all this I know to be your *case*, though not mentioned in it)—these disorders are now your present state for this reason, because it was not a priest, but the Quakers that have had the direction of your mind.

Everything must have a door of entrance according to what it is. Popery is to prevail against the objections of ordinary sense and understanding, and therefore it recommends to the mind such an humility, self-denial, and faith as keeps the eyes shutt, and so it gets an entrance. Quakerism is to prevail against the plain letter of Scripture, against the acknowledged institutions of Christ, and the most remarkable precepts of the Gospel, it is to prevail against all that the Apostles have writ and practised, against the authority of the Church of all ages, against the maxims of sober reason and prudence, and the doctrine of all the saints that ever lived either before, or since the coming of Christ ; and therefore if it is to prevail upon a *pious mind*, its business is to take soul and body out of their natural state, to prepare them both for convulsions, to make them both sick of strange distempers and full of unreasonable cravings, and to make the mind so desirous of a miraculous, supernatural state of hearing, seeing, feeling, tasting, and acting, that an outward Christ, outward sacraments, Gospel precepts, and every thing that is regular, or orderly, or prescribed either by God or man, may be disregarded as too low and carnal for its supernatural state.[1] And when an entrance is thus far gained, the very offices of the Church assembled together, the psalms and hymns of divine service, though made up of such as Christ and His Apostles used when on earth, and such as are even now sung by saints in

---

[1] Eighteenth-century Quakerism appears as a matter of fact to have been free, generally speaking, from the neurotic and morbid symptoms that have accompanied, but not necessarily discredited, most outbursts of religious " revival ". On the question how far the dominant " quietism " in the Society of Friends at this time was prejudicial to a life of healthy Christian activities, see page 190 ff., below.

Within a very short time of Law writing this letter, the first " revivalist " meetings of Whitefield and Wesley took place. Law disapproved of their emotional accompaniments, and indeed what he writes here of eighteenth-century Quakerism might more appropriately have been said of the Methodist movement, which was now on the eve of its first triumphs. In 1760 Law refers with disapproval to the "sighs, groans, swoonings, screamings of young and old," that often accompanied the Methodist and the Moravian preaching. (*Justification*, p. 224, and cp. *Address to Clergy*, p. 28, and Law's remark to Charles Wesley quoted in my note to page 57 below.)

Law dealt at considerable length in his *Regeneration* (1739, Sections 43 to the end) with the somewhat kindred subject of the value of a strong inward *assurance* of salvation, the necessity of which was upheld by many of the Methodists and Moravians. He points out how these feelings may be merely " worked up " by youthful passion or by " a sanguine imagination " or " a strong bias of self-esteem." There are, he agrees, " inward delights and enjoyments," " communications and impressions," which are of divine origin and indeed essential to the pious life of the soul, but it is dangerous to seek after them or rest in them. They are to be accepted, like outward blessings, as the good gifts of God and as great incitements to live wholly unto Him.

Law himself, though a mystic and full of a sense of God, had nothing of the visionary or psychic gift. (He expressly calls himself " a stranger to divine illumination " in a letter transcribed by Byrom [*Remains*, ii, p. 558] in January, 1735.)

heaven,[1] will seem like poison to such a soul, because they
nourish not its supposed supernatural state, and it will even
be afraid of being damned, if it should not renounce them.
And thus the poor soul is to judge of its spiritual growth
and progress, and to fansy itself become a saint, or very
near it, because the Spirit of Christ and His Apostles is
cast out of it, and because it has lost all regard to that
Church, those offices, institutions, and divine worship which
were appointed by God to keep up and preserve a perpetual
love, sence, desire, and practice of everything that is holy,
pious, and spiritual to the end of the world.

You know how much I am a stranger to you, but as soon
as I read your paper, I knew a great deal more of you than
you had there related, and was fully convinced that I could
send you a much deeper and fuller account of your self than
I have had from you.   But what is more and better than
this, I trust in God, that I see the method in which God will
releive you and give you His peace, as plainly as I do your
disorder, if you will but have patience.   But without
patience there can be no cure of any religious complaint.
Haste, impetuosity, and eagerness of mind are not from the
Spirit of God.   These tempers are the greatest part of
your disorder, and I can truly and with great assurance say
unto you in the words of Moses, " *Stand still*, and thou
shalt see the salvation of God." [2]   Your case is of a mixt
nature, and your disorder is both in body and mind ; but
for your comfort I can say to you, in the words of our
Saviour concerning Lazarus, " This sickness is not unto
death, but for the glory of God, that the Son of God may be
glorifyed thereby."   There are two spirits at combat
within you, and your unhappyness is that you mistake the

---

[1] Twenty years later, Law took a less exalted view of the Church
services, referring, *e.g.*, adversely to the cursing Psalms.   See pages 303
and 304 below.

[2] Exod. xiv. 13.   Law's advice here is, though he does not know it,
thoroughly in harmony with the quietism which was becoming characteristic
of the leaders of eighteenth-century Quakerism.   Compare his words in the
Spirit of Prayer quoted on page 331 below.

heaven,[1] will seem like poison to such a soul, because they nourish not its supposed supernatural state, and it will even be afraid of being damned, if it should not renounce them. And thus the poor soul is to judge of its spiritual growth and progress, and to fansy itself become a saint, or very near it, because the Spirit of Christ and His Apostles is cast out of it, and because it has lost all regard to that Church, those offices, institutions, and divine worship which were appointed by God to keep up and preserve a perpetual love, sence, desire, and practice of everything that is holy, pious, and spiritual to the end of the world.

You know how much I am a stranger to you, but as soon as I read your paper, I knew a great deal more of you than you had there related, and was fully convinced that I could send you a much deeper and fuller account of your self than I have had from you. But what is more and better than this, I trust in God, that I see the method in which God will releive you and give you His peace, as plainly as I do your disorder, if you will but have patience. But without patience there can be no cure of any religious complaint. Haste, impetuosity, and eagerness of mind are not from the Spirit of God. These tempers are the greatest part of your disorder, and I can truly and with great assurance say unto you in the words of Moses, " *Stand still*, and thou shalt see the salvation of God." [2]   Your case is of a mixt nature, and your disorder is both in body and mind ; but for your comfort I can say to you, in the words of our Saviour concerning Lazarus, " This sickness is not unto death, but for the glory of God, that the Son of God may be glorifyed thereby." There are two spirits at combat within you, and your unhappyness is that you mistake the

[1] Twenty years later, Law took a less exalted view of the Church services, referring, *e.g.*, adversely to the cursing Psalms. See pages 303 and 304 below.

[2] Exod. xiv. 13. Law's advice here is, though he does not know it, thoroughly in harmony with the quietism which was becoming characteristic of the leaders of eighteenth-century Quakerism. Compare his words in the *Spirit of Prayer* quoted on page 331 below.

state, to prepare them both for convulsions, to make them both sick of strange distempers and full of unreasonable cravings, and to make the mind so desirous of a miraculous, supernatural state of hearing, seeing, feeling, tasting, and acting, that an outward Christ, outward sacraments, Gospel precepts, and every thing that is regular, or orderly, or prescribed either by God or man, may be disregarded as too low and carnal for its supernatural state.[1] And when an entrance is thus far gained, the very offices of the Church assembled together, the psalms and hymns of divine service, though made up of such as Christ and His Apostles used when on earth, and such as are even now sung by saints in

---

[1] Eighteenth-century Quakerism appears as a matter of fact to have been free, generally speaking, from the neurotic and morbid symptoms that have accompanied, but not necessarily discredited, most outbursts of religious "revival". On the question how far the dominant "quietism" in the Society of Friends at this time was prejudicial to a life of healthy Christian activities, see page 190 ff., below.

Within a very short time of Law writing this letter, the first "revivalist" meetings of Whitefield and Wesley took place. Law disapproved of their emotional accompaniments, and indeed what he writes here of eighteenth-century Quakerism might more appropriately have been said of the Methodist movement, which was now on the eve of its first triumphs. In 1760 Law refers with disapproval to the "sighs, groans, swoonings, screamings of young and old," that often accompanied the Methodist and the Moravian preaching. (*Justification*, p. 224, and cp. *Address to Clergy*, p. 28, and Law's remark to Charles Wesley quoted in my note to page 57 below.)

Law dealt at considerable length in his *Regeneration* (1739, Sections 43 to the end) with the somewhat kindred subject of the value of a strong inward *assurance* of salvation, the necessity of which was upheld by many of the Methodists and Moravians. He points out how these feelings may be merely "worked up" by youthful passion or by "a sanguine imagination" or "a strong bias of self-esteem." There are, he agrees, "inward delights and enjoyments," "communications and impressions," which are of divine origin and indeed essential to the pious life of the soul, but it is dangerous to seek after them or rest in them. They are to be accepted, like outward blessings, as the good gifts of God and as great incitements to live wholly unto Him.

Law himself, though a mystic and full of a sense of God, had nothing of the visionary or psychic gift. (He expressly calls himself "a stranger to divine illumination" in a letter transcribed by Byrom [*Remains*, ii, p. 558] in January, 1735.)

Observations upon a Paper
of Mrs. F. H.

my Manner of Life from a child, none here are strangers
to; I shall therefore only give a faithfull account what of
late has befallen me. 'Tis now about a year & half since
God was pleased to declare to me his Will, wch He condescended to do in ye following Manner. That it might ~~~~ they
~~~~ the power as his Will, it would augment & make
me a Disciple of his beloved Son: But to attain this desireable
Blessing, He required yt I should entirely lay aside ye Vanities
and foolish Amusements of the World &c.

You should have told your Manner of Life, which cannot be unown, even
to them that knew you; viz. what kind & degree of Religion you practised, what sort of books you read, what sort of Devotion & Prayer you
sought after, whether you wanted or wished to know more of God &
his Will towards you, than is to be had in ye ordinary Way;
Whether you had read or heard of Persons that had been thus admonished by God, & hop'd & desired to have the same favour. Did you at
this time know nothing of the Quakers pretences to this kind of
communication with God? Had you then no knowledge of their
Books, or of their Opinions from any Personal Conversation wth
them? You say, God condescended &c. to declare his Will &c.
Do you only mean that such thoughts came forcibly into your Mind,
as when in other cases, a Person may say, the Devil tempted or prompted
him to do so or so? ~~~~~~~~~~~~~~~~ Was it any more
than certain thoughts in your mind? Did you hear a Voice speaking
distinctly these words to you, as you hear other sounds? If not, how can
you say, that God condescended to declare &c: If you heard such a
Voice, how did you know yt it was Gods, how comes it yt you was not
in some degree of astonishment & doubt about it? Was it not plainly
owing to this, because such things had been made familiar to you, &
& perhaps desired by you, from what you had & ye Quakers speak of the
frequency of such things among them, & ye mighty effects of them;
and of Gods declaring them to be his people by such Manifestations
of himself unto them?

In reading the Scripture you say, I seldom took up the book, but it
opend in ye 4th c. of St John, which happening so many times much
affected me &c. This shews me that you are upon the Watch for
things extraordinary, & therefore it is no wonder yt you often find
                                                    them

one for the other, and take the good to be bad, and the bad to be the good one. The piety of your mind and the goodness of God towards you has begun a good work in [your life. (?) The doctrine][1] of the Spirit you have received from the Quakers and their books, is the tares [that] is sown amongst the good seed. The work of God had gone on prosperously in your soul, and given you no sorrow but that of godly repentance, had you not been tinctured [2] with the spirit of this sect. But because you try everything by the spirit of this sect and are for governing your conversation by it, hence it is that you have raised this tumult in your soul and made the best state in the world, that of an awakened conscience, a state of torment and confusion to you. The Church with all its holy offices, orders, institutions, and services is the true refuge, releif, and sanctuary for distressed souls ; everything is there ready, prepared, and appointed by God to help the soul that feels the necessity of renouncing the world and living wholly unto God. Had Noah refused to enter into the ark for to save him self, when God had condescended to give him notice of the flood, he had acted just as you do, who upon God's condescending to bid you save your self from the world, refuse to stay in the Church, which is as truly and certainly God's appointed means of being saved from the world, as the ark was His appointed means of being saved from the flood.

You instance your trial, and in what it is [that ?] your courage and resolution ought to appear ; the spirit that is most boisterous in you calls for a hasty, speedy throwing your self amongst a people of yesterday, that have no name or being amongst the saints of God in any age of the world since the creation. Before them there never was a saint in the world without a Church, a sanctuary, a priest and divine ordinances ; this spirit terrifies and threatens your want of courage to declare for it ; but let me tell you, that if you will not mistake your trial, your courage is to exert itself in the

[1] The manuscript is frayed here.
[2] *i.e.* imbued, a term derived from alchemy, often used by Boehme.

contrary way, and resolutely turn your back upon that spirit, which with a strange extravagance calls you from the institutions of Christ in order to be a Christian. Everything that has yet happened to you, may and certainly will be made means of purifying your soul, if you will but be content to serve and worship God in such a manner and with such outward ordinances, as you must have done, had you lived with the glorious company of the Apostles, the goodly fellowship of the Prophets, the noble army of Martyrs,[1] and all the saints that have ever been in any age of the Church.

(To be continued in my next.)

[1] Law is quoting the words of the *Te Deum*, so familiar to all who know the service of Morning Prayer in the Anglican Prayer Book.

LETTER 2

Note.—This letter is also undated. It is marked, apparently by a contemporary pen, with a figure 2. The postmark is December 4th. The heading is Law's.

A continuation of the Former Letter.

There is no harm in your believing that God declared His will to you, as you imagin'd, since the matter of it was good in it self, and is His declared will to every one in the Holy Scripture ; but I am apt to think that the manner of it was not so extraordinary, as you think. You may do well to beleive, that it was God's good Spirit that gave you a strong and uncommon conviction of the necessity of renouncing the spirit of the world in order to be a true disciple of Christ. But what has made this admonition less beneficial, perplexing, and even dangerous to you, has been your regard to the doctrines of the Quakers, and a voluntary design to turn this admonition that way. You have no bad pain in you but what proceeds from this conduct ; no evil spirit possesses or torments you, but what has its birth and power from your endeavouring to make the Spirit of Christ lead you from the Church of Christ ; cast away this biass, and the evil spirit, you think so much of, will be cast out of you. Had you, when you received, as you say, this strong impulse convincing you of the necessity of a new birth, looked upon your self as the greatest of sinners, the poorest, meanest creature upon earth, that stood in need of every inward and outward help that all the united prayers, offices, institutions, and service of the Church could give to any penitent sinner, your conversion had been built upon a rock, secure from every

danger and delusion.   Had you then in this state of heart
turned your self to God in some prayer like this, " O my
God, I beseech thee, for thy mercies in Christ Jesus, to save
and deliver me from my self ; change, kill, and destroy
everything that ought to be changed and destroyed in me ;
quicken and bring to life all that ought to be made alive
in me," you had done well.   Nothing was proper at that
time, but such a prayer as this proceeding from such a
state of heart.   Had you done this and acted according to it,
the work of God had gone forward in your soul and room
had been made for all the happy progress of the new birth.[1]

But instead of this, instead of thus humbly thinking of
your self, and praying in this manner, you did that which
was the most improper, you reasoned with God, as you call
it, in this manner, " Lord, I ever found some of them to
be a very plain, and, I believed, sincere people, but they
allow not the outward institution of baptism and the Lord's
supper, which surely was commanded by our blessed Lord
and Master."

For what has all this to do with the impulse you had
received ?   What relation has it to the new birth which you
wanted ?   This reasoning so very improperly, where you
should not have reasoned at all, and turning your eye upon
the Quakers, when you should have had your eye only upon
God and your self, made room for all the uneasieness, perplexity, and mistake that has since fallen upon you.   Instead of submitting your self to an impression from God,
which only called you to an observance of the Gospel, you
try how to get an answer against [the] Gospel it self, that
your new birth may not be sought for and brought forth
upon the terms of the Gospel.   You, as it were, complain
to God, that this necessity of a new birth had brought you
into great streights, because these people (the Quakers)
renounce the sacraments which Christ Himself had instituted and commanded to be observed.   But how comes
this to be your case, who brought you into it ?   Who put

[1] The new birth in Christ Jesus was the centre of Law's teaching.

this difficulty in your way, but your self ? Why do you any more want to be united with a people, who reject the institutions of Christ, than to be united with those who deny Him to be the Christ ? Who hath required this of you ? Can you suppose that this call, which requires you entirely to lay aside the vanities and foolish amusements of the world, is equally a call entirely to lay aside the use of Christ's sacraments, as equally hurtful and dangerous to your spiritual progress ? Surely this is too shocking a thought for you.

And yet, if you did not think thus of the sacraments, that they are part of the vanities and amusements of the world, how comes the necessity of renouncing the one to put you under a necessity of renouncing the other ? Why could you not as well think of renouncing the Scriptures in order to obtain this new birth, as of renouncing the sacraments ? For the outward word and the outward sacraments are equally carnal and equally spiritual, they both stand upon the same bottom, and are both ordained for the same end, viz., for the sake of the new birth, and are both of them only and equally means of obtaining, preserving, and perfecting this same new birth in us to the end of our lives.

Every mystery of our redemption is more or less signifyed, represented, and offered to us by the Holy Sacraments of Baptism and the Lord's Supper ; every grace and degree of the new birth is rightly sought for, and certainly obtained by a faithfull, humble participation of them, and every expression of adoration, love, and gratitude due to Father, Son, and Holy Ghost for the work of our redemption, is in the plainest, openest manner set forth by our humble, faithfull, thankfull, reverential use of them.[1] No greater mark of the new birth's arising in us,

---

[1] With this exalted conception of the Holy Sacraments compare the following two passages, both written by Law within four years of this letter.

" For since they [the Scriptures] teach us a birth of God, a birth of the Spirit, that we must obtain, and that baptism, the appointed sacrament

than a reverential love and esteem of these institutions, and an earnest longing and desire to partake of them with all the sentiments of love, adoration, and thanksgiving that our hearts are capable of ; and the more the new birth advances in us, the more these tempers become real, essential, fixed, and habitual in us ; everything that Christ said, did, and appointed, becomes an object of love to the new-born soul. That new birth which either proceeds from or brings forth a contempt and renunciation of these divine institutions, is only being born again of our selves, by the will of the flesh, and by the will of man.

Strange is it therefore, that whilst you stand as it were under the voice of Heaven, called, as you think, by God Him self to be a disciple of Christ, you should be reasoning for liberty and watching for a voice, to authorise you to renounce the sacraments of Christ ! Stranger is it still, that you should imagine, that an evil spirit is sent into you and has possession of you, because you have not made haste enough in shewing your contempt and abhorrence of those holy ordinances, which have Christ alone for their author ! Should you have met with a sect of people pretending great simplicity, plainness of life, and communications with God, yet not suffering the words, *Christ* and *Jesus*, to be mentioned

of this birth, is to be done into the name of the Father, Son, and Holy Ghost, can there be any doubt that this sacrament is to signify the renovation of the birth of the Holy Trinity in our souls ? " (*Regeneration*, Sect. 16. It is one of Law's cardinal doctrines that man was originally created in the image of the Trinity.)

"And thus is this great sacrament, which is a continual part of our Christian worship, a continual communication to us of all the benefits of our second Adam ; for in and by the body and blood of Christ, to which the divine nature is united, we receive all that life, immortality, and redemption, which Christ, as living, suffering, dying, rising from the dead, and ascending into heaven, brought to human nature : so that this great mystery is that, in which all the blessings of our redemption and new life in Christ are centred." (*An Appeal :* last page.)

Similar words in praise of the "Holy Supper" will be found in the *Demonstration*, which Law was probably writing just about this time. (See *Dem.*, pp. 11 and 53. I have quoted the latter passage on page 228 below.)

amongst them, as pretending to such an inward spiritual union with their Redeemer, as will not allow of the use of such words, and if you was in pain till you had joyned your self to such a people, could you think that it was the Holy Spirit of God or the true love of your Redeemer, that made you want to be of a sect that had renounced the use of those names by which their Redeemer was called in Scripture, as hurtfull to the high state of their souls ? [1] Or can you think that, though there could be nothing bad in the names by which your Redeemer is called in Scripture, yet there may be something bad in those sacraments which He appointed to be observed, and even so bad, so contrary to the Holy Spirit of God, as to make it necessary to renounce them, in order to [2] the new birth ?

The poor woman in the Gospel that wanted to be cured of her grievous infirmity said within herself, " If I can but touch the hem of His garment, I shall be whole." [3] Such sentiments of love and faith had this poor woman, that she thought the very outward garments of Christ had something of a divine virtue in them, and that she could not touch them without receiving benefit from it. This faith and love our Lord highly approved and rewarded.

Pray see here, how different a way the spirit of the Quakers carrys you. See how different a faith they teach you, from that which our Saviour here approved and rewarded. They teach you to say within yourself, " If I could but renounce the institutions of Christ as useless, insignificant things and hurtfull to the spirit, if I could but turn my back upon that outward bread and wine, which He commanded to be taken and eaten as His body and blood, I should be whole."

[1] This is an example of the *reductio ad absurdum* argument which Law frequently uses in his controversial works.

[2] *i.e.* as a means towards.

[3] Matt. ix. 20–22. Law draws another illustration from this " poor woman that wanted to be healed of her infirmity " in his *Demonstration* (p. 130), which he was probably composing about the time he wrote this letter.

Let this teach you to reject the reasoning of a Quaker, as you would reject the reasoning of a Jew.   There can be no breach of charity in your avoiding or refusing the company of those, who would refuse and avoid an Apostle's company, if he administered the outward sacrament of the Lord's supper and authorised others to do the same (that is, if he did as our Saviour strictly commanded him to do).

You seem to place much in the fourth chapter of St. John ; but have you so read that chapter as to know that the spiritual worship of God is shut up amongst the Quakers, and that, though you need not go to Jerusalem or a mountain in Samaria to worship God, yet you must go amongst the Quakers ?   Does the light of that chapter shew you that, though you must renounce an outward Church, an outward clergy, outward sacraments and ordinances in order to be a spiritual worshipper, yet you *must* seek, adhere to, and unite your self with *outward* Quakers, men and women.   This is strangely extravagant.   The Quakers are as great offenders against the divine doctrine of that chapter, as the Scribes and Pharisees and Samaritans were.   They pretend to great spirituality, and yet as a sect they strike at the very heart of it.   For to renounce *outward* ordinances of *divine appointment*, because they are *outward*, and to set up their own *outward society*, full of *outward* distinctions invented by human fancy, in the room of them, is a degree of superstition and will-worship, not practised by either Jew or Samaritan.

The sect of the Quakers may be justly looked upon as carnal and Pharisaical in a high degree.   When our Saviour would shew us the spirit of the Pharisees, He gave us a parable of one praying in this manner, " God, I thank thee that I am not as other men are, fornicators, etc., or even as this publican ; I fast twice in the week, I give tithes of all that I possess." [1]   Our Saviour condemned the Pharisee and gave the preference to a poor penitent publican. If now we suppose a Quaker to pray in the spirit of his sect,

[1] Luke xviii. 11–12.

he will stand and say, " God, I thank thee that I am not as thy Apostles were, I practise not water baptism and the outward supper of the Lord, I pay no tithes, nor keep any solemnities of feasts or fasts, nor observe any outward ordinances of the Gospel."   This is as plainly the spirit of the Quakers, as the former was the spirit of the Pharisees.

Now what is the difference betwixt the Pharisee and the Quaker, how do they agree, and how do they differ ?   They agree in this, that they both of them trust in and boast of their works.   But they differ in this, that the Pharisee trusted in and boasted of his *good* works, for what he said of himself was good and according to the laws of God, but the Quaker trusts in and boasts of his *bad* works, of his not doing what the Apostles did, and renouncing institutions appointed by his Lord.   Now if our Lord preferred the poor penitent publican before the Pharisee boasting of his good and righteous works, I should think it plain that such a publican must be much more preferred before a Quaker, boasting of his bad works and disobedience to the express commands of Christ.[1]

You have no evil spirit, as that signifys a bad angel, that has possession of you.   And if I must tell you the matter, it stands thus with you.   Human nature is full of mysteries, we have the passions of beasts and animals, of devils and the Holy Spirit in us at once ;[2] when these are all in motion in a disturbed heart, we know not what to [make of them. (?)] If the least degree of spiritual pride has the [government of us][3] in this disorder, then the passions of the body, the passions of the soul, and the actings of the evil nature in us seem all to be holy, and every impetuosity whether of body or mind is taken to be a motion of the Holy Spirit, and we

[1] Compare page 208 below and footnote.

[2] Compare the title of the beautiful prayer of Law's, printed at the end of A. Whyte's *Characters and Characteristics of William Law* (p. 322) : " A Prayer for the destruction of the evil, bestial, and serpentine properties of the Old Adam and the quickening of the Divine Spirit of the Second Adam in the Soul."

[3] The manuscript is frayed here.

are sick of everything, impatient of everything that seems to check this supposed holy working of our souls. I don't charge you with any degree of pride, knowing it to be such. I daresay you both love and desire true humility ; but as the hearts of persons aged and experienced in piety are still deceitfull in some degree, so it is no wonder, if the heart of a person so young as you are should not be free from some deceit unperceived by your self. You don't know what a nature you are endued with and therefore mistake its workings ; your passions have not yet spent their fire, they have neither been baffled and disappointed by worldly objects, nor suppressed by heavenly ; you have not yet experienced their folly, their falsehood, their strength and cunning, and therefore it is no wonder that they betray you, deceive you, and perplex you in the work of your conversion.[1]

If you ask what is the remedy for all this and especially for your self, I can point you to one that is infallible, which neither men nor devils can prevent, if you will but faithfully take it. It is the *humility and contrition* set forth in these words, " I will arise and will go to my Father, and will say unto Him, Father, I have sinned against Heaven and before thee, and am no more worthy to be called thy son, make me as one of thy hired servants." Enter into the spirit of *humility and contrition*, leave it to the Quakers to be high and lofty [above] all ordinances and institutions, return you with this penitent, prostrate your self as low as he did, see no worth in your self, nor any fitness to be received as a son or favourite, beg only of the mercy of God that so poor a creature may have liberty to attend upon Him amongst His lowest servants. Open your heart for the reception of this humility, draw it into the depth and essence of your soul, that everything within you and without you

---

[1] Compare with this *Regeneration*, Sect. 44, where Law, enumerating various types of persons who may get harm through being taught to seek for " an absolute assurance of salvation " (see my note to page 31 above), puts first " all young persons, whose passions had not yet been much awakened or spent their fire ; who had but little experience of themselves and the deceitfulness of their own hearts."

may be governed by it, and then, though you had as many devils in you as Magdalen had, they must all depart from you.[1]   Hell is destroyed wherever such humility appears. By this humility the Kingdom of Heaven is let into the soul, the new birth gradually arises and Christ becomes formed in it, all wounds are healed, all sins forgiven, and the soul is delivered from its own captivity, the monstrous disorderly workings of its own corrupt nature, and is made a willing, thankfull captive of the holy pure Spirit of God, etc.[2]

(To be continued in my next.)

[1] This is a reference to Fanny's " Case ", where, with a Bunyan-like exaggeration, she had described herself as " a second Magdalen ".

[2] " This, this is the great end of God's raising a new creation out of a fallen kingdom of angels ; for this end it [the creation] stands in its state of war, a war betwixt the fire and pride of fallen angels and the meekness and humility of the Lamb of God : it stands its thousands of years in this strife, that the last trumpet may sound this great truth through all heights and depths of eternity, that ' evil can have no beginning but from pride : nor any end but from humility.' . . . Pride must die in you or nothing of heaven can live in you. . . . There is no other open door into the sheepfold of God. . . . Humility must sow the seed, or there can be no reaping in heaven.   Look not at pride only as an unbecoming temper : not at humility only as a decent virtue : for the one is death and the other is life : the one is all hell, and the other is all heaven." (*Spirit of Prayer*, Part II, pp. 73-4.)

LETTER 4

Note.—All that remains of this Letter is the final sheet, on the reverse of which the address is written. To the address the figure " 4 " has been added, apparently by the same contemporary pen that added the figures 1, 2, and 5 to the other Letters. It is therefore reasonable to suppose that this fragment is the conclusion of the fourth Letter, and that the third Letter has unfortunately been lost. (Walton was almost certainly mistaken in regarding this and the other incomplete Letter—my " 6 "—as both portions of Law's third Letter.)

This is the only Letter dated by Law—December 9th, 1736. The postmark gives the same date.

. . . grace is sufficient for you. Faith and patience and humble resignation to God seem to the hasty disordered soul to be too weak and slow a releif, and also too common and ordinary virtues to exspect so great a deliverance from ; she would also have something more extraordinary to appear in the manner of her deliverance, and also have some hand in it her self, etc. This makes it so hard to the soul at this time to be saved only by the ordinary virtues of piety. She had much rather take some strange extraordinary step than to have such great things, as she had fansyd of her self, to end in such ordinary virtues.[1]   But

---

[1] Compare *Regeneration*, Sect. 38. " To ask therefore by what *strange* or *extraordinary* effects the work of the new birth is to be known and felt to be done in the soul, is a very improper and useless question." Law deprecated putting trust in the efficacy or necessity of sudden conversion, rather than on the need of perseverance in a " gradual process of regeneration " through Christ. (*Op. cit.*, Sect. 48.)

she ought to know, that though these virtues are as it were the sinking down of the soul into its lowest state of annihilation before God, yet they are at the same time its highest exaltation. And though the words sound as if they left the soul in some uncertainty, yet it is not so, for by these virtues she becomes united with the omnipotence of God and must have a share of His superiority over hell and darkness.[1]

Let your affliction be what it will, hang patiently upon it, as upon your cross. You know how near our Saviour was to His total victory, when He hung upon the cross. Had He called to the Jews to take Him down, He had lost His victory. Call you not to the Quakers, for the same reason, that He called not to the Jews !

I have not time to add any more.

Your faithfull friend,

W. L.

Dec. 9, 1736.

[1] " Ask now what hell is. It is nature destitute of the light and Spirit of God and full only of its own darkness ; nothing else can make it to be hell." (*Spirit of Prayer*, Part II, p. 140.)

LETTER 5

Note.—This undated Letter is marked " 5 ". The postmark can be read as December 14 or December 24. The first date must be the correct one, as the letter is referred to by Law in his letter of December 17th to Byrom (see page 130 below). It may therefore be regarded as following closely on the preceding fragment.

Madam,

When you was reasoning about a certain difficulty which you had unreasonably raised up to your self, and wanting to have an answer against your fear of going over to a people that had renounced the sacraments, you say you " was, as though you heard a voice, thus answered, ' Obey my will, and thou shalt find my flesh is meat indeed and my blood is drink indeed. I am the Lord, I dwell not in tabernacles made with hands, my chosen temple is the heart. Remember my servant David's words, " Sacrifice and meat offering for sin thou would'st not, but a broken and a contrite heart, thou, O God, wilt not despise." What said my prophet Samuel to Saul, who spared of the flock for sacrifice ? " Obedience is better than sacrifice," etc.' " [1]

I will suppose (though I take it not [to] be so) that you heard an extraordinary voice, saying expressly these words to you. I grant also that the words here spoken are good and true, all taken from true Scripture.

But I will shew you, that you either falsely understood them, or else they were spoken unto you by a false spirit. The Scriptures, which the devil quoted to our Saviour, were true and good, but they were intended to betray Him

[1] The passages quoted successively in this utterance are—John vi. 55 ; Acts vii. 48 ; Psalms xl. 6 and li. 17 (combined) ; and 1 Sam. xv. 22.

into sin by a wrong application of them. The voice there-fore that spoke these words unto you is to be tryed by the end and design that was intended by the speaking of them. Now according to your own beleif, these passages of Scripture were spoken to you for this sole end and design, to convince you of the necessity of renouncing the Church and the use of the sacraments, and secondly of the necessity of doing this in order to obtain the new birth. For it is upon your conviction of the necessity of this new birth, that you wanted and received this answer, and upon receiving it you own yourself convinced, and only expostu-late with God about the difficulty of acting according to it. So that it is plain, that you own this to have been the *end* and *design* of these words of Scripture spoken to you. Now I will shew you plainly that either you falsely understood the voice, or that the voice intended to deceive you, by speaking these Scriptures for this end and design ; though it is my opinion, that there was no extraordinary voice, but only your own disturbed mind that spoke to itself.

You are here called to remember the words of David. I would have you also remember them, they contain excel-lent truths. But to prevent your misapplication of them, let me say thus much to you, viz., that which is *rightly* and *truely* taught in these words of David *now*, was rightly and truely taught in these words of David, *when* he first spoke them. And that which was not taught in these words *then*, is not taught in these words *now*. This is undeniable. If therefore, according to these words of David, God rejects outward institutions of religion now, then it was true according to these same words, that God rejected outward institutions when David spoke them, and that consequently David was more obliged to renounce the outward institutions of the Jews, than you can be by the hearing of these words obliged to renounce the institu-tions of Christ. For if this was the doctrine contained in David's words, he knew it better than you can, and therefore was more obliged to put it in practice, and might justly have feared a greater vengeance of God upon him [1] for not doing it, than you for not running away from Christ's institutions.   But that these words of David had no such meaning then, and that God did not in these words of His servant David reject outward institutions then, is beyond all possibility of doubt, because Solomon who succeeded David did by God's own order build a temple for the habitation of God, and set up a temple service of outward ordinances, which temple and service thereof was approved by God both by voices and miracles from heaven.   Therefore a spirit, that quotes these words of David as a proof that God rejects outward institutions of religion, abuses Scripture in the grossest manner.[2]   If the spirit that spoke

[1] In his later writings Law would not have used this expression.

[2] Isaac Penington (in a work written in Reading Gaol in 1671) propounds to himself and his readers in the most searching way similar queries as to how David could say in truth that " God desired not sacrifice, nor delighted in burnt offerings ", when God had in the Law of Moses desired and required the performance of these things from His people. " Ought not David to try this spirit, which spake thus in him, whether it was of God or no ? "

Penington's answer is a little vague, but it amounts to a belief that, though David continued to observe the sacrificial law, he looked forward in spirit to the day of its abolition and the passing away of all ritual observance. (The reference at the end of the quotation is to Hebrews xii. 26–8, a favourite Quaker text.) " David's aim," Penington writes, " was at another thing, and at other sacrifices. . . . He saw clearly that outward sacrifices were not the abiding thing, but significations of that which was abiding ; and this sight greatly shook them in his spirit. The Lord hath likewise shown us clearly that outward water, bread, and wine are not the substantial, the spiritual, the heavenly water, the heavenly bread and wine, but of the nature of such things as were to be shaken, that those things which cannot be shaken may remain in the gospel state and kingdom." (*Life and Immortality*, etc., in Penington's Works, 1761, vol. ii, p. 428.)

Many interpreters of the Old Testament would agree with Law's argument here, explaining the words quoted from Fanny's *Case* as only meaning that no religious ritual, however obligatory and divinely instituted, is a substitute for righteous conduct. It is possible, however, to hold that the two psalms which she quotes (being, according to this view, only attributed to and not written by David) form part of a repudiation by prophetic writers of the traditional ascription to Jehovah of the institution of animal

these words had no such meaning in them, then the error and misapplication of them is from your self. Which way soever it is, it matters not, the error is of the same danger and importance to you, and so equally to be renounced by you.

The next thing you mention in your *Case*, is a supposed threatening from God for not complying with the revelation and conviction you had received of the necessity of turning Quaker. But if, as appears, you have been erroneously conducted thus far, troubling your self, and from your self, with a supposed call to be a Quaker, then this is justly to be reckoned of a peice with that which had gone before. You are here also told of St. Paul's behaviour, and he is set before you as in the same circumstance that you are, but "not disputing," [1] as an example of what you should have done, and you are reproached for not obeying with the same speed as he did. But let me tell you, that you are here seemingly reproached with that, which really flatters you, and must in all likelyhood kindle the most dangerous kind of pride in you. For how can you look at St. Paul in that extraordinary time as an example for you, unless you think your self to be what he was at that time, *a chosen vessel* of God ? How much better had it been, when you was wanting to be so highly spiritual, as to have nothing to do with the outward Church and outward sacraments of Christ, had you then heard, as though a voice had said unto you, " Remember the poor Canaanitish woman, she begged only to have her share of the crumbs which fell to the dogs under their master's table. Remember the answer that Christ made to her, ' *O woman, great is thy faith, be it unto thee even as thou wilt.*' "

It is impossible to express the difference and the

sacrifice—of an insistence that "a perfect religious relationship is possible without sacrifice at all." (For the two views see, *e.g.*, Skinner, *Prophecy and Religion* (1922), p. 181.)

[1] These words, which Law quotes from Fanny's *Case* (page 90) are reminiscent of the words of St. Paul, " Whereupon, O King Agrippa, I was not disobedient unto the heavenly vision." (Acts xxvi. 19.)

different effects that must be produced in you, from your
looking at this woman as a president [1] for you to follow,
and from your looking at St. Paul in his extraordinary state
as your predecessor representing what God is doing to
you. By entering into the spirit of the Canaanite, you
will have Christ do to you as He did to her ; [2] but by
putting your self in the state of St. Paul, you will not be,
as he was, a chosen vessel of God, but a vessel chosen by
your self.

Moreover, what is there in your case, even as you
represent it your self, that has any likeness to that of St.
Paul ? The voice he heard was manifest enough by great
circumstances, yet he asked, " Who art thou, Lord ? "
And he was directly answered. He asked also, " Lord,
what wilt thou have me to do ? " And he was answered
in the most plain and particular manner. Did you ask
these questions ? Was you fully and particularly answered
as to both of them ? Did you ask whether the outward
Church and sacraments were to be avoided and renounced
by all the true disciples of Christ ? Was the Quakers
ever expressly mentioned in this whole supposed intercourse
betwixt God and you ? If not, don't you plainly see that
all this is an imaginary conflict about you know not what,
raised up by your self ? Further pray observe, St. Paul,
though he was chosen, called, and separated to be an
Apostle by as divine and miraculous a power as that which
called Lazarus out of the grave, yet after this miraculous
election and declaration of his being God's chosen vessel,
to bear His name before the Gentiles, etc., he was to go to
meet a man that was to lay his hands upon him ; by this
imposition of hands he was to receive his sight, and be
filled with the Holy Ghost. And after he had been thus

---

[1] *i.e.* a precedent.

[2] Compare with these references to the Canaanite Law's *Regeneration*
(Sect. 20) : " True Faith is a coming to Jesus Christ to be saved and
delivered from a sinful nature, as the Canaanitish woman came to Him and
would not be denied."

blessed by the imposition of human hands, the text says,
" he arose and was baptized." [1]

Can you possibly think that the same Spirit calls and
directs you, that called and directed St. Paul ? Can you
suppose that you are going to be of the religion that he was
of ? If he by these ordinances was led into Christianity,
are not you upon the very brinks [sic] of being led out of
it ? Must not you lose as much by renouncing these
outward means, as he gained by using them ? You might
indeed have received great instruction as to your case from
this conversion of St. Paul, but your eye was upon the
wrong part of it, for in his conversion this doctrine is writt
in capital letters visible to every willing eye, viz., that
*the most extraordinary gifts of God to His saints, the most
miraculous calls of the most sanctifyed persons, the highest
graces of persons particularly chosen by God, are not only
consistent with, but obliged* [2] *and directed to the observance of
outward ordinances as means and instruments of obtaining
their proper perfection.* This, I say, is writ in capital letters
in the history of St. Paul's conversion, where, after such a
miraculous and divine election and consecration, he was
directed to receive the imposition of human hands and
baptism. Further, let it be supposed that a voice pretending to be from God had expressly and positively
ordered you to renounce the institutions of Christ. Had
you not the same reasons to reject it, as our blessed Lord
had for rejecting the temptation of the devil in the wilderness ? Are you not as much obliged to abide by the
Scripture as He was ? Must you not, in imitation of
Him, say to such a voice, it is written, " He that beleiveth
and is baptized shall be saved " ? [3] And again, it is
written of the sacrament of the Lord's supper, " Do this
in remembrance of me." [4]

Have you not the authority of the Scripture to reject
an angel from heaven preaching another Gospel to you ? [5]

[1] Acts ix. 17–18.   [2] *i.e.* bound up with.   [3] Mark xvi. 16.
[4] Luke xxii. 19.   [5] Gal. i. 8.

Now the Apostle says that the change of the priesthood implys a change of the law,[1] therefore surely the annulling of the priesthood and sacraments of the Gospel must in a greater degree imply a changing of the Gospel, and therefore a voice requiring to renounce the priesthood and sacraments of the Gospel must be said to preach another Gospel to you.

I will mention but one passage of Scripture more, to confirm the doctrine that I said above was writt in capital letters, viz., " Then cometh Jesus from Galilee to Jordan unto John to be baptized of him.   But John forbad Him, saying, I have need to be baptized of thee, and comest thou to me ?   Jesus said unto him, Suffer it now, for thus it *becometh us to fullfil all righteousness*." [2]

John's baptism was only water baptism to repentance ; Jesus needed no repentance, yet He came to be baptized by John, not to please the Jews, not to avoid giving offense to any, but for this *one reason*, thus it *becometh us to fullfill all righteousness*.   The difference betwixt Jesus and John the Baptist, was the difference betwixt heaven and earth ; " He is from above," saith the Baptist, " I am from beneath." [3]   Yet this person from above, divine and high beyond all expression or comparison with any human creature, came to John, to him that was from beneath, to be baptized of him, for no less reason than this, " thus it becometh us to fullfill all righteousness."   Can darkness be more contrary to light, than the spirit and practice of the Quakers is to the spirit and practice of our blessed Lord ?   I desire you to open but half an eye to see the miserable delusion you have given in to.   The Son of God, your Lord and Saviour, humbly and under a sense of duty, as a thing that became Him, received the sacrament of John the Baptist, you are too high, too sublime, too spiritual to condescend to receive the sacraments of Jesus Christ, they

[1] Heb. vii. 12.
[2] Matt. iii. 13–15.
[3] A paraphrase of John iii. 31.   (Cp. John viii. 23.)

become not that degree of righteousness which you are to fullfill.

Do you think that Jesus Christ knew not what He said and did, when He thus spake and thus called for baptism? Or do you think that He said and did so, because He was in a lower degree of spirituality than you and the Quakers are arrived at? Will you say that He said and did right, that He owed this duty, reverence, and regard to the sacrament of John, but that you are more independent of Him than He was of St. John, or that He wanted that from John's sacrament, which you don't want from His?

John was only " a voice of one crying in the wilderness," yet Christ for the sake of righteousness owned, esteemed, and partook of his baptism.[1] Jesus Christ is the Way, the Truth, and the Life, but His sacraments you disown, disesteem, and renounce for the sake of righteousness. The Scripture says, " He spake the Word and they were made, He commanded and they were created." Now this same Word and command which made the sun to be a light by day and the moon and stars by night, hath instituted and commanded the sacraments to be *spirit* and *life* to all that faithfully, piously, and humbly make use of them.[2] Surely

---

[1] Barclay is able to meet the foregoing argument in the following manner. "Some object that Christ, who had the Spirit above measure, was notwithstanding baptized with water.

"I answer, so was He also circumcised. It will not follow from thence that circumcision is to continue; for it behoved Christ to fulfil all righteousness, not only the ministry of John, but the Law also; therefore did He observe the Jewish feasts and rites, and keep the Passover. It will not thence follow that Christians ought to do so now; and therefore Christ (Matt. iii. 15) gives John this reason of His being baptized, desiring him to *suffer it to be so now*; whereby He sufficiently intimates that He intended not thereby to perpetuate it as an ordinance to His disciples." (*Apology*, Prop. XII, Sect. 8.)

Law does not allude to the baptism of Christ by John in the drafts which deal with the Quaker view of baptism below.

[2] With this passage compare page 6 of Law's *Demonstration* (probably written about the same time), where Law quotes the same verse from the 148th Psalm, and observes : " Now the Word, which thus speaking created

I need say no more to convince you of the danger and
delusions you have been contriving for your self, and to
fill you with a pious, just, and zealous care to avoid and
renounce the conversation and society of those that wish
to have you tyed and bound in this blindness and delusion.

But I must add one word more. Let it be supposed
that you was in a highly spiritual state of divine communications, revelations, etc., born again from above
to a divine life ; that the clergy and outward sacraments
were, like John the Baptist, things from beneath ; let it
be supposed that the clergy, compared with you, were
not worthy to touch your shoes ; suppose this was so
visible, that they themselves should say unto you, " we
have more need to receive spiritual gifts of thee ; and
comest thou to receive sacraments by our hands ? " Yet
even then, according to this extravagant supposition, if
you would have any regard to the example of Christ, if you
would not think His practice too low for your imitation,
you must be obliged to say, " Suffer it now, for thus it
becometh us to fullfill all righteousness."

After this supposed threatning from God and reproach-
ing you with the behaviour of St. Paul, you say, " I could
not make use of the forms of prayer I used to do, by reason
they suited not my condition, and, as medicines wrong
applyed, rather augmented than eased the conflicts my soul
laboured under ; I then truly knew my own weakness,
that of my self I knew not what to pray for, but the Spirit
truly helped my infirmities in sighs and groans unutterable, etc."

I should make no remark upon this passage, there

all things, is not more extraordinary . . . than that Word which in the
institution of the sacrament spake, and it was done ; commanded, and it
was created.   For it is the same omnipotent Word that here speaketh, that
spoke the creation into being. . . . And it is impossible for anyone to show
that there is less of divine power and greatness, less of mystery and miracle
implied in these words spoken by the eternal Word in the institution of the
sacrament, than when the same eternal Word said, ' Let there be light, and
there was light.' "

being nothing of moment in it, were it not that I apprehend you consider it as a direction to change your old religion, from whence you had these helpless forms, and to go over to the Quakers, who make great pretences to this new kind of prayer which you have found in this perplexity. But if you look upon it in this view, you see it no more according to truth, than a man in a jaundice sees things in their proper colours.

The matter admits of this plain and easie solution. I have shewn you before, that you have introduced a strange fire into your soul ; you have so opened your heart for the reception of it, that all your passions have their heat and motion from it, all your instincts of piety and awakenings of conscience are forced into its flame. What wonder is it therefore, if your old forms of prayer, like sober moderate proposals to an impatient passion, seem rather to augment than to ease your pain ?   What wonder is it that it should be so sweet and agreable to you to let your heart speak and work in its own way ?   Is not this the case of every disorder and of every passion of the mind ?   What so agreable to a mind overwhelmed with any passionate distress, as to indulge it self in hearing, feeling, and following all that its passion can inwardly suggest unto it ?[1]   Is not this more liked and relished than either to call to mind the former maxims of reason and prudence that it used to delight in, or to hear other people proposing only lessons of discretion and prudence to it ?   Do not the dictates of sober reason and the wisest maxims of morality, when offered to a person in the anguish of complaint, often seem to be as medicines wrong applyed, and to augment, instead of easing, his distress ?   But when is it that such a person is said to be releived and cured ?   Is it not, when he comes

---

[1] With the above compare *Regeneration*, Sect. 37.   " When religion is in the hands of the mere natural man, he is always the worse for it : it adds a bad heat to his own dark fire, and helps to inflame his four elements of selfishness, envy, pride, and wrath.   And hence it is that worse passions, or a worse degree of them, are to be found in persons of great religious zeal than in others that make no pretences to it."

to acknowledge and submit to the rules and maxims of reason and prudence, and to feel and delight in the goodness, justness, and fitness of them?

Thus much upon a supposition (which I suppose to be a true one), that you consider this change in your devotions as a sign that you are to join yourself to the Quakers. For had you said this of your self upon some other occasion, or had another person said the same things of himself, as you have here done, I might have found reason to have remarked very differently upon it. For there may a time happen to devout souls, merely through the goodness of their devotion, and from the very excellency of those forms that they have used, that a change in them becomes necessary, as having fitted and prepared the soul to enter into a nearer and more intimate kind of application to God, than that which consists in their former prescribed and settled forms. And the devout soul is thankfully to accept this progress in prayer, and carefully to endeavour in all its private prayers to turn all its adoration into spirit and life. It is also exceedingly proper and beneficial in all our private prayers to follow the present state and want of our hearts, and to pray according to them.[1] You must not therefore think that I would censure, undervalue, or endeavour to quench any degrees of inward and spiritual prayer, or turn you to dry forms instead of it. No, had I it in my power, you should have no thought or word or action, either in prayer or out of prayer, but what proceeded from and was directed by the Holy Spirit of God. But

[1] In the *Serious Call* (ch. 14) Law says that, though a form of prayer seems very necessary for public worship, yet praying *without* a form will be usually more helpful in private devotion, unless the heart is in a dull and unawakened state. He shows beautifully how we may suit our prayers to "the present state of our heart." Compare the passages quoted from the *Spirit of Prayer* in Chapter IX (Part II) of this book; and from the same treatise (Part II, p. 126): "But if your heart knows its own plague . . . knows what it wants to have removed, will you not let your distress form the manner of your prayer? or will you pray in a form of words that have no more agreement with your state than if a man walking above ground should beg every man he met to pull him out of a deep pit?"

know this, that when the soul is thus the instrument of the Holy Spirit of God, not only outward forms of prayer, the hymns and psalms of the Church, but all the actions and occurrences of life become harmonious to it, everything that touches this instrument strikes musick out of it. But no more of this.

The next paragraff in your case is the most extraordinary of all, and I hope the re-consideration of it will be of great service to set you right. Here you say Mrs. Drummond happened to come into your neighbourhood, that she preached there in her journey, and that you happened to refuse to go amongst others that went to hear her.[1] But the self-condemnation that followed for this neglect, you say, was "inexpressible." "After this time," say you, "in vain were all the reasons I could urge in my behalf, my own heart condemned me as guilty of a great error, as did God, who is far greater. My concern was so great, it shewed it self in all my actions, in so much that all that saw me enquired what could be the reasons; which I no longer scrupled to discover." Now, Madam, take patiently, consider seriously, and strive not to disbelieve that which I shall here say to you. All the disorder, that you here mention, is justly to be looked upon as meer nature, the meer workings of human, young, unexperienced, and disturbed passions. I know that there are at the bottom of all this certain kindlings of piety, goodness, and an awakened conscience, but the gross violent workings here mentioned are the workings of meer nature.[2] To see this

---

[1] For an account of Mrs. Drummond see the Note appended to this Chapter.

[2] With this ruthless analysis of Fanny's spiritual leadings we may compare Law's similar verdict on the experience of one of the early Methodist converts (who had had considerable share in Charles Wesley's own discovery of Christ). Charles Wesley tells us how on August 10, 1739, he took his pious friend, John Bray, the poor brazier, to see Mr. Law at Putney, " who resolved all his feelings into fits or natural affections, and advised him to take no notice of his comforts, which he had better be without than with."

It is worth remarking (in view of Law's strictures upon the preaching

in the plainest manner, take only this short review of what you have said of your self.

When God Him self, as you suppose, charged you to renounce the vanities and foolish amusements of the world, you was not disordered with any sense of guilt for having lived in them. When God also convinced you of your wanting a new birth, you knew how to bear the want of it, it threw you into no greif, but such as you could manage and govern. But when a woman-preacher, forbidden by the Apostle to preach, came into your neighbourhood,[1] the guilt of this great sin did that to you, which never had been done before ; your pain, remorse, and self-condemnation became impossible to be expressed, excused, or concealed, and so all burst out. Can there be plainer marks of meer nature and human passions ?

If you should see a person, that had been admonished by God of his neglect of certain weighty matters of the law and of his want of some virtues essential to piety, quiet and tolerable to himself under this reproof ; but some time after half distracted at the horrour of his sinfull condition, for having neglected to wash the outside of a cup and platter, would you not easily know that human nature, sickly passions, and a disordered imagination had kindled that fire within him ? Now it is impossible for you to shew, that you committed a greater sin in not going to hear Mrs. D. [Drummond] than in neglecting to wash the outside of a cup and platter. It is also impossible for

of women) that on the same occasion Law blamed Whitefield's way of preaching, and " was fully against the laymen's expounding, as the very worst thing both for themselves and others." (Charles Wesley's Journal, quoted in Jackson's *Life*.)

It is necessary to remember that by " mere nature " Law meant something much more worthless than most of us would mean to-day by such an expression. It was fundamental to the theology of both Law and the Quakers that human nature had become hopelessly corrupt and devoid of God. I find in an unpublished fragment of Law's that "no religion can be true and good that is merely natural ", and again that " mere nature in the creature is mere want ".

[1] Sc. " and you did not go to hear her ".

you to shew, that there could be any more goodness in going to hear her, than there is of goodness in having those " itching ears " condemned by the Apostle.[1] The Apostle absolutely prohibits women to preach in the Church,[2] yet you feel the horror and amazement of a dreadfull guilt for not having gone to hear a woman preach. Is this a sign that the same spirit awakens your conscience, that directed the Apostle's doctrine ?

You want to know whence your pain and distress has arisen. I have said enough already to shew you the cause and the cure of it. When your greif was at its greatest height, you have known and confessed the cause of it, that it arose to that height because of your not going to Mrs. D. [Drummond]. Here, I say, the cause is owned and confessed, which is more than you was aware of. Now the cause, which produced this height of pain in you at this time, was no new thing in you, it had been in you from the beginning of your disorder, and was only now worked up to this height, because it had been working so long in you before. This I told you in my first,[3] that God had begun a good work in your soul, but that, by your endeavouring to turn it to the sectarian spirit of the Quakers, all this tumult was raised in your soul, and the passions of your body drawn in to have a share of it. And you see to what extravagance this spirit has proceeded. At first it only told you of submitting to the voice of God Himself, and reproached you with not doing as St. Paul did, but now, after a longer possession of you, it ventures to tell you anything and charges you with the greatest of sins, for not having gone to hear a woman preach ; and you stand trembling under the terror of such an accusation.

As you have asked my opinion and advice concerning your state and circumstances, so you ought not to be displeased at the plainness of my expressions, or that I speak things that may seem to reproach you. For if you are in

---

[1] 2 Tim. iv. 3.   [2] See note on page 71 below.
[3] See page 33.

any mistake, how can I any other way assist you, or what fuller proof can you have of my sincerest charity for you, than by setting [all] nakedly before you? I have not the smallest spark of enmity towards the persons of any one sect in the world, and would and do as willingly and gladly commend whatever is commendable in them, as in the Church it self. I am in full charity with the Jews, every blessing that my heart can think of I wish unto them, and would no more exercise any acts of enmity towards them, than I would towards an Apostle. But if your inclination and supposed call was towards them, and I should shew you the danger and delusion of joyning your self to such a miserably deceived people, you would perhaps think that my heart was too hardened towards them and that I spoke too much against them.

Your faithfull friend,

W. L.

LETTER 6

Note.—This document stands on a different footing from the rest. It is in William Law's handwriting, covering exactly six large sheets and breaking off in the middle of a sentence. Its form shows that it is either a preliminary draft for a subsequent letter or a copy of the letter actually sent.

On page 130 of this book will be found a letter which Law wrote to Byrom on December 17, 1736, after hearing of a certain decisive step taken by his impetuous correspondent. In this communication he refers to a fifth letter meant for Miss Fanny, and he continues, " When yours came, I had almost finished another long letter, which I intended should be the last, unless fresh matter appeared ; at the receipt of yours I took off my pen. . . ."

It is, in my judgment, practically certain that we have here the draft on which Law was then engaged (and not, as Walton thought, part of Law's missing third letter).

The different paper on which it is written, the frequent cases of omitted or superfluous words in the manuscript, the unfinished endings of one or two of the paragraphs, all suggest that it is a preliminary draft. We know, from other papers in Dr. Williams' Library, that Law was in the habit of re-writing his manuscripts, rather than correcting them.

Again, though there is no absolutely decisive evidence whether this letter was intended to be read before or after Letter 5, the contents suggest that it comes after the other letters. In the other letters Law makes systematic references to and quotations from Fanny's *Case*. By the time he wrote this letter, he seems to have finished dealing directly with the *Case*, and alters his manner of argument considerably. (He refers specifically to a passage in his first Letter, just as he had done in Letter 5.)

Moreover, the fact of our having this letter alone in draft is well accounted for, if we suppose that it is the last letter, which he never copied out or sent. It is even possible that the concluding words " the Quakers glory " (which end the page in the original manuscript) represent the exact point where he " took off his pen ", though it is more likely that there is a final sheet missing. In any case it is somewhat trying that the letter should break off in the middle of an interesting discussion on the lawfulness of women-preachers !

Madam,

Consider seriously what it is that you propose to your self, and what it is I propose to you ; and then you may best judge how you ought to receive my advice.

Do you desire to take up your cross and follow Christ in the most perfect manner you are able ? I exhort to it with all my heart. Do you desire to dye to your self and all the workings of your corrupt nature, that you may be born again in the spirit of Jesus Christ, I hold this so desireable, that I say, that it is better not to be born at all than not to be born again.

Do you desire to renounce the world and all its worldly tempers, and to live in it as a pilgrim, a stranger to all its cares and pleasures, having all your conversation in heaven, I should be glad to say or do anything that [may] help to render this desire effectual in you. Do you desire to have all that poverty of spirit, humility of heart, strength of faith, pure and unmixt love of God, which ever any devout soul attained to, I wish you all the zeal in the world after these virtues, and that every day of your life may be a day of growth and progress in them.

Do you desire to renounce everything that divides or diverts your heart from God, every thing that cools the ardour of your soul towards Him, everything that takes the eye of your mind from Him, everything that hinders you from hearing what God inwardly speaks to the humble attentive soul, no one can recommend this with more earnestness to you than I would. Do you desire to mortify every sense of your body and every passion of your mind, to resist and kill every motion of self-love and self-seeking, and to suffer no love or affection to have any place in you, but so far as it is a true branch of the pure love of God, I pray God help you to this perfection. Do you desire to avoid even the smallest appearance of sin, to live in a continual watchfullness over every inward thought and outward word and action, to do everything as in the presence of God, and purely from a sense of piety and duty to Him, as His servant and looking only to His will in all, even the smallest actions of life, I would do all that I could to keep alive this desire in you.

Do you desire to practise every virtue according to its greatest purity, to give all you have for the purchase of it, to resist and renounce every thought, care, and inclination, that seeks for any worldly profitt or pleasure? Do you desire to avoid and renounce the ordinary allowed imployments of life,[1] the unnecessary use of any bodily ease, worldly convenience, or satisfaction, that you may be a better, fuller sacrifice to God, you have my good wishes in all this.

Do you desire and resolve to look upon all your temporal goods as the sacred things of God, to take only your necessary share of them with fear and reverence of Him, whose they are, and to consider your self only as one amongst other poor people, that are to have a necessary subsistence out of them?[2] Do you desire and resolve to renounce and

---

[1] He probably means "diversions", most of which, if not actually harmful, he would regard as "impertinent".

[2] In the picture Law drew in his *Serious Call* of *Miranda*, the ideal maiden lady, we read, "This is the spirit of Miranda, and thus she uses

avoid all world[ly] honour, respect, esteem, and distinction, to take the lowest plaice everywhere and in every thing, to beleive your self to be the poorest and meanest of the servants of God, the greatest of sinners, unworthy of every thing you enjoy, justly deserving to be trod under the feet of all your fellow creatures,[1] to prefer everyone to your self, to esteem everyone as your superiour, and to practise every kind and degree of humility, submission, obedience, and servitude to every person that you are any way concerned with, thankfull to God for everything that humbles you in your own eyes, and in the eyes [of others ?], you have my prayer that these desires and resolutions may proceed from the bottom of your heart and bring forth fruits suitable to them.

Do you desire that everyone would drop all human respect towards you, forget that you are anything or have anything or deserve anything or have a right to anything but that which cannot be refused to the lowest and meanest of human creatures ? Do you desire that no one may acknowledge or commend any virtues in you, but that all the falseness of your virtues, the imperfection of your graces, the deceitfullness of your heart, the disorder of your passions and most secret inward failings, may be discovered, censured, and condemned ? . . .

Do you desire and resolve to have the coarsest, cheapest, meanest cloaths to cover your body, the coarsest, cheapest food for your diet,[2] the coarsest, cheapest bed, lodging, or

the gifts of God : she is only one of a certain number of poor people that are relieved out of her fortune, and she only differs from them in the blessedness of giving."

[1] Law argues powerfully in the *Serious Call* (ch. 23) that each person who examines his own heart " may justly look upon himself to be the greatest sinner that he knows ", inasmuch as, in the case of any other great sinner, " you can never know that he has resisted so much divine grace as you have, or that in all your circumstances he would not have been much truer to his duty than you are ".

[2] Miranda's one rule in dress was " to be always clean and in the cheapest things " ; and she takes just so much food " as gives a proper strength to her body and renders it able and willing to obey the soul ". (*Serious Call*, ch. 8.)

house to live [in], chusing rather to serve than to be served, I could readily grant these desires and resolutions to proceed from a truly regenerate spirit. Do you hate all manner of shew and superfluity and love all manner of poverty, plainness, and simplicity of life, manners, and conversation, I would willingly promote this spirit in you.

Do you know that there is a spiritual pride, a religious self-love, a desire of spiritual significancy, singularity, and distinction more dangerous to the soul than any outward claims to respect and distinction, do you watch more against all that may raise, nourish, and support this turn of the soul, than that which may betray you into any outward pride, do you know that this pride is rather diabolical than human, does a deeper mischief than that of patches and paint,[1] I would do all I could to strengthen this right judgement in you. Do you desire and resolve to treat your self as your greatest enemy, to look upon your heart as your most deceitfull companion, your passions as your most dangerous counsellors, your own flesh and blood as your continual snare and temptation, to reject everything that flatters and elevates you and receive everything that humbles you, I should readily own that you stood[2] . . .

Do you desire and resolve to be as humble, innocent, obedient, simple, and unpresuming in the Church as in the State, to meddle no more with the defects in the one than in the other, to stand quietly in your lot in the one as in the other, to leave the order [and] government of both to God, equally the founder, supporter, and gouvernour of both, looking upon [it] as a greater sin against the God of order to destroy distinctions, despise authority, neglect

[1] Law often refers with reproof to the eighteenth-century fashion of "patched faces". Compare Lady Mary Wortley Montagu, writing in 1715, "Hours . . . passed in deep debate, how curls should fall or where a patch to place."

[2] The unfinished sentence is one of the indications that this document is a draft made before the actual letter was written. The whole letter up to this point, both in manner and in matter, follows closely the style of the Christian Perfection and the Serious Call. The next five paragraphs, however, are skilfully framed with special reference to Fanny's Quaker leanings.

E

commissions, usurp offices in the Church, than to destroy distinctions, despise authourity, neglect commissions, and usurp offices in the State, I dare confidently affirm that such a desire and resolution neither proceeds from, nor can ever lead you into any error.

Do you desire and resolve not to put your trust in any of your outward works, not to rest in the outward profession of Christianity, trusting in forms of godliness, depending upon the privileges and benefits of Church communion and outward ordinances of religious worship, there is nothing that I would than [*sic*]. . . .

Do you desire to live in the world with your heart and spirit out of it as much as possible, as a person devoted to prayer, to the love and contemplation of God ?   Do you desire and resolve to seek God inwardly by prayer and purity of heart, making room for the manifestation of His holy presence in your soul, that so you may enter within the veil and see and know and feel and experience all that is inward, spiritual, and divine [in] the work of our salvation ? There is nothing that I would have you, etc.

Do you desire and resolve to watch over and be tender of those instincts of piety and kindlings of an awakened conscience, which God has stirred up within you ; to lend an attentive ear to what the inward monitor [1] continually and faithfully admonishes ?   There is nothing that I would recommend to you with more earnestness than this.   For the Light within you is the most precious thing in the world, it is the pledge of our redemption, the possibility of our salvation, it is the pearl of the Gospel, the Kingdom of God hidden in the soul, and it must be all your care and endeavour to remove everything away that hinders its rising up within you.[2]

Do you desire and resolve to commit your self to the guidance and direction of the Holy Spirit, to beleive in and

[1] Fanny uses this expression at least once in her autobiography.

[2] Compare with this the passage about the " pearl of eternity " (from the *Spirit of Prayer*) which I have quoted on page 296.

hope for His continual influence and inspiration, to give light to your mind, purity to your heart, and to be the sanctifying principle of all your thoughts and inclinations, words, and actions? All this is of the essence of the Gospel, for the inspiration of the Holy Spirit is as necessary to the life, is as necessary to the birth and preservation of the new man in Christ Jesus, as the outward air is necessary to the outward birth and preservation of the outward [man] of flesh and blood.[1]

You may here see by my mentioning all these desires and resolutions and declaring my fullest approbation of [them], that I wish well to your perfection, that I have no desire to quench the Spirit of God in you, or to lead you to a religion of outward forms and dead practices. I have no desire but to add wings to your devotion, and quicken everything in [you] that tends to God. If you have these desires and resolutions in any degree of reality, I may confidently affirm it to be impossible for you to turn Quaker, the bare proposal of such a thing to you, must appear to you to be more absurd than anything [that] can be well imagined.

It was with this view that I said in my first letter, that I foresaw the way in which God would help you to peace and quiet [in] all the difficulties that are struggling in your soul. For I imagined upon good grounds, that if you was really in earnest and [if] this disturbance was really the disturbance of a pious soul, only wanting such helps as it

---

[1] This comparison is probably not a mere figure, but part of Law's nature mysticism (which he was just learning from Boehme), according to which every material thing is a representation of some spiritual reality. Thus he often emphasizes in his later works the correspondence of material light and air to the Son and the Spirit respectively in the Holy Trinity.

Compare *Address to the Clergy*, p. 8 : " Now as no animal could begin to respire or unite with the breath of this world, but because it has its beginning to breathe begotten in it from the air of this world, so it is equally certain that no creature, angel or man, could begin to be religious or breathe forth the divine affections of faith, love, and desire towards God, but because a living seed of these divine affections was by the Spirit of God first begotten in it."

thought it had not in the state it was in and which were in all probability to be found in this supposed change, that then a plain demonstration, that the Church you was in proposed, allowed, and encouraged everything that any pious soul could want or wish, must necessarily set you at ease. And on the other hand [if you received] a plain demonstration that the change you had thought of making cannot be done without renouncing not only the plain letter but the whole current of Scripture, the practice and sentiments of the saints of all ages, there could be no room left for any further doubt ; since everything, that could affect a pious, tender mind, might be said to engage your continuance and everything, that could convince any one sober person of sin, might be said to deter you from uniting with the Quakers.

I say not only the plain letter of a few texts, but the whole current of Scripture is directly opposed and set at nought by the fundamental ground on which this sect is built. For besides the plain texts of Scripture instituting and commanding the holy sacraments, there is scarce a chapter to read in it [without] something that either directly teaches, supposes or depends upon this truth, viz., that there is an outward Church, with outward authourity and outward ministers of different powers and outward offices, neither to be confounded, neglected, nor usurped, but all of them, Church, ministers, and offices modelled, formed, and governed by stated rules derived from the authourity of that God who is a God of order.

Now take all these places out of Scripture that either directly teach, suppose, or depend upon these things, concerning an outward Church, ministers, offices, and what relates to them, and you leave it scarce intelligible ; for these things are so intermixed with every part of Scripture and enter so much into almost everything that is related, that almost every part would be destroyed, if such passages were to be blotted out and declared to be no longer of force either for doctrine or instruction. And therefore it is, that

I say this sect is fundamentally built and stands upon a ground inconsistent with the whole current of Scripture, because all those parts of Scripture that directly teach, suppose, or depend upon anything that relates to an outward Church, offices, rules, ministers, etc., as well as those texts that relate to the sacraments, must be all taken out of Scripture, before the ground on which this sect stands can be said to be according to Scripture. For all that is descended to us from the Apostles to this time, that relates either to Church, ministers, sacraments, offices, rules of government, obedience, etc., are by this sect wholly rejected, though they keep the Scriptures that authourise, teach, and contain all this, just as the Jews retain the Old Testament that describes and points out and proves that Messiah which they will [not] acknowledge.[1]

You may perhaps, when you was looking towards a change, have imagined that, [by] your proffessing (as you call it) the faith and doctrine of the Quakers, you was only going to a people that seemed more zealous in asserting the Light within and the assistance of the Holy Spirit and also the spirituality of religion it self, than the Church of which you are a member.[2] But let me observe to you, that this is nothing of the matter, the merits of the cause does not [at ?] all lye here. If you would have the doctrine and faith of the Quakers as they are a sect seperated from the Church, you must renounce all the authourity of our blessed Lord, so far as He has instituted sacraments, erected an

[1] This is the fourth or fifth passage in these letters where Jews and Quakers are compared. The comparison seems to be made on theological grounds only, not (as in the case of a similar comparison by the malicious Cobbett in his *Rural Rides*) on the grounds of their love of acquiring wealth. Compare the reference to a similar juxtaposition in Law's first book (page 236 below).

[2] Compare the passage in Law's *Address to the Clergy* (pp. 27–8), where Law defends himself against the charge of preaching Quakerism, by pointing out to the clergy, how " collect after collect in the Established Liturgy [*i.e.* the Book of Common Prayer] teaches and requires them to believe and pray for the continual inspiration of the Spirit ". In the *Spirit of Love* (Part II, p. 47) he quotes from some of these collects.

outward Church, appointed ministers, offices, and promised
to be with them to the end of the world.   You must reject
the faith and doctrine and practice of all the Apostles, so
far as they have owned an outward Church, ordained
distinct ministers in it, practised outward ordinances,
taught doctrines concerning them, observed sacraments,
enjoyned the observance of them, gone from place to place
teaching and baptizing, declaring the duties of governours
and the duties of the governed, asserting superiority and
inferiority in the Church, etc.   All this and all the Scriptures which contain any thing relating to these things must
all be disowned and rejected, before you can profess that
faith and doctrine which distinguishes the sect of Quakers
from the Church.[1]

A bold step surely for a person whose conscience is
awakened !   You had need have much more courage than
I have for such an undertaking as this.   For my part, I
can't see why you should fear anything, if you are not afraid
of renouncing so much as is here mentioned.

In the Apostles' days spiritual gifts, prophesys, revelations, miracles were very common ;   yet in these very
extraordinary times it was, that ordinary stated ministers
and offices in the Church were appointed and settled.   All
outward means was then most strictly observed, most
regularly performed, and the rules and directions and
doctrines relating to the observance and continuance of
them most particularly given, when the Church seemed to
be all spirit and life and abounding with all sorts of extraordinary gifts.   What a contradiction is this to the spirit
of the Quakers, who, upon pretence of certain secret
workings and gifts of the spirit within them (known only
to themselves), reject the sacraments, ordinances, offices,
ministrys of the Church, which were instituted, appointed,

---

[1] It is perhaps as well to remark here, that the Society of Friends in
the eighteenth century recognized *ministers*, *elders*, and *overseers* as holding
important offices in the Church, and that they would have claimed that
such were more directly ordained by the Holy Spirit to these positions than
any Anglican clergyman or Roman priest.

and observed, when all the extraordinary gifts of the Holy Ghost were visibly common in the whole Church !

The Apostles in those days of miracle and extraordinary gifts were strict and regular in the observance of outward ordinances and the distinction of Church offices and officers, but [and ?] they ordained others to do as they had done. The Epistles to Timothy and Titus are full of instructions relating to this matter ; they are charged to " ordain elder[s] in every city ";[1] and to " lay hands suddenly on no man." [2] But if the doctrine of the Quakers had been then known, how could there have been any discourse about ordination, or why need anyone have staid till human hands were laid upon him ?

In the days of the Apostles the liberty of prophesying [3] was at its greatest height, because the Holy Spirit was then in an extraordinary manner poured forth both upon men and women, so that in their Church assemblys a liberty of speaking in unknown tongues by interpreters and of prophesying one after another, as anything was revealed unto them, was under certain rules and orders then allowed ; yet in this very time (which is well to be marked) the Holy Spirit of God excludes women expressly from having any share in this liberty of speaking in their assemblys. " Let your women keep silence in the churches ; for it is not permitted unto them to speak, but they are commanded to be under obedience, as also saith the law . . . for it is a shame for women to speak in the church." [4] And again (1 Tim. ii.) " Let the woman learn in silence with all subjection. For I suffer not a woman to teach, nor to usurp authourity over the man, *but to be in silence*," etc.[5] Here

---

[1] Titus i. 5.   [2] 1 Tim. v. 22.

[3] This is the title of Jeremy Taylor's famous book of 1646, with the main conclusions of which Law would no doubt agree, though he would much dislike its constant allusions to pagan writers.

[4] 1 Cor. xiv. 34–5.

[5] Barclay refers to the two passages here quoted, asserting (and this was the usual Quaker explanation) that Paul meant only to "reprove the inconsiderate and talkative women among the Corinthians," and that other

you see in the time of this greatest liberty of speaking in the publick assemblys, the Holy Spirit in the greatest solemnity of words excludes women from it, as a thing unlawfull, shamefull, and against the very order of nature.[1] When therefore the Quakers glory . . .

passages (*e.g.* Acts ii. 17 and xxi. 9, and 1 Cor. xi. 5) make it quite clear that women preached and prophesied in the Church in New Testament times. But the real consideration on which the Quaker view in this matter was based is that given by Barclay in the following words : " And lastly, it hath been observed that God hath effectually in this day converted many souls by the ministry of women ; and by them also frequently comforted the souls of His children ;—which manifest experience puts the thing beyond all controversy." (*Apology*, Prop. X, Sect. 27.)

Similarly George Fox, after quoting Scripture passages to justify women's religious meetings, concludes thus : " And if there was no Scripture for our men and women's meetings, Christ is sufficient, who restores man and woman up into the image of God, to be helps meet in the righteousness and holiness as they were in before they fell : so He is our rock and foundation to build upon." (*Epistles*, p. 388, quoted from a long letter entitled *An Encouragement to all the Faithful Women's Meetings in the World, who assemble together in the Fear of God*.)

[1] Compare with Law's argument here a strikingly similar twentieth-century pronouncement on this subject. " We record the fact that the restrictions of the ministry of the priesthood to men originated in a generation which was guided by the special gifts of the Holy Spirit." (Archbishop of Canterbury's Committee's Report on *The Ministry of Women*, 1919, quoted by A. Maude Royden in *The Church and Women*.)

M.ʳˢ MAY DRUMMOND.

MAY DRUMMOND IN MIDDLE LIFE

NOTE ON MRS. MAY DRUMMOND

Mrs. (*i.e.* Miss) May Drummond was a very remarkable woman. She was born about 1710 of a " good " Scotch Presbyterian family, her brother being Provost of Edinburgh in 1731. In that year she was convinced of Friends' principles through the preaching of one of the greatest and most cultured of Quaker evangelists, Thomas Story. She began to preach almost at once among the Scottish Quakers, and in 1735 crossed the border and held great public meetings in the West and South of England. The next year she repeated the tour with still greater effect. A contemporary newspaper records that " Mrs. Drummond, the famous Quaker preacher, came to town on Thursday night, having been the admiration of the countries, where she made her progress ". (It was probably in the course of this journey that she spoke at Manchester and came within reach of Fanny Henshaw. A copy of a letter, which she wrote to Fanny about this time—it was dated 1736— was in existence a few years ago, but is now unfortunately untraceable.) Her social position and the report of an interview which she had had with the Queen, excited special interest in her, and she apparently possessed both an eloquent speech and an attractive presence of a kind that was rare in Quaker woman preachers. At this period (*i.e.* until women began to preach among the Methodists) public speaking by women was, as far as I can discover, unknown except among the Quakers.

We are told that " many thousands flocked to hear her ", and that " more of the gentry and nobility than ever was known before " attended Quaker meetings.[1] Doubtless many of the same persons came to her who three or four

[1] *E.g.* when she preached at Chester with Thomas Story and Fanny Henshaw's friend, Joshua Toft. (*Thos. Story's Journal*, folio edition, pp. 714, 719–20.)

years later were crowding to hear the more soul-stirring open-air preaching of George Whitefield or John Wesley. An acute Quaker critic, who had taken pains to see a good deal of May Drummond in Devon and Cornwall in 1744, when she was still drawing crowds (and especially the " young folks "), speaks highly of her private character, and for her preaching his only criticisms are that " her style is rather too learned " and that she became at times slightly theatrical. He adds (and this is significant of the " quietist " spirit of the day), " she makes inward silence and attention of absolute necessity . . . she dares determine nothing about the disposing of herself (in her journey, for instance) without this internal influence ".[1]

In later years she confined her ministry more to regular Friends' gatherings. By 1765 she had developed certain failings that caused Edinburgh Friends to cease to recognize her as a Minister. She died about 1772 at Edinburgh, still faithful to Quaker principles, though fallen into some disesteem.[2]

The preaching of May Drummond may surely be accounted a landmark in the Women's movement. So it was at the time by at any rate one enthusiastic feminist, who wrote in praise of her in the chief literary magazine of the day,[3]

" No more, O Spain, thy Saint Teresa boast—
There's one outshines her on the British coast ",

and much more in the same strain. Before the nineteenth century I doubt whether a woman speaker ever swayed audiences of the size she is said to have held. We may well believe that some at least of her many hearers became better men and women and less nominal Christians through

---

[1] *Memoir of William Cookworthy*, pp. 10–16.

[2] The above account is chiefly based on two articles by W. F. Miller in the *Friends' Historical Society Journal* for 1907. Numerous other references to May Drummond are scattered about the volumes of the same Journal.

[3] *Gentleman's Magazine* for the year 1735, p. 555.

her preaching, even if conversions in the usual sense of the word did not result.   As far as I have been able to discover, she seems to have been entirely neglected by the historians.

In a curious apocalyptic book, *The Great Crisis*, published by Richard Roach in 1725, there is a passage in which the author emphasizes the age as one in which women are beginning to draw men up to heaven ; and instances the influence and writings of Antoinette Bourignon, Madame Guion, and Mrs. Jane Lead (of the " Philadelphian Society") together with " the appearance of the she-preachers among the Quakers ".

CHAPTER II

FANNY HENSHAW ON HER DEFENCE

THE reader of the preceding letters will perhaps have occasionally winced, as I did, at the ruthless manner in which the confessions of the erring damsel, to whom the letters are addressed, are dissected by her formidable spiritual adviser and antagonist. It is therefore only fair that we should now make ourselves as fully acquainted as possible with Fanny Henshaw's side of the argument, if only to judge how equitably Law has treated it. In this section I am accordingly reproducing an autobiographical statement, which Fanny has left on record. It appears to date, in its present shape, from about the year 1754, when the writer had already become a mother and a widow. As printed in its pamphlet form,[1] it is preceded by a preface,

---

[1] The pamphlet has a curious history. Fanny Henshaw (then Frances Dodshon) died in August, 1793, at Macclesfield. Before the close of that year her tract of 1744, *A Serious Call, etc.* (see page 171 below), was reprinted in that town by the agency of her son William Paxton, her sole executor. In a prefatory note, dated September, 1793, he stated that he " thinks it his incumbent duty to mankind, as well as the Author's desire, for most of her manuscripts, etc., to appear in print; which, when copied in order to meet the approbation of the Society [of Friends], are intended for the press as soon as they can be got ready."

Now it was for a very long time (actually from 1673 to 1860) the rule in the Society that all Friends, or at any rate all Ministers, wishing to publish anything of a religious nature should submit them for examination to the " Second Day Morning Meeting of Ministers and Elders " in London, who in this way exercised a very real censorship over such productions. The *Narrative of Frances Dodshon's Convincement* was duly submitted to this body in 1794, was set up in type, and then at its proof stage was, so it is said, " suppressed for some discoveries of a certain kind of spiritual pride ", which had been made by the two Friends appointed as correctors of the press. (This statement emanates from William Phillips, the son of one of these correctors.) How far this statement is justified by the contents of the *Narrative*, I must leave the reader to judge. The son of the writer seems at the time to have accepted this decision, but notwithstanding

" To the Reader ". Herein, after some general exhortations as to the need of more messengers to proclaim the
truths of the Christian life, the writer states that, though
she would rather choose to " bury in oblivion " her past
history, she is publishing it for the instruction and encouragement of her fellow-creatures "in the course of their
Christian warfare against the powers of darkness and delusion ", and in token of praise and thanksgiving to God.

It is important to remember that all that Law had
before him, when he wrote his letters, was the so-called
Case (without the " additions " [1]) to be found above Fanny's
signature on pages 87 to 91 below, together with some
more or less biassed and scrappy account of her situation
and past behaviour, with which Byrom had probably fur-
nished him.   If Law had been able to read the full narrative
here printed, he might perhaps have been less severe in
some of his strictures.   Indeed, he may be considered as
open to blame for venturing to deal so intimately and exact-
ingly with a tender spirit, whose case was of so complex a
nature, without having any personal knowledge of her.
If as regards his published works he could truthfully claim
that " I never wrote upon any subject till I could call it my
own ", [2] it is to be feared that he sinned against this principle
in this series of letters.

Compared with Law's terse and pointed arguments,
Fanny Henshaw makes but a poor show.   She was evidently

in 1803 he or some other person caused the document to be reprinted and
published at Warrington (not far from Macclesfield).   Evidently some
Friends were impressed by it, for in the same year it was reprinted again in
a slightly different form, and in the next year a third edition was published.

In reproducing the *Narrative* I have as a rule followed the 1794 edition,
except in Fanny Henshaw's so-called *Case* (pp. 87–93), where her own
manuscript copy is available.   The 1803 and 1804 editions have been
edited slightly, but except in the case of one short passage (which I have
annotated) the variations are not important : and no attempt has been made
by the later editors to eliminate or alter those passages which might be
conceivably suspected of implying "spiritual pride" in the writer.

[1] See Byrom's letter of December 21, 1736, to Law.
[2] *Answer to Dr. Trapp* (1740), p. 204.

a great student of the Bible, and many readers of the following account of her spiritual experiences will probably feel that it loses some freshness and power, through being expressed for the most part in language that is strongly reminiscent of Scripture, if not direct quotation from it. This was the pious custom of the day among simple folk, and the Scriptures were the mould which conditioned their spiritual life.   And it seems to me impossible to doubt the profound reality of the crucifying experiences through which the writer of this narrative passed.   To Fanny, as to William Law, her own soul was felt as the scene of a tremendous battle between the forces of good and evil— between God and Satan, compared to which all the ordinary events of social life sank into insignificance.   And concurrently with this conflict, there was present in her an overpowering, though largely subconscious, craving for religious fellowship, such as might give her freedom to express her inmost thoughts, in a way that seemed impossible under the forms of the Church of her upbringing.   These two features redeem from dullness, as it seems to me, the following narrative, imparting to it a quality of spontaneity and intensity, which every now and then breaks through the somewhat conventional language in which it is expressed. Let Fanny now tell her own story.

Narrative of the Convincement and Religious Experience of Frances Paxton [*i.e.* Fanny Henshaw]

As there is a possibility that this may fall into the hands of some who may be altogether strangers to my manner of life, it appears to me expedient, by way of introduction, to give some account of it, as briefly as I can.

I was born in Staffordshire, at Cawdenhall [1] near Leek in the Moorlands, in the year 1714 ; but Providence seeing meet to take away my mother about two years after, my father, being left with a daughter about four years old and myself, left Cawden and resided at Leek during his life, which was about three years after the decease of my dear mother ; but Providence was pleased to favour my sister and me very highly, in directing my father to choose for our guardian one whose care, fidelity, and tenderness was so great, that it supplied in all respects the loss we should otherwise have sustained, in being so early deprived of our parents. [2]

Our trusty guardian was brother-in-law [3] to my father, through a marriage between his father and my father's mother, but by his affectionate conduct to my father and to us, ever since we came under his care, he might be

---

[1] Probably a variant for Cauldon Hall. Cauldon or Caldon lies eight miles S.E. of Leek. Mary Howitt (see my note to page 162 below) described it about a century later as "the slumberous village of Caldon, lying under Caldon Low, the highest point of round green hills" ; she wrote a delightful poem, *The Fairies of Caldon Low*, which has recently been reprinted in *After Tea : a Nursery Anthology* (Ernest Benn's Sixpenny Series).

[2] We are informed (in the "testimony" issued after her death in 1793) that Fanny's parents "possessed a considerable estate and were respectable members of what is called the Church of England". The Henshaws are stated to have been "Nonjurors" like William Law.

[3] *i.e.* half-brother. The guardian was Thomas Sutton.

esteemed a much nearer relation ; his concern for our future happiness was demonstrated in placing us with such persons as might be confided in and also be instrumental to implant in our tender age a love of virtue and abhorrence of vice. The education he gave us was liberal, being equal with that of many of much greater affluence, though, through the goodness of Providence (and my uncle's care), we had more than sufficient, and rather abounded than suffered want. We were instructed in reading, writing, working, and other things—as music and dancing—which by some were thought expedient for our sex and fortune and which I had naturally [1] a great life in, and which in my more mature age cost me much sorrow to lay aside ; together with other follies of the like tendency, viz. singing, playing at cards, etc., which in the course of this little history I may further treat on.

At our removal from boarding-school, after being there instructed as above, we came into Cheshire, where we boarded with an acquaintance of my uncle's, a person of great understanding and prudence, who had married an acquaintance of ours : and for upwards of six years we lived together, I think it may truly be said, in as great harmony and friendship, as if our happiness depended on each other's welfare ; being all of us esteemed sober and religious, more than some of our acquaintance of the same profession, viz. the Church of England ; being diligent not only in frequenting the public worship, but in private prayer in the family, and after that apart in our closets, where (more than in public) I was often favoured with the warming beams of divine love, which being sweetly infused and shed abroad in my heart, animated me with a secret love for retirement, feeling the serenity and calmness it brought me into. In which situation great was the con-descension of Divine Goodness to me ; He being nearer to me than I was aware, to strengthen and encourage every good resolution in me, and also to judge and suppress every

[1] *i.e.* in my unregenerate nature.

thing that tended to my hurt, giving me distinctly to discern between the one and the other ; and like a tender father, speaking peace to me when I chose the good, and following me with the reproofs of instruction, when I joined with any presentation, that engrossed too much of my time and was in danger of being a competitor with Him in my affection. For I oft found a struggle in my breast betwixt religious inclinations and a too great propensity to such earthly pleasures, as are esteemed innocent by many, but ceased (after conviction) to be so to me. And as I duly regarded my inward Monitor, I found with the Apostle the friendship of the world to be in its nature enmity with God ; but I yet knew not how I should be enabled to renounce it, or be redeemed out of it, often lamenting that my affection should be divided, or drawn too much from the Creator into the creatures, and wishing I had been a companion with the Apostles and primitive Christians, who followed Christ in a holy self-denying life and con-versation ; and [I] longed to know, if there were in this present age any that were like-minded.

And in these serious reflections I was led to consider the profession and conduct of mankind in general, and compare it with the practice of the primitive believers, and often in secret bemoaned the great disparity and declension in life and conversation, which I evidently saw in our conduct when compared with theirs ; and sometimes the people called Quakers were brought into my remembrance, as a plain, simple, honest-hearted people, that were separated from the follies and friendship of the present world, demon-strating both in their apparel, conduct, and language, as also by their loving one another, that Christ was their Lord ; and that in the main their actions were more corre-spondent with His doctrine and example, than ours of the Church of England, or any other people of my acquaintance. But however just and impartial these reflections were, they gave me considerable concern to think that any should in reality go beyond the members of the Church of England,

in conformity of life, etc., to the example of Christ and
His Apostles, as I could not in truth deny the Quakers did.
And as I kept in a humble frame of mind, I felt a secret love
and approbation of their simplicity and godly sincerity,
though I had no great acquaintance with them, nor was
much conversant with their writings, neither had been at
more than two of their religious meetings, and those when
I was very young ; but the inward sense given me of them
as a people, so conscientious in the converse and commerce
amongst men, kept me from prejudice against them, nor
durst I, like some of my acquaintance, (though in other
cases I had as quick a satyrical disposition as most) make
this people the subject of ridicule, nor speak lightly of the
spirit they professed, feeling in the interior of my mind, it
would be at my own peril, if I should so daringly and im-
prudently indulge my wit.   Thus through many snares
in company and conversation, I was by attention to my
secret Monitor taught to do by others as I would they
should do to me and preserved in a degree of innocency ;
feeling the reward in my own breast of faithfulness to
divine instruction to be peace and joy in the Holy Ghost.
And thus at an age when the world and visible objects
sought most to allure me, it pleased the Almighty in an
eminent manner to visit and separate me from my former
beloveds, relations, acquaintance, customs, and manners.

    In the year 1734, being just turned twenty, I was
brought into a very serious state of mind, owing to a sudden
indisposition seizing my dear sister, who with myself had
to that time been favoured with a great share of health and
prosperity, harmony and concord.   But this was not always
to last ; for the sudden stroke of sickness which my poor
sister had deeply affected us both ; and it lying heavy on
her spirits made her apprehensive of sudden death, which
terrified us all and was as a sword piercing through my
heart, till I was brought to calmness and consideration of
the innocence and sweetness of her temper and past life,
from which I hoped she needed not dread the approach of

death : but should it prove her end, which I did not apprehend it would, I hoped there was no room to doubt her
happiness. Yet grieving to see her so afflicted, and being
naturally of a bolder spirit than she, I was ready to petition
the Almighty in the secret of my mind, that she might be
relieved if it were consistent with His will, and, if one of
us must suffer, that it might rather be myself than she,
judging myself less timorous. But in the midst of these
considerations, I was informed as certainly in my own
conscience, as if it had been told me by a person of un-
questionable veracity and authority, that I must undergo a
great work and know a thorough change, before I could be
prepared for a happy death. A query arising in me what
this could import and what this change must be, I presently
had an answer uttered to my breast with great weight and
solemnity to this effect, " the change is this : thou must
with others bear the cross in the closest way, and become a
Quaker ! "

Words cannot express the situation of my mind in this
critical juncture. Hope and fear, both for my sister and
myself, successively took place. But I endeavoured as
much as I could to surmount the conflict I was under, and
aid my poor sister ; whose illness still increasing and in a
little time reducing her to a very weak state, my thoughts
and time were pretty much engaged on her account ; and
being mostly abstracted from worldly views of any kind,
I had the better opportunity in that retirement to adhere to
the reproofs of instruction, and impartially weigh every
presentation. And great indeed was the condescension of
Divine Wisdom to me in this solid disposition of mind ;
many passages in the Scriptures were unfolded to me in
so lively and affecting a manner, that my understanding was
enlarged and my heart more powerfully affected with the
teachings of the heavenly Instructor in a few days, than
ever I had witnessed by outward means or instructor,
though from my childhood I had been diligent in attendance of religious duties, both public and private, and was

by some thought to have profited therein more than many of my age or sex. . . .

When I obeyed the heavenly vision, in shunning what it disapproved and doing what it required, I was filled with peace and joy in the Holy Ghost. But when, through human weakness or the opposition of my relations and acquaintance, I suffered myself to be diverted from my attention and obedience to the ingrafted word of divine wisdom and began to reason with flesh and blood, I lost my strength, and was bereft of my joy and heavenly consolation, . . . and had not the invisible arm of divine power secretly preserved me, I had certainly fallen a victim to the power of darkness, in that hour of close temptation, wherein through the suggestions of Satan, I esteemed myself utterly abandoned and forsaken of God. And in such a circumstance dreading the continuance of my days on earth, least I should be suffered to fall into evil practices, I earnestly sought death and resisted unto blood striving against sin ! My life being a burden unto me when bereft of the light of life, I refused my natural food, thinking I might by that means gradually compass bodily dissolution with the least imputation of reproach. But my relations, especially my dear sister, having a watchful eye over me and being greatly concerned least I should by my abstinence shorten my life, obliged me sometimes to take food ; but it was so little they could prevail with me to take, that they said, and I have often since thought, that it was a wonder I pined not away ; which was what I secretly aimed at. But the grand enemy of souls was frustrated in this his attempt on my life. I was also preserved in a wonderful manner by the interposition of Divine Providence screening me from death in another shape ; and I plainly saw that I should not be suffered, however desirous of death, to be my own executioner.

Thus the enemy was again defeated of his purpose ; and finding he could not touch my life, laid his baits another way ; and in order to make the way of truth I had been convinced of appear despicable to me and my acquaintance, he secretly injected a supposition into one of my nearest intimates, that possibly it might be the good opinion I and our family, especially herself, had entertained of a neighbour of ours, who had sometimes been at the house and done many acts of friendship for us, that had biassed my judgment in favour of the Quakers' principles ; he being a strict Quaker and very conscientious in his whole conduct and conversation, which I thought was praise-worthy both in him and others. But I was very far from any personal liking or affection to him, though a report was soon spread that I was in love with him ; how little ground there was for such a conjecture and in what degree he was instrumental in my convincement, the sequel of this little history shall, as briefly as I am capable, honestly set forth.

The cross being so great, and the divine influence in great measure obscured through my disobedience, I fell in with my acquaintance in resisting the spirit of grace and wisdom in its reproofs, convictions, and instructions, and passively gave way to the persuasions of my intimates, to try if the strictest life in the way of the Church of England would not excuse me in the sight of my Maker and meet with His approbation. O the forbearance of a merciful Father to me in that time of probation, that He did not consume me by the breath of His displeasure ! For indeed it was justly kindled against me and burnt inwardly as an oven ; and I was brought to experience in the words of David, *Sacrifice and meat offerings thou wouldest not accept,* nor anything short of perfect obedience to the divine manifestation ! But my way, as the mournful prophet expresses, was made up as with hewn stone,[1] and all attempts to open it proved ineffectual, until it pleased infinite Wisdom to favour me again with light from on high, which overcame the darkness and in time wrought my deliverance through manifold afflictions, inward and outward, that would have overwhelmed the stoutest of mortals, had not Divine

[1] Lam. iii. 9.

aid interposed and secretly preserved [me] ; to the praise
of His own name, who with the temptation made a way to
escape, after I had continued about a year and nine months
in this precarious halting state, thoroughly convinced of
my duty, but striving to evade it, and seeking peace where
I was made sensible it was not to be found : which made
the cross I had to take up in giving up to the heavenly
vision much greater, and my way to the kingdom straiter
than it would have been, if I had not made my bonds
strong by opposition.

In the course of this proving season much pains were
taken by my relations for the restoration of my health
and tranquillity of mind : but all proved ineffectual, till the
great and good Samaritan appeared for my help and in His
own time administered the wine and the oil to my tortured
and wounded soul, that had been tossed with tempest and
not comforted ! [1]   In this interval I made a visit to my
dear uncle, my trusty guardian, whose care over me was
great ; and I have reason to believe, from his own expressions, the Almighty made him sensible in a good degree
of the necessity I lay under of making this great change
before hinted at, and also of my regard to him, as my uncle
and guardian, and my timorousness of offending him, on
the one side, and my heavenly Father, on the other, by
my repeated delays of coming up in the way of divine
manifestation.

The Searcher of hearts, who knew the strait I was in,
wrought upon my uncle in my favour and made him plead
my cause with *them that strove against me*, and with a courage
becoming his station assert and plead for my just liberty of
worshipping God in the way I believed to be right ; saying,
I had as good a title to this liberty as any person and none
should abridge me of it, and he stand by ; at the same time

[1] In the 1794 edition of this *Narrative* the following footnote is here
inserted, with reference to the letter from Thomas Smith, which I have
printed on page 94 below.   " See a letter from T. S., p. 20, who appears
to have been an instrument in the hand of Providence to convince her
uncle's judgment."

requesting I would give in writing, for his vindication, the reasons that induced me to embrace the principles of the Quakers. Which in the simplicity and integrity of my heart I immediately committed to writing, as the Holy Spirit opened my heart and directed my pen, as followeth.[1]

It is about a year and a half since God was pleased to declare to me His divine will, in the manner following.

That if I would obey and be governed by His will, He would accept me and make me the disciple of His beloved Son ; but to attain to this desirable blessing, He required that I should entirely lay aside all the vanity and foolish amusements of the world, which are a great hindrance to our spiritual progress and suffer not His word when received to take effectual root in the heart. This I had experienced to be very true, therefore I implored His divine assistance to enable me to lay aside whatsoever was contrary to His will or might hinder my performance of it acceptably, resigning myself entirely into His hand, as clay into the hands of the potter, desiring to be what best pleased my God. In order to which He gave me an inexpressible satisfaction, in humbly reading His holy word, which plainly sheweth us the way, the truth, and the life Himself taught us. I seldom took up the book but it opened in the fourth chapter

---

[1] Fanny is most scrupulous in desiring to minimize the extent of her guardian's interference with her liberty. It is clear, I think, from statements made in Byrom's Journal that he was still continuing to put very material obstacles in her way, or at least allowing his wife to do so, when he made this request for her reasons. See pages 122 and 124 below.

The statement that now follows, down to the point (on page 93) where Fanny has appended her signature for the second time, represents what is known as her *Case* with the " additions ". (The latter, however, Law apparently did not have before him.) Three manuscript copies of this have survived besides the printed version. I have as a rule followed the version in the *Toft* collection in the Friends House Library, which appears to have been made by Fanny herself. The variations in these written versions are not important.

of St. John's gospel ; [1] which happening so many times
much affected me, as I am persuaded it would have done
any serious person, who, obedient to the Gospel, had a
desire to work out their own salvation with fear and
trembling, which it behoves all very zealously to do, it
being a work none is permitted to do for us.

I happened about this time to see a person, a Quaker,
from whose opinion the world imagines I conceived mine ; [2]
how far I did, I will shew in as faithful a manner as I am
capable.   He, seeing me more thoughtful than usual, asked
if I was well or if it was for my sister (who was then ill) that
I was in so great a concern.   If it was only on her account,
he begged me to be content, believing, he then said, her
illness would not be fatal, but would be removed in God's
good time.   If my concern was upon my own account, he
said I must apply to God and His holy word for assistance
and relief and submit myself entirely to Him, who is all
powerful to relieve the afflicted and distressed.

What fault could I find with this advice ?   I knew it
to be agreeable to Scripture and right reason, and had it
proceeded from the mouth of a Turk, I should have been
desirous to put it in practice ; but how great was my
concern when I found, not from him, but by a secret impulse till that time unknown to me, that, to be a disciple
of Christ, I must make a thorough change in life and
manners, become a new creature, be born again, to be
made an inheritor of Christ's kingdom.   Unwilling still
to entertain a thought in favour of the Quakers, I thus
reasoned—" Lord, I ever found some of them to be a plain
and, I believe, a sincere people, but they allow not the

[1] The chapter containing the verse about worshipping God in spirit
and in truth, which Law elsewhere describes as " the foundation of
Quakerism " (page 206 below).

[2] This appears to be the same individual as the one mentioned by Fanny
previously (page 85) with whom she was reported to be in love.   It is
just conceivable, though hardly, I think, likely, that this person was one of
the brothers, Joshua or John Toft, of Leek, with whom she was on terms
of friendship in later years (see page 161).   Otherwise there is no means
of identifying the acquaintance in question.

outward institutions of baptism and the Lord's supper, which surely were commanded by our blessed Lord and Master." To which, as though I heard a voice, I thus was answered—" Obey my will, and thou shalt find my flesh is meat indeed and my blood is drink indeed, and I am the Lord ! I dwell not in temples made with hands, my chosen tabernacle is the heart. Remember my servant David's words, ' Sacrifice and meat offering for sin thou wouldest not, but a broken and contrite heart thou wilt not despise.' What said my servant Samuel to Saul, who spared of the flock for sacrifice ?—' Behold obedience is better than sacrifice, and to hearken than the fat of rams.' "

Confuted, as it were, thus far in my opinion, my troubled soul thus expressed her grief : " Is there, Lord, no way but this, wherein I may live agreeably to thy holy will ? Must I wholly renounce the opinion it pleased thee I should be brought up in, which as my natural mother claims me as her child ? Oh ! most severe and fiery trial ! I have read thy word is sharp and piercing, yea, sharper than any two-edged sword ; and so indeed I find it to be even to the dividing asunder of soul and spirit, joints and marrow. What will my friends and all the world say of me, if I profess the opinion of a people so much despised ? Oh ! that when I was born I had given up the ghost, then I had been at peace."

After these reflections I endeavoured to compose myself, but in vain. My soul, like a troubled sea, found no rest, and I heard as though a voice had pronounced these words—" Knowest thou, O weak woman, whose will thou thus disputest ? Consider and dare not to offend me— remember I am God, able to kill and make alive. Wilt thou then, to please the world and thy own will, disobey me, who can destroy both body and soul in hell ? Obey my will, and thou shalt find it shall be well with thee. As to what the world may say of thee, remember it is enmity with Christ, that they, who are of it, have no part in Him ; thou canst not serve God and Mammon. If thou wisely makest choice of my service, adhere to this the day of thy visitation, and thou shalt assuredly find my grace sufficient for thee.   Otherwise it will be hard, thou wilt find, to disobey and cast my words behind thee.   Remember Paul, he stood not disputing."

In this circumstance my whole desire and prayer to God was, that He would speak no more to me in wrath, lest I should be consumed with the breath of His displeasure.   I could not make use of the forms of prayer I used to do, by reason they rather augmented than eased the conflicts I laboured under, like medicines wrong applied.   I then truly knew my own weakness, that of myself I knew not what to pray for ; but the Spirit greatly helped my infirmities, with sighs and groans unutterable. Still unwilling to reveal the conflicts I laboured under on account of my sister's illness, I strove as much as possible to keep my concern to myself, well knowing it was God alone and His holy word, that could relieve me ; unto which I ever fled as the anchor of my hopes and solver of my doubts.

There was at this time a person in the neighbourhood (her name is Drummond), who professed the opinion of the Quakers, whom as a stranger many people went to hear speak, I amongst the rest being asked if I would go : which I refused, unwilling to leave my sister in her illness ; but 'tis impossible to express the self-condemning thoughts I laboured under.   After this time in vain were all the reasons I could urge in my behalf, my heart condemned me as guilty of a great error, as did God who is far greater than our own heart.[1]   So great was my concern that it shewed itself in all my actions, insomuch that all who saw me enquired what could be the reason—which I no longer scrupled to discover.   Upon which they immediately sent

[1] This and the previous sentence referring to Mrs. Drummond have been omitted by the Editors of the 1803 and 1804 printed versions of this document.   They have also omitted the reference to " my dread companion " a little later on.   For Mrs. Drummond see page 73 above.

for the clergyman of the parish, who took much pains to convince me of what he thought so groundless an opinion. But in vain are all arguments against matter of fact. Disputes may quench, but cannot baffle the Spirit of God, nor the mind once convicted by its influence : it is a bosom friend, a faithful monitor, impartial and not to be biassed. Which since I by disputes have vexed and quenched, I have been (Oh! grief to tell!) a second Magdalen ; but Christ on her sincere repentance received and cured even her. And as God has been so merciful [as] to spare my life hitherto and has done great things for my soul's deliverance, I am not faithless, but believing (if these are His chosen people, as sure I by experience must believe they are) that through faith in Christ and His name God will at their request rid me of my dread companion, thereby making known His glory and power, that He is the same God that ever He was ; whose hand is not shortened, that He cannot save, nor His ear heavy that He cannot hear ; but it is my iniquities that separate betwixt me and my God, and my sins and disobedience that have caused Him to turn His face from me. But though I should incur the disesteem of the whole world by obedience to the discovery of the truth, God forbid I should conceal it any longer from any, for should I lie against the light, my wound would be incurable. But I will declare it, that I may be refreshed. Yea, I will open my mouth in defence of the truth ; which I have delayed long to do, or I had not been given up into the hand of the enemy, whose malice seeks my life. But his power goes not farther than God permits, who has mercifully spared me, and I hope will in His good time set my soul at liberty to bear testimony to the truth and be His faithful penitent, entirely devoted to His service.

FRANCES HENSHAW

I dared no longer accept any man's person, neither give flattering titles to men, for in so doing my Maker would soon take me away.   For what indeed am I that I should dare to stand in opposition to the Almighty ?   Shall the clay say to Him that formed it, why hast thou made me thus ?   God spake once, nay twice, but I perceived it not, in a dream, in a vision of the night, when deep sleep fell upon me ;   when I was slumbering upon my bed, then opened He mine ears to receive instruction, to withdraw mine heart from vanity, and to lead me in the way ever-lasting, to keep my soul from the pit, and my life from the enemy's power.   But He hath chastened me with a multi-tude of pains and afflictions, so that my life abhorreth bread, and my soul dainty meat, because I have rebelled against the will of the Lord, I have not followed the commandments of my God.[1]   But my soul has indeed experienced His mercies to be boundless and unlimited.   Therefore doth she greatly love and fear Him, for she to whom much is forgiven, gratitude demands she should love much, for this is the only return we can make, or that God requires of us. And sure it is a pleasing task.   For love makes all things easy, and we love not our own souls, if we love not God, even to the laying down our lives, if His service require it, for His sake, who spared not His own Son for our sake, to reconcile lost man and His offended Father.   Oh ! let not any therefore delay returning to God or despair of His mercies on their sincere repentance ;   since I, who have drank of that bitter cup, have through mercy received some glimmerings of hope, that God will not cast off for ever, nor shut up His old loving kindness in displeasure, so as not to pardon.   How did he receive the prodigal ?   Nay He tells us there is joy in heaven over one sinner that repenteth, more than over ninety and nine just persons that need no repentance.

If I am not understood by the terms of a second Mag-dalene, I desire farther to explain myself in this matter. God has, for reasons best known to Himself—I hope for His own glory, been pleased to permit me for a year or more to

[1] Compare Job xxxiii. 14–20.

be grieved, nay even possessed with an evil spirit ; whose power over me for some time was so absolute, that it drove me to the utmost extremity and despair. It was with the greatest difficulty that I strove to refrain myself from committing violence on my own life. What unfeigned thanks therefore am I bound to return to my merciful God, who gave not my enemy power to touch my life, though with malice he sought my destruction. But God, casting an eye of mercy and compassion on my lost and deplorable condition, has miraculously preserved my life from the enemy's power, and given me also a hope that by sincere and unfeigned repentance He will bring my soul out of bondage, and, on my hearty obedience, restore the wandering and lost sheep to His favour. Indeed I know not wherein I have so highly offended my gracious God, to incur this heavy punishment, except in rejecting the doctrine and opinion of the Quakers, by refusing to join myself in their way of worship, when opportunity offered, which I rejected. Upon which account began my affliction and trouble, which daily increased, until of late that God is pleased to offer me to open the gate to them that knock, and by seeking to be delivered from my enemy, to serve Him in freedom of spirit.[1]

I leave to your discretion to publish or keep private my present case, as ye judge may tend most to the glory of God and the good of all people.

I commit myself to your charity and prayers and all of us to God and His Christ, and desire to be His and yours.

FRANCES HENSHAW. Farewell.

*   *   *   *   *

[1] One manuscript adds the following words at this point : " In her copy of this, which she sent to some friends, she has underwrit it ".

The whole of the present paragraph, to this point, reappears in Byrom's letter of December 21, 1736, in an almost verbally exact rendering. See note on page 135.

The preceding pages represent much the larger part of Fanny Henshaw's narrative of her life, as she wrote it down soon after the death of her first husband. The remainder is postponed until we have introduced the reader to the third person of the drama, the amiable Dr. John Byrom, whose entertaining Journal will probably come as a relief, after the somewhat intense atmosphere in which we have been moving hitherto. It is moreover in connection with Byrom's Journal and correspondence that it is most convenient to attempt a reconstruction of the events that followed the writing by Fanny of the statement immediately preceding.

In addition however to the autobiographical record, three contemporary letters have fortunately survived (in the collection of manuscripts left by Fanny's friends the Tofts of Leek, and now in the Library of the Society of Friends), each of which in different ways and from a different standpoint puts the case for liberty of conscience and for the Quaker view of Christianity. For any expert marshalling of arguments they will not bear comparison with William Law's letters, but they contribute materially to justify the position which Fanny had taken up.

The first of these three documents is a letter from a Quaker acquaintance of hers, Thomas Smith of Balby, near Doncaster.[1] It is referred to, in the editorial footnote which I have quoted on page 86, as having contributed to convince Fanny's uncle of the desirability of respecting her freedom of choice.

Balby, near Doncaster, 8th Month, 27th, 1736.

Friend Sutton,

Though I am entirely a stranger to thee, I crave thy favour candidly to read over the following lines, without

[1] See footnote to page 141.

prejudging me ; then I hope thou wilt excuse the freedom I have taken, and wilt, I presume, in some measure join with me. The occasion of my giving thee this trouble is on account of thy niece F.H., who I understand has been a considerable time under great dissatisfaction of mind on a religious account, being persuaded in her own conscience it is her duty to dissent from you in [the] form of worshipping God. From her own words (for she always speaks of thee with much gratitude and esteem) I draw the conclusion, that thou hast not only performed the part of a friend and relation to her, but also that of a tender parent too, in her education to this time, and I doubt not hast a respect for her and wishest her present and future welfare. In return perhaps thou mayst be ready to say, she is undutiful, and slights thy care and advice. But if thou wilt bear with my freedom a little, I hope thou wilt be otherwise minded, when thou hast considered the reasons she gives thee, and especially that it is a matter of *conscience* to her ; which I understand " is that persuasion of mind that arises from the understanding's being possessed with the belief of the truth or falsity of any thing." So that, if a man acts against his persuasion or conscience, his act or offering is no ways acceptable to God, for the apostle says (Rom. 14th. 23), *whatsoever is not of faith is sin.*

Now as thy niece firmly believes it her duty to dissent from you in way of worship, it gives me true concern to find thou art so strict with her, as to deny her that liberty thyself expects from all mankind, a liberty the government thinks good to allow us, a liberty entirely consistent with right reason, and consonant to that maxim and advice of " doing to others as we would they should do unto us." I have nevertheless the charity to believe, that if thou wert sensible what affliction and anxiety of mind she undergoes at times (considering the respect and esteem I'm persuaded thou hast for her as a near relation) thou wouldest not debar her from that reasonable liberty ; for what sorrow, what grief and trouble, can equal that of a wounded spirit ?

*   *   *   *   *

Then, after a long paragraph setting forth how alien to Christianity is compulsory conformity, the writer continues :

Give me leave to acquaint thee, it is not our practice to persuade any persons to join in community with us, who do not first believe it their duty to do it ; nor can I apprehend we deviate at all from right reason and Christian charity, in giving our advice freely to such as may be under doubts and dissatisfaction on account of religion, when they apply to us for our advice.   Would my friend only suppose a Quaker, or any person of a different community from himself, laying all his scruples respecting religion before him, and desiring his kind admonition and counsel, would he not contribute as much as in him lay to the inquirer's satisfaction ?   From the idea I form to myself of thee, I readily believe thou wouldest.

I suppose thy chief reason for preventing thy niece from joyning with us is the disuse of water baptism and the outward supper ; ceremonies which we believe are not necessary to salvation.   In proof of which I should have advanced something, notwithstanding the length I have already run to, if Robert Barclay had not long since done it for me.   And if I mistake not thy character as a man of sense and a gentleman, I need not doubt thy readiness to consult his *Apology* [1] on those heads, rather than any longer (upon supposition barely and taking the question in dispute for granted) deprive her of that liberty the law has designed to secure to her, as a free-born subject and a Protestant.   A breach of which law in any person I doubt not but thou art sensible is not justifiable.   Such an infringement upon one's property [2] might by a resentful person be called in question : and if thy niece is of a disposition quite the reverse, should she therefore, my friend, meet with less condescension ?

I have wrote to thee with much freedom ; what a reception it will meet with I know not, but I depend upon

[1] See note on page 211.
[2] I think the writer means "propriety", *i.e.* "individuality", "personal independence".

A LONDON QUAKER—FROM A PRINT OF 1711

thy favourable construction of the liberty I have taken, for
be assured it is no other than the effect of my great goodwill
to thy niece, to whom be pleased to present my respects,
and believe me, with due regard to thyself,

Thy well-wisher and friend,

THOS. SMITH

The letter which I print next is somewhat of a
riddle. It consists of four quarto sheets in close, neat
handwriting, with a contemporary inscription, " For
John Toft—copy of letter ". A later pen has added
the heading " Letter on behalf of Frances Henshaw,
about 1736 ". The handwriting has the appearance
of being that of Thomas Smith, the writer of the preceding letter. If so, it is probable that a copy of the
letter was sent by the writer to Fanny, while she was a
guest (in 1737) in Thomas Smith's house, and that her
host made this second copy.

The letter is unsigned. Its writer was certainly
not a Quaker, and was probably (from its reference to
" our Church ") a member of the Church of England.
The mention of " your parish " together with other
indications suggest that it was written to a clergyman of
that Church. In any case it was in reply to a letter from
a person who had received a " paper " in defence of
Fanny's action. This paper is almost certainly the
Case, printed on pages 87 to 91 above, which was
also sent to Law : I have mentioned in my notes specific
references to parts of this. It seems therefore most
probable that the letter was addressed to some clergyman—perhaps her parish clergyman,[1] with whom
Fanny had previously been having a discussion and who
had written traversing portions of her Case in a similar

[1] Or else the Rev. Mr. Hoole of Manchester. See pages 126 and 147.

manner, though doubtless much less effectively, to
William Law.

Who then was the anonymous writer of this epistle?
The reader will have noticed that Fanny stated in her
Narrative that her uncle (who is elsewhere spoken of as
having at first tried hard to make her change her intentions) became favourable to her and went so far as
to " plead my cause with them that strove against me,
and . . . assert and plead for my just liberty of
worshipping God in the way I believed to be right ",
etc. Is it possible to imagine that the extremely
vigorous pleading in this letter came from the pen of
Fanny's uncle and guardian, Thomas Sutton? If so
he must have been a Churchman very dissatisfied with
his Church—a very comprehensible state of mind in
eighteenth-century England, but also one who had in
a short time acquired an extremely favourable view of
the Quakers and some amount of insight into the
grounds of their beliefs. (Had he perhaps read
Barclay's *Apology*, in accordance with the wish expressed in the last letter?) Indeed the estimate of the
Society is so high, that it is a little difficult to suppose
Lawyer Sutton can have indited it. Still the suggestion
is a tempting one, and at that we must leave it. We
have not the knowledge to suggest any alternative
name. I have somewhat abbreviated the letter, which
in places is rather discursive.

Sir,

I had an opportunity of seeing your letter to Miss
Henshaw which I have perused without prejudice ; and
take the liberty to answer it ; without either flattery or
animosity, for (to use your own expression), " Charity
obliges me to suppose " that in writing to her your motive
was good. Had your arguments been so, you had found

her readier than perhaps you imagined to have conceded to them.

What you suppose in your first paragraph concerning that part of her life you say you are a stranger to,[1] I believe is true, as far as her station in that time and the way of thinking of her directors would allow it. And I believe it to be her conscience instructed by God's Spirit, that has spoke to her in the manner exprest in that paper, to which your letter was designed an answer.

*   *   *   *   *

I believe Miss Henshaw is ever willing to acknowledge she is desirous of doing God's will, that she takes those, who endeavour to serve God in spirit and truth, to be God's people (call them Quakers or what else you please) ; that therefore, to do God's will, she must imitate them in all essential points ; and why not even in the plain decency of their speech and dress ? And why, I pray, may not she be desirous of hearing either Mrs. Drummond or any other servant of God, in the ministry of revealing His will to mankind, provided that according to God's special command, they deliver it as freely as they have received it.

*   *   *   *   *

After having long dwelt upon Miss Henshaw's account of her extraordinary dispensations etc., you ask, " How far, and to what a degree she asserts matter of fact ? " I own I don't well understand your meaning. The only demonstrable proof of divine revelations being matter of fact, to me, is self-sensation. I ask you, Sir, whether your feeling the inward dictates or impulses in your conscience be a matter of fact or no ? . . .

" The impulse," you say, " the [answer], as by a voice, and the dream [2] will be considered as of little moment

---

[1] This evidently refers to the first words of Fanny's *Case* or " paper ", in the form in which William Law had it : " My manner of life from a child, none here are strangers to ". (See page 26.)

[2] Fanny in her *Case* speaks of a particular secret impulse, of a compelling voice, and (in what Byrom calls the " additions " to the *Case*) of a

amongst sober Christians, who all, ' not in types and shadows ' etc."—Pray, what great affinity have impulses, voices and dreams, with types and shadows ? But, of all people in the world, you cannot charge the Quakers with dealing in types and shadows ;[1] neither can you deny, that " with open face and in full day they behold the glorious wisdom, mercy, and power of God, displayed in the redemption of mankind by His Son," as well as the best of us.

*   *   *   *   *

But since your repetitions require repetitions, I tell you again, I know Miss Henshaw reads the Scriptures, imploring God's mercy, grace, and spirit, that she may be acceptable to Him by the unfeigned practice of vertue ; from whence she hopes eternal happiness, as I am well assured she dayly finds more and more, that Christ's yoke is easy, and His burden light indeed. I have already told you what I suppose the Quakers, Mrs. Drummond, and all other good people in the world are to her.   I hope you are not so selfish and so uncharitable as to regard no body, because you don't know their hearts !   If so, I pray God turn yours ; but till then, pray, for the publick's sake and your own, forbear exposing your sentiments.

" ' But,' say you, ' they renounce the vanities of the world, and therefore you must by experience believe them to be God's people,'[2] and here I must ask you what experience you mean ? "   Your question is impertinent.[3]   Don't you understand English ?   " The tree is known by its fruits."

" It is the peculiarity indeed of the Quakers to distin-

dream or vision of the night, as having been determining factors in her decision.   Law refers specifically to the impulse and the voice, but not to the dream.   He had not the "additions" before him, as apparently this clergyman had.

[1] Passages such as Col. ii. 16–22, referring to the law of ordinances as a "shadow" of the life in Christ, were often quoted by the Quakers.

[2] This sentence appears to be a quotation by Fanny Henshaw's opponent of her letter to him.

[3] *i.e.* irrelevant.

guish themselves more by attending [to] the private
mammon, than the public divertions or fashions of their
neighbours." If by this private mammon you mean their
worldly business, I ask you what harm you find in that?
Even yourself must be the better for it, if you have Quakers
in your parish. I find that making recreation of business is
a pleasure you are not yet acquainted with. Do you know
a society in the world that makes a better use than they
do of the blessing God gives to their honest industry?
Have you ever seen one of them beg or want? Who is it
relieves their poor? Does our Church? Nay, but they
often serve ours at their doors, to our shame it may be said !
This I must say on their behalf, that they are not very social
in following the fashions of their neighbours : but those
who are acquainted with them know they don't lay such a
stress upon their uniformity of dress, as you say in order to
make them appear ridiculous. Pray, Sir, who seem most
to imagine that God's will lies in such or such a fashion
of cloaths—the clergy, or the Quakers? Suppose an
American [1] of good natural sense, who had never heard of
the customs of Europe, nor ever seen anybody dressed, was
brought into a room, on one side of which should stand a
few Quakers, and on the other side as many of our clergymen in their canonical dress according to their degrees ;
and having been told beforehand that the Quakers' dress
would divert him much, as the honest Indian is turned into
the room, which, think you, would he take for the Quakers?
For my part I think he would take the clergymen. And
yet you cannot deny, but they must needs be dressed in
some of them cloaths [sic] to perform any part of divine
service.

If St. Paul were now alive and was to write an Epistle
to the English, I don't at all doubt but he would mention
Mrs. Drummond or any other faithful woman preacher,
in the same manner he did formerly Phebe and Priscilla
(Rom. xvi.). What do the prophets mean by saying,

[1] *i.e.* a Red Indian.

"Your sons and your daughters shall prophesy," [1] etc., and St. Paul (1 Cor. xi. 5), "But every woman [praying or prophesying] etc."? When he forbids women speaking in the Church, it was concerning the regulation of Church affairs, where it seems they were not admitted to hear what was done. Otherwise I don't see what occasion they could have to ask their husbands at home. Neither religion, reason, nor common sense can exclude women from uttering what the Spirit of God dictates to them. Who can deny that in spiritual things they are the same as men, unless it be a Mahometan? Why then should they not have the same privilege?

As to what you say concerning the Lord's supper, I shall only repeat what Christ said to His disciples, when they murmured (John vi. 63), " 'Tis the spirit that quickens, the flesh profits little, the words that I speak unto you, they are spirit and they are life." If you believe we are really obliged to eat bread and drink wine in remembrance of Christ, why do you not believe, with the Papists, the bread to be His body and the wine to be His blood? For those are His own words.

Had a thorn of doubt given Miss Henshaw any uneasiness, you had, I'm persuaded, removed it indeed, confirming her in her late choice by your arguments.   I hope you'll excuse the freedom I have used ; and permit me to recommend you also to the abundant mercy of an all-wise God, who knows best why so many differ in their articles of faith, though all agree in those of morality.

I am, Sir,

etc., etc.

Our last item in the present collection of documents is a contemporary letter from the hand of Fanny Henshaw herself. The surviving copy of this is undated,

[1] Joel ii. 28.

but from the fact that she uses the " thou " and " thee " language (which she had not yet adopted in the letters transcribed by Byrom), as well as from other indications, it must have been written after she had, in a manner that will transpire later, made her escape to a Quaker household.

The document bears two insciptions : (1) " Copy of Frances Henshaw's correspondence with her Guardian who very much opposed her coming amongst Friends ", and (2) " Copy of l̄re F. Henshaw to Sutton—or Cripps." There is no form of address at the beginning.

In view of the reference to " my Aunt Sutton " in the opening sentence, it would be natural to suppose that the letter was intended for her Uncle Sutton. But this is rendered improbable because it is written to somebody who was evidently violently antagonistic, as one superscription states, to her action, and we have Fanny's word [1] that her uncle had become very favourable to her by the time it was carried through. On the other hand we know that she had another uncle of the name of Cripps, with whom she was staying (not for the first time) at Doncaster, at the time of her final decision,[2] and it is quite reasonable to suppose that, not knowing her precise address, he may have written to her, through Mrs. Sutton, a strong letter of protest. (We know that Mrs. Cripps at least was much opposed to Fanny's ideas.) If so, it would appear that he had some kind of responsibility for Fanny's religious upbringing.

The letter (or rather the copy we have) is remarkable for its entire absence of stops, and occasionally the grammar is defective. I have added punctuation, and inserted a few words which appear to have dropped out.

[1] See page 86.   [2] See page 144.

Inclosed in a letter from my Aunt Sutton, I received thine, which, as thou says and [I] believe was kindly meant, I take kindly ; for realy, Friend, what idea soever thou may have conceived of me, I have not so learned Christ as to want that eminent virtue that shone so conspicuously in His exemplary life when upon earth, viz., charity and meekness, not only to them that acknowledged Him the Messiah, but to His most inveterate opposers and the worst of sinners ; among whom thou having ranked me and my Friends, I could have rejoyced to have found in thee some demonstration of a truely Christian spirit [or] compassion —at least if we were indeed such a people as thou unkindly and without proof represents us, which I may safely affirm in very truth we realy are not ; neither canst, I believe, prove against us any one of the things thou lay'st to our charge, although thou hast pas't condemnation on the whole Society, of which I believe not a member would hurt a hair of thy head.   Neither will I retort, but as one amongst the many thou hast already passed sentance on.   [I] intreat, for thy own safety for the future, thou would'st be more cautious how thou judgest, least for shewing no mercy thou should'st at the great tribunnall meet with judgment without mercy.   Remember how the great Apostle queries in the like case, " who art thou, O man, that judgest another ? " and " to his own Master let him stand or fall "—

I accuse neither thee nor any one of neglect with reguard to my soul, knowing assuredly that no mortall can either purchase or dispose of it for me ; having already considered that religion is not to be caught or cast like a ball, the Scriptures assuring me that neither Noah, Daniel, or Job should save any but themselves.   I know not that I have the least room to accuse myself of any breach of what thou say'st was my duty.   For what I have done was not secretly or in a corner, but openly and with the knowledge of all parties concerned. Neither am I in the least confounded or ashamed to confess the faith of Christ crucifyed, and manfully and in reality to fight under His banner, viz., the truth as it is in Jesus, against sin, the world, and the devil.

Thou say'st it is highly blameable in me by my act to proclaim, as if all my forefathers and persons to whom I owe my being and every other person, who hath died in comunion with the Church of England, had nothing but misguided notions of religion, etc. With the same justice may the Church of Rome accuse my forefathers and the whole Church of England of haveing proclaimed, by dissenting from them, all the Popes, Cardinals, and Nuns to be scarcely within the pale of salvation. But I hope better things boath for many of them and also of the Church of England, knowing of a truth that God is no respecter of persons, but in all nations and societies, whosoever fears Him and works righteousness, will most assuredly be accepted of Him, who is just and holy in all His ways and will not receive or approve a wicked person because he is called a member of the Church of England, neither reject a just man because he is called a Quaker, but will reward every man according to his works—

Wheather I be endued with the Christian temper of humility or no, I'll leave ; but that I know, I was and still am very far from imagining my own judgment superior to every one's that lived before me or thousands yet living. But as the grace of God has appeared to me and all, and as that Divine Teacher instructs [I] endeavour in all things to act. And as a measure of the good and unering Spirit of God is given to me and everyone to profit with all, I endeavour to improve the measure granted unto me in doing what I believe to be my duty, keeping, as much as in me ly's, a conscience void of offence towards God and towards man. For that I take to be true religion, as saith the Apostle James : " pure religion and undefiled before God the Father is to visit the fatherless and the widdows and to keep thyself unspoted from the world." And they who do so I take to have the power of godliness as well as the form, and consequently [they] cannot be the saducers which the Apostle foresaw would arise ; [they] are not such as think the gift of God can be bought and sold for money or purchased with a few years study at Oxford or Cambridge and afterwards sold to the highest bidders for as much a year as any body will give for it.[1]

Is it not matter of grief that men should be thus blind and not suffer their eyes to be opened ? Did the Apostle do thus ? No, he laboured that the Gospell might be without charge. Now permit the question, who corresponds most with his example, your Church, or ours ? Who "doate most about questions and strifes of words "— they whose worship is never performed without a form of words composed by men as fallable as themselves and teaching such for doctrine, or they who worship as the spirit of God dictates and have no more form than decency and order ?

What the Apostle says concerning women keeping silence in the Church, I presume he meant respecting the discipline of the Churches ; otherwise I think he would not immediately after have given directions for a woman praying or prophesieing to have her head covered, etc.[2]

The true supper of the Lord I have learnt is to be made true spiritual pertakers of His body and blood, to refuse entrance to sin and keep our bodys as temples fit for the Holy Ghost to dwell in, to open the door of our heart at the first knock of our Redeemer, who will not fail to sup with such, receiving them to sup with Him, when bread and wine shall be no more and the eliments shall be disolved with fervent heat. To which everlasting supper of the

[1] Compare what William Law says in *The Spirit of Prayer* (Part II, p. 115): "almost everywhere you see . . . the Church trading with the Gospel, as the old Jews bought and sold beasts in their temple " ; and in the passage quoted on page 303 below.

[2] See 1 Cor. xi. 5 and xiv. 34. " Immediately after " is incorrect.

Lamb, slain from the foundation of the world, I desire thou and all people may come, haveing on the weding garment.

As to baptism, I believe with the Apostle there is one Lord, one faith, one baptism ; " for we," says the same Apostle, " who were baptized unto Christ, were baptized into His death ; and how shall we who are dead unto sin live any longer therein ?   Circumcision is nothing, uncircumcision is nothing, but a new creature ; and he who is in Christ is a new creature, old things are done away, behold all things are become new."

Thou mayst, if thou please, inform thyself by history of the lives, sufferings, and barbarous deaths of many of our worthy elders, and what was it [that] enabled them without any assistance from the powers of this world to profess the truth before all the world, and at last to seal their testimony with their blood.   Doubtless the arm of Divine Goodness was their protector.   Now this cloud of witnesses haveing gone before me, 'tis them I hope to follow, that I may be made a pertaker with them in glory.

Amen says my soul, F. H.

CHAPTER III

JOHN BYROM'S NARRATIVE

IT is now our task to turn from the two saintly and intense personalities revealed in the foregoing pages to the very different and very versatile genius, who forms the third character in our drama. Had it not been for Dr. John Byrom, Fanny Henshaw would not have been brought into contact with William Law. And Byrom himself is such an attractive figure and one so little known to this generation, that some account of his life and his literary remains should not be out of place here.

John Byrom was Law's junior by some six years, having been born in 1692, the son of a prosperous Manchester linen-draper and merchant. He received a good education at the Merchant Taylors School, London, and at Trinity College, Cambridge, where in 1714 he gained a fellowship. A little later he took advantage of the peace with France to spend about a year studying medicine at the University of Montpelier, where Sir Thomas Browne had studied about a century before him. In 1720 he fell in love with his cousin Elizabeth and married her. It was a very happy marriage. Byrom's frequent and affectionate letters to his wife are full of tenderness and charm. Though he was called *Doctor*, he hardly practised physic at all, having (as he once wrote to his wife) " neither health enough, nor interest, nor experience, nor consequently inclination enough for the profession ". He had some private income, and this he supplemented by teaching shorthand. He invented a system, which became very popular in his lifetime ; he even secured (in 1742) an Act of Parliament reserving to himself the sole right to teach it for a period of twenty-one years. After his death in 1763 the system was printed, and to it the more convenient modern methods are said to owe a considerable debt. His most distinguished pupils were John and Charles Wesley, and (what a contrast !) Horace Walpole. He gave lessons also to several prominent members of the House of Lords, though these were by no means satisfactory clients ; they were as often as not " abed " when he called—he " began to find that the lords would require a deal of waiting on ". Byrom's home was in Manchester, but the necessities of his profession required him for many years to spend a greater portion of his time in London and Cambridge.

We owe it in part to Byrom that John Wesley has left us such a full and continuous record of his crowded life. For from the year 1736, when Wesley was in Georgia, until his death in 1791, the greater part of Wesley's Journal and private manuscripts were written in Byrom's method of shorthand, which he had learnt on the advice of his brother Charles. Charles Wesley used it too, even sometimes for letters to his brother.

Byrom himself kept a private shorthand journal from about the year 1722, when he was thirty years of age. It enables us to reconstruct his life and feelings between that date and the year 1740 in a marvellously vivid way.[1] Day after day he sets down his hours of rising, the details of his meals (he was largely a vegetarian, though by no means a teetotaller), his visits and his conversations, his business and his recreations, his purchases of books, his constant charities, and (more rarely) his reflections on life and on persons. The Journal is supplemented by many valuable letters. Moreover Byrom was an industrious versifier, whose productions occasionally rise to the level of true poetry. In his own day his title to poetic fame rested principally on one pretty pastoral lyric, " Colin to Phebe ", published in the *Spectator*, and on several witty epigrams. To-day he is especially known as the author of the lovely

---

[1] After 1740 only a few fragments, unfortunately, of the Journal have survived. But we have a volume of his correspondence extending to within a few months of his death.

Christmas hymn, " Christians, awake, salute the happy morn ".[1]

Byrom's reflections naturally ran to verse, and he versified almost every conceivable subject, especially religious ones.   He was fond of turning into rhyme striking passages from the writings of his revered Mr. Law—a rather regrettable occupation, though it seems to have given pleasure to Law, who once wrote to him, " You sing for me so sweetly, that you may (for ought I know) sing my prose out of date." Perhaps the chief merit of his poetry is that it reflects (like his Journal) the simplicity, purity, and lovingkindness of the man, as well as his wide intellectual and literary curiosity, and his childlike interest in every aspect of human life that was not morally repulsive or degrading. Among the many journals that have been thought worthy of publication, Byrom's Journal appears to share with that of Samuel Pepys the distinction of entire artlessness, of being written with scarcely any thought of a possible reader, other than himself.   Like Pepys' famous Diary (which Byrom actually came across at Cambridge, but did not decipher), its shorthand character was calculated to conceal its contents from the ordinary reader.   Byrom wrote of it (in 1726) :

"What I set down in this kind of journal is nonsense for the most part, yet these nonsenses help to recollect times and persons and things upon occasion. . . . When I consider that it is the most trifling things sometimes that help us to recover more material things, I do not know that I should omit trifles ; they may be of use to me, though to others they would appear ridiculous ; but, as nobody is to see them but myself, I will let myself take any notes, never so trifling, for my own use."

Byrom appears to have had a marvellous memory, thanks to which we possess long, detailed records of his conversations and discussions ; these, so far as they can be

[1] See the Note on Byrom's poetry at the end of this chapter.

checked, give the impression of great accuracy. The opinions, for instance, which he puts into the mouth of William Law harmonize for the most part admirably with what we otherwise know of that great man.[1]

This is not the place to set out any full account of the genial John Byrom and his doings. But something must be said of his religious views and connections, and of his relationships to the little world of Quakerism and to his future " Master ", William Law.

Byrom's father was a pious Churchman, a devout student of the Bible, who endeavoured to shield his son from the deistic and other heresies of the time. The son, if not the father, was attached to the Nonjuring branch of the English Church, and had Jacobite sympathies of a mild kind.[2] But this attachment must have been very

[1] The only edition hitherto printed of John Byrom's Journal is that published by the Chetham Society of Manchester in four volumes during the years 1854–57—*The Private Journal and Literary Remains of John Byrom :* edited by Richard Parkinson, D.D. May some enterprising publisher be inspired before long to bring out a new edition !

Byrom's poems were first printed in 1773, ten years after his death, when John Wesley tells us that he read them with much enjoyment. They were reprinted in 1814, and again in 1895 and 1912 by the Chetham Society, in a sumptuous edition of five volumes, with elaborate annotations by A. W. Ward. The fourth volume also contains a missing portion of the author's Journal (for the years 1730 and 1731).

Since completing this chapter I have become acquainted with Arthur Ponsonby's entertaining volume on *English Diaries* (Methuen, 1923). Mr. Ponsonby only gives a notice of some two and a half pages to Byrom's *Journal,* and he falls very short, in my opinion, of doing justice either to its manifold interest or to the character of its author. The same criticism may be passed on the eight-page notice which he allots to the diaries and journals of John Wesley.

[2] *Nonjurors* was the name given to the clergy and others of the Established Church who refused to take the oaths of allegiance to William and Mary or to George I, as well as the oath of abjuration to the Stuart dynasty, and became therefore ineligible for any position in Church, State, or University. (Byrom actually took the oaths, though his sympathy was strongly with those refusing.)

The Nonjurors had unauthorized chapels of their own, where the services were held for the most part in accordance with the Church liturgy, except that the office of the Eucharist tended to gather round it more ritual and solemnity than was to be found in other Anglican churches of this period.

loose, for he chose as a rule to attend the Established Church instead of a Nonjuring place of worship, and indeed on some Sundays he missed church altogether.[1] During the early years of his married life he took remarkable interest in learning the opinions and practices of the different sects and schools of thought ; he was friendly with Dissenters and Romanists, he consorted with Deists, and we have records of his attending the gatherings of several of the Nonconformist bodies.

Thus twice (in 1723 and 1725) he goes on a Sunday to the " Anabaptists' meeting " (missing church apparently). When Count Zinzendorf was in London in 1739, he went to hear him preach at a Moravian gathering. He almost certainly took part in some of the early Methodist assemblies (which were just beginning in 1737). Later on, at any rate, we hear of him as a listener to Charles Wesley's preaching, and again to Whitefield's at a family service in the residence of the Calvinist Countess of Huntingdon, who had invited him to dinner. To the Methodist movement in general Byrom unhappily preserved like Law an attitude of rather cold neutrality, but he kept on friendly terms with his old pupils the Wesleys, in spite of his outspoken protests against their attacks on Law and Boehme.[2] Generally speaking, we always find Byrom on the side of tolerance, maintaining " the absurdity of persecuting one another for differences of opinion ".

His general attitude is well expressed in the following ironical verses, which form a remarkable indication how he anticipated the " superdenominational " spirit to which William Law was then only gradually attaining. (They

---

[1] The following entry is thoroughly Byromic. " Sunday, 23rd [March, 1735] : rose at 8 ; went to go to St. Clement's Church, but as I went through Lincoln's Inn called at Taylor White's, and stayed there all day. Mem.—to resist the little temptations in order to avoid greater which [are] consequent upon them."

[2] Thus, when Charles Wesley visited Manchester in 1756, he records in his Journal, " I dined with my candid friend and censor, Dr. Byrom ". (Jackson's *Life*, ii, p. 128.)

John Byrom

JOHN BYROM AT CAMBRIDGE UNIVERSITY

occur in the *Journal* for November, 1730, and may be taken as typical in quality of most of his less inspired theological verse.)

Churchmen are orthodox, Dissenters pure,
But Quakers are God's people to be sure ;
The Lutherans follow evangelic truth,
But all the elect are Calvinists forsooth ;
The Baptists only have regeneration,
While out of them there can be no salvation.

We form a Church [compacted ?] of the seven ;
" Lo, here is Christ ! lo, here the way to heaven ! "
Thus do the sons of England, Rome, Geneva,
Adjure by Jesus like the sons of Sceva—
Wanting the love that should enforce the call,
An evil spirit overcomes them all.[1]

Combined with this wide tolerance was a persistent longing for an intimate knowledge of the God of Love, and a desire to do His will in daily life.   This it was that drove Byrom to some of the fountain-heads of mystical religion, though it must be confessed that his choice of sources was somewhat erratic.   His first prophet was the French philosopher-monk Father Malebranche,[2] who was superseded ere long by an eccentric Flemish visionary, Antoinette Bourignon, whose influence over quite a number of distinguished men of the period is something of a riddle.   Finally Byrom fell under the spell of William Law and Law's

[1] These four lines refer to the incident related in Acts xix. 13–16, where the seven sons of Sceva, a Jewish priest, tried to exorcise an evil spirit with the mere name of Jesus, with the result that the possessed man attacked and wounded them. [Byrom's *Poems* (Chetham Society), Vol. II, Part I, p. 71.]

[2] *Nicolas Malebranche* (1638–1715) was a mystic and a follower of Descartes, who spent much of his life in the religious house of the Oratorians in Paris.   His guiding conception that " We see all things in God " fascinated William Law, when an undergraduate at Cambridge, and he " kept his act " (*i.e.* wrote a thesis) upon this theme.

master, Jacob Boehme,[1] and to their guidance he appears to have remained true till the end of his long life. The stages of this evolution can be traced in the pages of the *Journal*.

Byrom was a younger contemporary of Law at Cambridge University, where he knew him by name, but apparently not otherwise. Law came to the front as a writer in the year 1717, but we have no indication that Byrom took any interest in his controversial writings, whether directed against the latitudinarian Bishop of Bangor, or against the sceptical Mandeville. But he bought Law's great work, *A Serious Call to a Devout and Holy Life*, immediately on its appearance in 1729, and its austere precepts evidently made a deep impression on him. Most of his easygoing friends were naturally unconvinced by Law's severe warnings ; poor John Byrom was three-quarters convinced, and yet incapable of following his prophet. Thus Law insists on the duty of early rising. " Rising this morning (*i.e.* at 7 a.m.) ", writes Byrom in February, 1729, " makes me sleepy ;[2] but I must rise every morning soon, as my friend Law says, for it is a shame to lie a-bed." But alas, he cannot keep his resolution, and three weeks later we read, " Monday, 11th : rose at 12—why not sooner ? God be merciful to me a sinner ! " Again, in January, 1730, we have the record of a supper party at the Mitre Inn : " talked about Hebrew points, happiness, Law, stage plays, we paid 2s., I two bottles— too much for a defender of Law to drink." He was shaken too in his views of the lawfulness of theatre-going for a Christian, though it is doubtful how far he eventually abandoned the practice, so reprehensible in the eyes of the great moralist.

Meanwhile Byrom was seeking for opportunities of personal contact with Law,[3] who was at that time (and for

---

[1] See page 268–70 below.

[2] He usually wrote his journal last thing at night.

[3] We are reminded of Boswell and Dr. Johnson some thirty years after this. The Mitre Inn mentioned in the last paragraph is presumably the Mitre Tavern in Fleet Street, which was Johnson's favourite place of resort.

some ten years after their first meeting) chaplain and tutor in the house of Mr. Gibbon, the historian's grandfather, at Putney. Several of Byrom's acquaintances knew Law, and it was with one of these that in March, 1729, Byrom went to Putney to pay his first call. At the Bull Inn, where they were eating mutton chops, Mr. Law came to them, and we have the first of several long conversations recorded with the great man. Byrom had from the outset an extraordinary veneration for the author of the *Serious Call*, and it was years before he was at his ease in approaching him. "I longed", he tells a friend in November, 1731, "to write to Mr. Law, but it seemed so like invocation of saints, that I know not how to venture". During the next few years he meets Law at a book-sale (both men were enthusiasts for buying up old copies of the mystical writers), in the street, in college rooms at Cambridge, and elsewhere. Their last recorded interview, before Fanny Henshaw appears on the scene, was in June, 1735, at Putney.[1]

Byrom's interest in Quakerism began some years before he came under the ascendancy of Mr. Law. In April, 1725, on a Sunday, when he missed church in London, as some compensation he visited first a Baptist and then a Quaker meeting. This is the solitary record of such attendance, though some years later (1731) in the course of a remarkable journey taken on foot from London to Manchester he stopped by the town of Henley to "hear a piece of a Quaker woman's sermon".[2] In the year 1729,

[1] On this occasion Law did his best to wean Byrom from his infatuation for his admired Madame Bourignon. Both were at the time coming under the influence of their future guide in theology, the "Teutonic philosopher", Jacob Boehme or Behmen. Whether Byrom, without Law, would have adopted him as prophet, may be doubted, though he seems to have bought and read a volume or two of his mystical writings with appreciation before Law did, *i.e.* as early as January, 1731. And he was discussing "Behmen" in 1735 with his Quaker acquaintances, Vigor and Penn, at the *Three Tuns* over a supper of radishes, cheese, and white wine, and two pipes, "which made me very sleepy".

[2] Perhaps I may recall here the witty but rude remark made by Dr. Johnson, when Boswell told him (on Sunday, July 31, 1763) that he had

during the course of a party at the King's Arms in London, where " we were very merry ", Byrom records that " we had the *Friends' Yearly Epistle* ¹ which I read to them, and Salkeld said it was stupid, and we that it was very good ". Two years later he was reading Barclay's *Apology*,² if not with approval, at any rate with understanding and interest.

Byrom had found a very congenial acquaintance in a certain William Vigor,³ a Quaker, though evidently a rather nominal member of his religious society.   He was an occasional traveller on the Continent and an interesting talker.   Vigor, himself a shorthand pupil of Byrom's, secured him another pupil in William Penn, eldest grandson of the founder of Pennsylvania, who, after paying Byrom the usual five guineas, had his first lesson in the Pennsylvania coffee-house.⁴

been hearing a woman preach " at a meeting of the people called Quakers " : " Sir, a woman's preaching is like a dog walking on his hind legs. It is not done well ; but you are surprised to find it done at all."

¹ From the latter part of the seventeenth century to the present day the Society of Friends in " Yearly Meeting " assembled has invariably issued an Epistle of advice and exhortation addressed primarily to their own members.   When Byrom read this Epistle (June 9, 1729) it was only ten days since the Yearly Meeting in question had been held.

Salkeld seems to have been somewhat of a sceptic.   At any rate on another occasion he introduces Byrom to a poem by a deist writer.   In this 1729 " Epistle " there are earnest exhortations to Friends to prevent their children and servants from reading either " plays, romances, and all such books as have a tendency to lead their minds from God and draw their youthful affections to a love of the world ", or " such vile and corrupt books as manifestly tend to oppose and reject the divine authority of the Holy Scripture, and to introduce deism, atheism, etc.".   This may very well have seemed " stupid " to Mr. Salkeld, and " very good " to a would-be disciple of William Law.

² See note on page 211 below.

³ I can find nothing of interest in regard to William Vigor, except the references in Byrom's Journal and the fact of his being the third husband of a lady (previously Mrs. Ward), of whose letters an entertaining volume from Russia was published anonymously in 1775. (Her other two husbands had been representatives of Britain in Russia.) Byrom's friendship with Vigor can be traced from about 1728 till 1748 at least.

⁴ This William Penn, third of the name, was born in 1703 and afterwards went to live on the family estate in Ireland, to which he succeeded and where he died, after an unhappy married life, in 1746–7.   His first

Shortly afterwards, as the result of an invitation from Will. Vigor, Byrom had the unusual experience of attending a Quaker gathering, though one of by no means a solemn kind.

"Went to Pen's coffee-house, and W. Vigor was there, and presently William Penn came to us, and we went to the White Lion, and sat by ourselves a little talking shorthand, and then went into the next room, where Friend Aubrey (uncle to William Penn),[1] Friends William Read and John, and Friend Jos. Vigor [2] came to us after; we had two quarts of peas to supper, three of us; we staid till two o'clock or near it, three of us [*sic*], W. Vigor, Read and I; we were very merry and talked much about religion, manners, etc.; Read invited the two Vigors and me to dinner tomorrow at two o'clock."

It is evident that most of the Quakers with whom Byrom came into close contact were of a somewhat worldly and pleasure-loving sort. This undoubtedly diminished his respect for the Society. We are fortunate in possessing a (slightly defective) transcript of a document which sums up the judgment which Byrom had formed in regard to Quakerism by the year 1730. It provides also a very characteristic picture of his religious outlook. A certain E. Lampe [3] had written asking him to engage in a disputa-

---

wife was a granddaughter of Robert Barclay of the *Apology*, which may in part account for Byrom's interest in that book. (In Byrom's Journal for June 19, 1729, he is described as "nephew" to the founder, but this must be a mistake, as indeed appears from another entry—March 31, 1737—and from the reference to William Aubrey quoted on this page.)

[1] William Aubrey married Letitia Penn, daughter of the "Founder," in 1702. He died in 1731.

[2] He married a cousin of Byrom, and was probably a brother of W. Vigor.

[3] This Quaker is perhaps to be identified with Ephraim Lampe (born 1705), son of Dr. Henry Lampe (1660–1711), a remarkable German, who suffered with the French Huguenots, came to Canterbury, where he joined the Society of Friends, and finally settled as a physician at Ulverston in Lancashire.

tion against Quakerism in the town of Stockport.   Byrom
replied as follows [1] :—

Dear Sir,

I do remember a dispute you had with Mr. Deale ;
and I have been told that you had a dispute with him,
whether he would or not, which appeared as a police-report.
But, as you are asking me to oppose in conjunction with
him any person who would take your part in defence of
Quakerism, [this] obliges me to tell you that I had no
dispute or controversy to take, to have, or to hold with
any person whatever—Christianity being always more
injured than advantaged by such means.

I am desirous to enjoy my own way of thinking to
myself, and to receive or communicate any sentiments that
may tend to promote true Christian duty, charity, [self- ?]
mortification and self-denial, and cure that vanity, love of
pleasure, of riches, of any created thing, in short, that
[passes ?] with all our fine talking.   But, as for disputing,
as far as I can perceive, 'tis the evil of our pride and self-
conceitedness that tempts us to it oftener than anything
else ;   which obliges me to resist any temptation thereunto.
Besides, would you have me dispute against the principles
of Quakerism, before I know what they are ?   I had a
letter from you to explain them to me.   But I am never
the wiser ;   and all that I can learn concerning the Quakers
is either :

1st.   They do say that every man has the light of faith
in him, if he would walk by it ;   that we must follow the
light within, and be led by the Spirit of God.   For want
of obedience to Him many and great corruptions have been
brought into Christianity ;   and stairs lead up [?] towards
matters which belongeth rather to inward . . . ;   and
herein I agree with them.

2nd.   That they wear particular habits and use particular

<hr />

[1] This letter is taken from Byrom's shorthand copy transcribed and
printed in App. V, p. 592 of Vol. II, Pt. II, of the Poems (Chetham Soc.).

pronouns, avoiding the custom of lifting the hat off, and such-like ceremonies of gesture and speech ; and these things, supported from no faction about them, I suppose to be matters of indifference, which a man may use or let alone, as he finds it suitable to himself.

3rd. That they abolish Baptism and the Lord's Supper, two positive institutions of Jesus Christ, without any particular revelation or command from Him to lay them aside, and in general [feel ?] contempt at all outward ways used in all Churches of Christians of showing our willingness to obey and communicate with the governors and members of Christian societies.   And in these things I cannot justify them, neither have I any authority to call upon them to do it, being myself none of [their] number, but baptized according to the Church of England, wherein I think I can be edified [sooner than in] another profession, if it be not my own fault.

I am far from being an enemy of the Quakers because of their name " Quakers."   It is their life, their love of the world, their wisdom as to this generation, their luxury and neglect of that Spirit which they particularly pretend to, which I blame in a Quaker as well as in myself and others.   I exhort you, upon the whole, Friend Lampe, [to] curb that spirit of dispute that will engage you in talking and spluttering about Christianity, while you should be manifesting it in the quiet spirit [by] prudent and serious behaviour at all occasions.   In taking this advice, reason will justify. . . .[1]

Your humble Servant,
J. BYROM

I have no doubt that Byrom was perfectly sincere when he wrote in the above letter that he blamed *in himself* luxury and the love of the world.   From the time when he read the *Serious Call* and began to make William Law's ideals of life and faith his own, he was a man of a constantly

[1] The concluding sentence is unintelligible.

divided and penitent mind, never succeeding in living up to the very austere standard of Christian conduct which he had set before him. His life was on the whole pleasant and comfortable, if we allow for a certain measure of ill-health and the long absences from his beloved wife and children ; he seems to have spent as a rule much more of the day in recreation and congenial society than in work. But we may admire him for his constant cheerfulness, his kindly, affectionate disposition, his unfailing sympathy with poor folk in distress, his honesty with his own feelings, his generous tolerance of opponents, and, last but not least, for his accurate observation and industry in keeping records —qualities which have preserved for us one of the most vivid and valuable series of pictures of the early Georgian epoch.

It is now high time that we should turn to those portions of the *Journal* which bear upon the episode of Fanny Henshaw and William Law. The origin of Byrom's intimate acquaintance with this young woman is veiled in impenetrable obscurity. On October 14, 1736, Fanny makes an abrupt first appearance in the *Journal*, though she is referred to familiarly and as an acquaintance of some standing, under the initials " F. H."

" Thursday, 14th : came from Damhouse, the third time of my being there, Mrs. Hilton of Park being there a-visiting, whom I did not see, choosing to come away *incog*. We should have all a-ridden out, that is Mrs. Sutton and F. H., to Mr. Leigh's, but this visit prevented Mrs. Sutton ; and F. H. behind William [1] brought me part of the way and returned back to tea, and I came to Kersall,[2] where I drank tea and went to

---

[1] *i.e.* on horseback (pillion).

[2] Kersall Cell (two and a half miles north-west of Manchester) became John Byrom's property and residence not long after this, by the death of his elder brother in 1740. Here his extensive library remained almost intact for over a hundred years after his death, until it was removed to the Chetham Library in Manchester, where it is now to be seen.

Manchester and went to see brother Josiah, who had been ill and was bled a day or two ago ; I supped there upon apple-tart and milk and talked with him much about F. H. ; he thought Mr. Law's a proper way."

From this passage we gather that Fanny was at the time residing with her uncle and guardian, Thomas Sutton, and her aunt, Mary Sutton, at the mansion of Dam House in the parish of Leigh, about seven or eight miles from Byrom's residence in Manchester.[1] The last words no doubt refer to the scheme just devised by Byrom to get the author of the *Serious Call* to try his persuasions upon the young woman, whose leanings towards Quakerism had been made known to Byrom at his visit to the family.

On the following day, October 15th, Byrom records a long conversation (covering some six pages of his *Journal*) which he had at the Manchester Exchange with one Abel Strethall,[2] who had apparently been commissioned to approach him by the Manchester Friends' Meeting, with members of which Fanny was in touch. It reads like a

[1] From Fanny Henshaw's autobiographical statement (see pages 82, 86, and 87) it seems probable that her stay with the Suttons did not begin before the earlier months of 1736. From a letter of Byrom's to his wife in 1733, we know that Byrom and his family were friendly with the Suttons, as well as with a Mrs. Mort, who was connected with them and living at Dam House (where Byrom visited her in 1730) till 1734, when her husband died and Thomas Sutton came into the property. Mrs. Mort was acquainted with a married sister of William Law, who lived at Derby. Thomas Sutton died at Kensington in 1759.

Dam House is a handsome Elizabethan Manor-House now much restored and originally surrounded by a moat. It is now called Astley Hall, and has been converted into the municipal hospital for the borough of Leigh.

Overton, probably following Walton, in a very brief reference to F. H. (he had not seen the letters) describes her as a *relative* of Byrom's. I have not been able to discover any evidence of this relationship. It is probably a mere guess or error of Walton's, due to his desire to account for the remarkable intimacy which existed (as their correspondence will show) between the good doctor and this attractive young woman.

[2] This Abel Strethall was probably a member of the well-known Quaker family of Strettell, who were then carrying on an extensive trading business in Dublin.

faithful and marvellously well memorized record of a verbal duel between the pertinacious Quaker and the writer, who did all he could to justify Fanny's relations and give his questioner as little information as possible, while remaining scrupulously polite. Abel Strethall asserted that Fanny was confined like a prisoner " as much as if she were in Lancaster Castle", brought back like a criminal when she had escaped in order to visit the Quakers, her letters to them intercepted, etc. Byrom disclaims knowledge of most of this, but appears to justify some kind of restraint, though (speaking doubtless from his sympathy with the Nonjurors) " he hates persecution as much as any Quaker can do ".

Abel Strethall further stated that Fanny's friends give out that she is mad and melancholy, and that her uncle must have sent for Byrom to refute Fanny's reasons for leaving the Church of her fathers. All the cautious Byrom will admit is that she had said that " if the truth did abide with the Quakers, she hoped to do so too", that he had seen " a writing of hers " [1] about the matter (which her uncle had asked her to draw up), that " she is a very good girl and I hope will judge for herself and do that which is best ".

So the interview ended, and the next day Byrom sat down to write to Fanny the following letter :—

" Saturday afternoon.

" Dear Miss Fanny : How do you do ? [Here follows a passage relating to an obscure legal matter.] . . . Since I saw you last, the man who spoke to my brother asked me the same question—what I intended to do with F. H. ?— and many others of much the same pertinency, which I endeavoured to answer in such a way as might give the least offence to any one, the least intimation to him that might be improper, and the least occasion of any uneasiness to you. He talked much of confinement, persecution, etc., which I imputed to his zeal and his ignorance of the true

---

[1] Presumably F. H.'s *Case*. See page 87.

state of your case.   I perceive that if I was subject to the inquisition of these good people I should be poorly off.

" Oh, dear Fanny, be content and thankful for all things! You cannot probably do all at once ; but endeavour to recover from a long unprofitable [infliction ?] of these people, and employ that humility which your afflictions have acquired you in conversing meekly with your domestic friends ; let them know that you are sensible of their love and kindness, and that you hope to do your duty among them.

" This man talked to me of a letter, that was the property of Lydia Miller, and taken from the person to whom it was delivered contrary to law, etc.,—rare stuff this in so tender a case as yours.[1]   I am glad that letter is not Lydia Miller's property, though Lydia might have known that you would not have jumped into their meetings so readily as she was pleased to propose.   You was glad yourself, I dare say, that this letter went not, and will take care how any do for the future.

" I desired you to select your known acquaintance among them, if you would write, which had better not be. But I believe I need not be so scrupulous, for, if you write to one, you write to all ; they are so spiritual that they act all in a body on these occasions, as far as I apprehend. And I commend their diligence and would imitate it in preserving you among your present cordial friends, who will, I hope, always rejoice to see you act the good Christian —Oh that I might do it at last myself !   I have not time to say a thousand things ; write me if I say wrong."

This fatherly epistle crossed one of Fanny's, which Byrom received just before starting to church on the Sunday.   He found time hastily to compose an answer before going, from which the following is taken :—

" I am sorry that you should be denied joy and satisfaction in going whither I am going just now.[2]   When I see

---

[1] Fanny was at the time in her twenty-second or twenty-third year.
[2] *i.e.* to church.

the harm on't, I shall forbear ; when I see the good, I will to your joy and satisfaction—who can help wishing it ?

" Remember, I neither urge nor will urge you knowingly to do anything against your conscience.   But at the same time I suppose that we may be mispersuaded ; and that which has given you joy and satisfaction appears to me preferable to that which has given you sadness and disquiet.

" Your letter to L. M. [Lydia Miller] is in my hands, and the others—nobody has or shall see them without your express orders.   I keep all your papers they light on, that none may see them or talk of them ; if I am wrong in this, command it otherwise.   I do as I would for my own child, but am sensible that I may miss it ; therefore I desire to stand corrected, but because of my infirmity, I would engage as little with a multitude as possible.

" I have but little time now.   I repeat my service to you as long as acceptable and useful, and no longer ; I will see you whenever you shall desire it.   I will do my best, and if I err, God and my neighbour forgive me !   I pray you to have a good heart and to put as good a construction upon that which once did (and again will, I hope) give you satisfaction as upon other things.   Adieu, and be happy ! "

Evidently Fanny's uncle and aunt were reposing great confidence in the Doctor—" I keep all your papers they light on ", that is, intercept ! Certainly she was being treated at the age of two-and-twenty as a child, though there may have been some degree of justification for this in the intense and dangerous mental depression, to which she herself confessed (see page 84).   The surprising thing is that Miss Fanny, however much humiliated she secretly felt, seems to have taken all this in good part.   For in her next letter, a few days later, to Byrom, she writes, " Continue still to do for me as a child, nay, even allow me the satisfaction to esteem you as a parent ".   (Byrom had the advantage that he was earning her gratitude by repre- senting Fanny in some legal proceedings, to the exact

nature of which we have not the key.) Fanny's letter
ended as follows :—

" May I hope to see you in a few days ?   I much desire
that favour, for I want to talk with you and consult with
uncle and aunt how we may best order for this journey.[1]
O that we were on the road !   Time seems long ere we
set about it.   Pray let me see you.   I was very ill last
night, and am yet but poorly.   It is late, and wishing you
a good night, I must at present bid adieu.   My love to
all, my aunt sends hers.

" Yours, F. HENSHAW."

Then immediately follows in the Doctor's Journal the
following account of Fanny's attitude in the face of her
critical friends.

" It seems Mrs. Sutton had read my last letter to her
in a tone as if I was angry ; so she told me before F. H.
And I said that I was not angry, but that one must be
careful not to be deceived by too good opinion of folks.
She was very well in health this time of my going, and had
a pretty good night.   She would not be persuaded to go to
the chapel,[2] and the last thing I said to her, when I came
away on Saturday after tea-time, was about that, that I
thought she had better go to the chapel, because, to preserve
her impartiality now, she had taken the best course to
satisfy herself ; but this forbearance seemed like a determination on one side, and I appealed to her if I could
say less.

" She said once, when I said something about this
matter, that ' she must ' (or ' one must ') ' see for themselves
in some things ' ; and once, when I was talking to her
alone, she seemed to say that she was willing to have others

---

[1] This journey (on horseback), for which Fanny will shortly be ordering
a riding-habit, was to visit her uncle Cripps at Doncaster, as appears below.

[2] Probably the Nonjurors' Chapel, of which there were two then in
Manchester.   Fanny's relatives were Nonjurors, like Byrom (in sympathies
at least) and William Law.

satisfied as well as herself (in such a manner that she struck me silent, it looked so like a resolution to be a Quaker), but that she would do what should be thought necessary for the satisfaction of others. And [she] always expressed herself as if sure that it was God that spoke to her, that, if it had not been for baptism and communion, she should have gone to the Quakers long ago. When I said once that the Quakers would be angry at me and say things, etc., she said that would nettle her more than anything.

"She used the expressions, ' I often told them,' and ' they often told me,' so that I told her she had conversed with them more than she thought for. But she still thought that it was not from them, but from herself or something within her, that she had such and such notions. She called the service of the Church ' prayers made ready for her,' and when I urged her to give me reason why she could not go, she said, ' How could she go to prayers that were not fit for every condition ? ' ; and instanced one, that of thanksgiving (' O come let us sing,' [1] I suppose), which she thought in her condition not right. To which I replied, that it was our duty in all times and places to thank God. Mrs. Sutton mentioned a young woman at Doncaster that turned Quaker, as one that she had been acquainted with, when I mentioned to her having been acquainted with them ; and F. H. said that she admired her courage always, because her aunt used her so.

"We could not persuade her that she had a partiality for the Quakers, though it seemed so to us both [that] whenever anything was said about them, she construed it so favourably for them. She mentioned often a paragraph in the news, about a clergyman at Minehead going into the Quakers' meeting. She read in Isaiah and Jeremiah, and thought them very plain and easy. I desired her not to enter into dispute with Mr. Maudsley,[2] hinting to her

---

[1] *i.e.*, Psalm xcv. in the Morning Prayer service.
[2] The parish clergyman (of Astley), to whom the letter printed on page 98 above may possibly have been addressed. Cp. also page 147.

that it was not so decent. I told [her] I hoped I should never hear of her preaching in a Quakers' meeting, calling it an indecent thing.

" F. H. writ a letter by me to Mrs. Worral to make a riding habit, that she should want it soon. [On] which I saying, ' Why need you say so ? ', she said, ' Why, she will not make it else.' And she had writ at the bottom, ' Your Friend, etc.' ; and I said, ' Why cannot you write " Your humble servant ? "'—what harm, Miss Fanny ? Do not see harm where there is none in words.' [1]

" I mentioned a religion no older than Damhouse, 1650. And as I was riding home, it was strongly upon my mind about ' the stones out of the wall would speak ' ; before the year 1650 no Christians ever did so and so, rejecting baptism, the Lord's prayer, have silent meetings, etc.[2]

" She expected her sister and Miss Haynes home from Mr. T[rafford's] on Saturday night ; but Phe.[3] told me when I came home that they had sent a letter to stay three weeks longer, which I thought would surprise F. H.

" She talked very prettily sometimes, when she turned the discourse to serious ; and that, if it would please God that she might do His will and not her own, it was all that she wished for, everything else being indifferent.

" Mr. J. Walker,[4] who had called upon me the Friday

[1] Barclay observes that " in this last age he is esteemed an uncivil man, who will not to his inferior or equal subscribe himself *Servant*". He mentions especially " Your humble servant " as one of those flattering titles the use of which has accustomed Christians to lie. (*Apology*, Prop. XV, Sect. IV.)

[2] George Fox began preaching about 1647. There is a reference here to Habakkuk ii. 11 : " For the stone shall cry out of the wall ". Probably the date 1650 was inscribed on a stone in one of the walls of Dam House, where Fanny was living. It is remarkable that (according to the *Victoria County History of Lancashire*) the date " A.D. 1600 " is still to be seen inscribed on an oak timber in the wall of Dam House. The mansion was altered and restored at different dates subsequent to this.

[3] *i.e.* Phebe Byrom, his sister.

[4] For J. Walker, see page 150 below, from where and elsewhere it appears that he was a reader of mystical writings, and an admiring acquaintance of William Law's from an earlier date than Byrom.

morning that I went, and had his notes and [a] note of
£100, drank a dish of tea with me and asked me why the
Quakers denied baptism, etc. ; and I asked him if they had
said anything to him, and he said that Abel Strethall had
spoke to him, to know if he had heard anything of her,
and wondered at my going there and thought it very odd
that I should converse with a young woman of twenty-one,
which I thought a little carnal of Friend Abel. But I
would endeavour to give no offence of this nature, though
I hope God will preserve me from doing anything in His
sight that is sinful ; for however imperfect my endeavours
may be, I hope that I have no other [aim] but to assist her
as one Christian should assist another. If I was to
consider my own wretchedness, I should indeed forbear ;
but, as I hope that God can employ even me if He pleases,
I will not hide my talent under a napkin. And I hope God
will bless the event, to whom I shall esteem the good effect
due just as much as if it was a miracle, so little do I think
there is in me, but rather the contrary, to procure any good."

On November 2nd Byrom wrote again a brief note to
Fanny, and was meditating sending her a tract on " Regeneration". Moreover, about this time, though he does not
record it, he must have written, no doubt with great reverence and expectation, to the Reverend William Law at
Putney, expressing to him the desire that he should write,
for the sake of her soul, one or more letters to the misguided
damsel. While the last passage quoted from the privacy
of his Journal leaves no doubt, I think, that the good doctor
was sincerely anxious to preserve from a false step his
attractive and strong-willed protégée, he was also happy
in having an excuse for getting into closer acquaintance
with Mr. Law, with whom he was not as yet, in spite of
his devotion to him, on terms of any intimacy.[1]

Apparently Fanny's consent to receive the epistles had

[1] He had probably not seen Law for nearly eighteen months. Even in
1739 we find him writing that " he was not acquainted with Mr. Law, but
had seen him now and then ".

been obtained,[1] and, as an introduction to her, Byrom sent to Law a copy of the document known as her *Case*, of which, as we have seen, Law makes great use in his letters.

Towards the end of November Byrom's heart was rejoiced by receiving the following letter from Law :—

Putney, Nov. 20, 1736.

Dear Sir :

I received yours. I wish you had wrote sooner. What you call her *Case*, is very far from being so : as plainly appears from your letter. I will write some reflections upon it, and then give the best directions I can for her conduct, both with respect to the Quakers, etc. But this I can do only upon this condition, viz., that what I write be given to her entire and unaltered, and that what she has to say upon it, be under her own hand. If this be accepted of and you will let the correspondence be through your hands, I am ready to do all, that God shall enable me to do for her assistance.

My best respects to all friends,

I am your most affectionate humble servant,

W. LAW

To this Byrom replied by return of post.

Reverend Sir :

Going to answer yours, I just now receive this note from F. H. And a man and horse [are] come for me, and the man says there are two or three Quakers come hither, and I must go without any direction from you.

I would have writ sooner, but it was agreed that she should see you privately in person ; so much did I mistrust myself, and thought that then you would see how it was with her really.

Pray, sir, favour me with your assistance. I had never any thought of other conditions than those just and reason-

[1] See her statement quoted in Byrom's letter to Law on page 135 below.

able ones which you propose. I will absolutely comply with your directions to me in everything, by God's help. If God has given you talent to help at this time, hide it not from us. I commit myself to Him, for I know not how to behave with these people. Her " Case " was her own writing before I saw her at her uncle's.

Whatever it really be, I hope it may please God to prevent my being an hindrance to her relief, which is what I shall be as careful of as I can ; but I should have been glad of an hint from you how to behave on this point. I suppose it best for [her] not to turn Quaker, that a good spirit calls her to be a good Christian, and a wrong spirit gives a wrong turn to it. If I am wrong, please to set me right ; it is necessary for and will oblige

Your obedient humble servant,

J. BYROM

Tuesday evening.

The hesitation and want of self-confidence displayed in this letter of Byrom's is significant. We see, too, that the wide tolerance he had shown of recent years towards Quakerism and other forms of religious belief did not prevent him being distressed when someone intimate with him was bent on leaving the Church of England.

Here follows an interval of about three weeks, during which Law's letters to " Mrs. F. H." were written. Meanwhile, not to anticipate by saying more, a crisis in Fanny's affairs had arisen. The news was duly communicated to Law, with a brief outline of the facts contained in Byrom's letter below. Hence Law's further letter :—

Putney, Dec. 17, 1736.

Dear Sir,

I suppose before this you have received another letter from me, which makes the fifth on this occasion, and is the second not yet seen by her.

When yours came I had almost finished another long

letter, which I intended should be the last, unless fresh matter appeared ; at the receipt of yours I took off my pen, but perhaps may finish it and send it to you. If she could see these letters in the manner she has seen the others, I like it very well, but not in any other way, because I have nothing of them here.[1] I leave it to your discretion to let anybody see them that has a mind, or to whom you think they might be of any benefit ; only no transcripts.

I plainly foresaw M. Guion [2] at the bottom, and intended to have said something to that point, though she had concealed it in her *Case*. I am not sorry that they intend to print it. Pray take care of that copy of it which she drew up for me, and which your sister has, and let it be dated, if it is not already.

I forgot once or twice to speak of the expense you put yourself to in the letters you send, I desire that may be omitted, I am willing to bear my part in it. All blessings be with you all.

Yours,

W. LAW

To the above letter of Law's we now have Byrom's lengthy answer.[3]

To The Revd. Mr. Wm. Law
    at Putney
        near London.
                Manchester, December 21, 1736.

Revd. Sir,

I received yours of December 17 this day, and the second letter not seen by her, before. I told you that I

[1] This seems to mean that he had not kept any copies of the letters, and that he wanted the originals back, so that Fanny must not keep them. See page 231, where Byrom writes returning them to Law.

[2] *i.e.* Madame Guyon—see note on page 137 below.

[3] This letter, hitherto unpublished, is preserved in Dr. Williams' Library. Up to this point, the correspondence and narrative recorded in this chapter (*i.e.* from October 14, 1736—see page 120 above) is almost wholly taken from Byrom's *Journal*, Vol. II, Part I, pp. 64–82.

had writ to her to Doncaster to know if she had a desire to see that which I had received first. This afternoon her cousine that went with her returned through this town to her unkle's and gave us an account that she was for going to Balby to the Quakers from her unkle Cripps's, but was opposed in that design by her aunt who was much concerned upon her account ; that upon that denial she grew fretfull and passionate, to such a degree that her unkle, seeing his wife so much disturbed and her so much resolved, thought it as well for the peace of the family to let her go, if she would, to the Quakers at some other place, and not to Balby so near them. And so Leek, as I apprehend, is now to be [the] scene of her open entrance into outward Quakerism, and that in a few days—Leek in Staffordshire, whereabouts she was born and where some Quakers for whom she had contracted an esteem were neighbours.

My letter reached her at Doncaster, and by her young kinswoman she returns an answer in these words, after saying how she left her unkle's : " I trust in God the affliction which all my friends have had on my account will end in the satisfaction and benefit I seek and trust in God to receive. I shall at any time be very glad to see so kind a friend as I ever found in Dr. B., and hope I shall never forfeit the esteem and respect due to so much merit and friendship. I am greatly obliged both to you and Mr. L., and should wish a continuance of so good correspondence and, although I cannot in all respects agree in your sentiments, it does not in the least lessen my respect for your goodness.

" My reason for professing the Quaker faith and worship is that I find it (to me at least) the most agreable to Scripture doctrine, in perticular the Epistle to the Hebrews and Gallatians.[1] Again I cannot find peace or satisfaction out of this way.

---

[1] These two Epistles were great favourites with the early Quakers, inasmuch as they emphasize the contrast between the religion of the Spirit and the law of ordinances.

" Here I hope to imitate Thomas a Kempis and also to follow the same pattern he so lively represents and followed. And do my best to live Miranda's [1] Life, for I have a great desire to be pleasing to God, as she undoubtedly is.

" My dearest love and sincerest thanks attends all my good friends, Dr. B. in perticular, who I hope believes me his most obliged

" F. HENSHAW."

I write her name in greater letters, that being her manner since she received Mrs. Drummond's letter, who does so, and she I suppose in humble imitation ; for she did not before that time.

She writ a letter to Mr. Smith (which was to have gone by the post to him, but did not [2]) in these words, " How did I fear I had taken a wrong step in seperating from my dear friend ! [meaning when she came with me to my brother's, instead of going quite away with this Mr. Smith] I was greatly afflicted in soul and body and passed the whole night in severe conflicts and distressed agitations of fear."

Yet this poor creature, when she had recovered her cooler thought a little, told my sister, who asked her why she was so much concerned, that it was for fear she had not done right in not going with the Quakers ; but that she thought it was better too that she had not gone with them and was glad that she had not. And so upon every rightish step she has been afraid at first and glad upon consideration ; and if the Quakers would have let her been at leasure, she would have acted, I believe, more considerately than she has done. And it seems as if they had been somewhat aware that they should lose her, if they did not,

[1] Miranda is the ideal Christian lady of Law's *Serious Call*, of whom there are reminiscences in Law's last letter to Fanny. (See notes on pages 63–4 above.)

[2] *i.e.* it was intercepted and sent to Byrom to read, like previous letters of poor Fanny !

by insinuating the danger of delay, prevent her consulting and considering, though she had determined to do so. She had an impulse that they were in the right, and they had an impulse that she was in the right ; and so what need of any further consideration ?   She goes on :—

"But tho' heaviness endured for a night, the God of our hope sent joy in the morning, [the very morning that she was in the greatest distress I had seen her in, when she writ me that strange note which I then sent you] O Israel, let us love Him, obey Him, and ever trust in Him, for with the Lord there is mercy and with Him is plenteous redemption.   O when shall the outcasts of Israel be united to the body to serve the Lord in freedom of spirit with an enlarged and thankfull heart ?   I greatly desire to be with you ere long, etc."

In the *Case* delivered to my sister, that was to have gone to you, the additions which I hinted to you are these.

"If I am not understood by the terms 'a second Magdalen,' I desire farther to explain myself in this matter.

"God has (for reasons to Himself best known), I hope for His own glory, been pleased to permit me for a year or more to be tormented, nay even possessed with an evil spirit whose power over me was for some time so absolute, that it drove me to the utmost extremity and dispair.   It was with the greatest difficulty that I strove to restrain myself from commiting violence on myself ; what unfeigned thanks therefore I am bound to return to my merciefull God, who gave not my enemie power to touch my life, though with malice he sought it. [I have seen a letter from the gentleman of the house where she was in her despairing way, that says she had attempted violence upon herself.]   But my God, casting an eye of mercy and compassion on my lost and deplorable condition, has miraculously preserved my life from the enemie's power and given me also hope by sincere and unfeigned repentance that He will bring my soul out of bondage and on my hearty obedience restore the lost sheep to His favour.

"Indeed I know not wherein I have so highly offended my gracious God to incur this heavy punishment, except in rejecting the doctrine and oppinion of the Quakers, by refusing to join myself in their worship, when opportunity offered, which I rejected ; upon which account began my affliction and troubles, which daily encreased, until of late, when God is pleased to offer me to open the gate to them that knock and by seeking to be delivered from mine enemie to serve Him in freedom of spirit." [1]

And then follows the paragraph, which I mentioned, relating to her going to you, thus.

"Notwithstanding I know it's the general oppinion of the profession of the Church of England that miracles are now ceased,[2] yet I go first to one [3] of the most worthy professors of this Church, to try if God will please through his assistance to give diliverence and free me from mine enemie, if it so please Him ; His will be done.

"Otherwise I must seek a remedy from the fountain of my affliction, and with Naimon be glad to wash in the river I disdained, and thereby experience who are the true prophets in Israel ; for my soul faithfully hopes such there are to be found, nor can she have rest untill she find them."

So that you see it must be a miracle if you do her any good. How differently did she talk to me, when she her self proposed you for the good Samaritan, etc. ! Her cousine tells me that she said she wished to see "the letter that Dr. B. told of"; nay, once she was almost consenting

[1] The whole of the above "additions" is to be found at the end of Fanny's *Case* (see pages 92–3 above).

[2] This statement of Fanny's may be held to indicate that she had come across many "deist" opinions among Churchmen, and also to refer to the Quaker insistence upon the continued operation of the Holy Spirit; and she may have perceived that William Law was coming to share their belief in this matter.

[3] "Mr. Law" is Byrom's own marginal note here.

to go to you overnight, but quite altered again next morning. I would have writ to her again, and offered to bring her your letters if she would, but that post goes not out till Fryday morn[ing]. If you think anything can be done or properly tryed, I will go to Leek or any place to finish this affair to the likeliest advantage to her.

The night after the Quakers had been to fetch her and been disappointed, two of them came to my house, and the maid came to tell me, where I was at another house, that two Quakers wanted me.[1] I judged at that time from the presumed nature of their errand that it was better to let them know that I was in company and, if they had any particular business, desired that they would leave a note. They sent word back that they had no business but came only to pay their respects, and left their names and went away exceedingly, as I since hear, offended. Which I was sorry for, designing rather to avoid than give offence, by any disputes that might or must have happened, I thought, between us. It was their Mr. Smith of Balby and Mr. Moss of this town who has resented it so heinously as to threaten (as I am told, but how to guess at such extraordinary menace I know not) to bring the whole body of the Quakers upon me, who, he says, are slow, but weighty ; and moreover to print the *Case*.[2]

I am most concerned at present for the poor bequakered party, whose unhappy case it is to be so infatuated. I cannot imagine that they will print the *Case*, till the *Case* is altered from what she has written it ; whose copy I shall take care of, according to your directions. I thank you for the liberty of showing the letters to particular friends. I will not suffer any transcript without order from your self, and if she sees any more, I will show them to her myself. It was impossible to conceal the correspondence ; but in whatever I have in my power your instructions shall be

[1] This was evidently the occasion when Byrom wrote, in considerable perplexity, his reply to Law's letter of November 20th.
[2] This of course refers to Fanny's statement.

punctually followed. I believe they may be usefull to others, if not to her—which yet they may some time or other. However you will perhaps finish them and touch upon M[adame] Guion, whom the Quakers pretend to have been a Quaker, and use her name in quakerizing such as they can prevail upon. F. H. has had a pamphlet about this lady put into her hands sometime ago.[1] I thought her mistaken in the text she told of, which I thought was " the Kingdom of God is within you." There is much talk here of a converted Quaker at Halifax, who is well known in this town, and of this young perverted lady, who, if you pursue the means which appear so proper to bring

---

[1] Jeanne Marie de la Mothe Guyon (1648–1717), the friend of Fénelon and the victim of Bossuet, had only died comparatively recently. Law at this period was very critical of her (see page 146), but his admiration of her increased in his later years. With Molinos and Fénelon she is the leading name among the continental Quietists.

The pamphlet referred to by Byrom is probably a twelve-page quarto tract entitled *A Letter to J. O.*, which consists mostly of extracts from the " Lady Guion's " writings, bearing on the way of inward prayer and of finding Christ in the heart. It is signed " J. M.", 1727, and is the work of Josiah Martin.

With Byrom's statement here compare the following words of Martin at the end of a long " Apologetic Preface " to his translation of Fénelon's *Dissertation on Pure Love* (p. cxxvii) :—

" Some perhaps may say this lady [*i.e.* Madame Guion] was a good Catholick, because she took the sacrament every day : but we take the universal love and charity she breathes in her writings, even towards strangers and those too out of the pale of her Church, to be a much better criterion and token of her being a good Catholick."

For an eighteenth-century Quaker this is a very broadminded statement, and it is remarkable that the writer does not take the opportunity to emphasize the very real similarity with Quakerism of Madame Guyon's teaching in regard to the life of the spirit. Madame Guyon was of course a faithful, if independent, Catholic to the end of her life. There is no reason to think that she had any knowledge of the Quakers.

Martin's pamphlet describes Madame Guyon as having become settled in the possession of God's love in the *twentieth* year of her age. This was just about Fanny's own age at the time of her conversion. I cannot explain Byrom's reference to " the text ", but the one he quotes is emphasized in the pamphlet.

For Josiah Martin and his interpretations of the quietists, see the second note at the end of this chapter.

her to a better sence of things, will, I would fain hope, perceive, acknowledge, and renounce her mistake.

My brother Josiah desired me to-day to give his service to you.

Your much obliged,

J. B.

The foregoing report of Byrom to Law, with its copious quotation from Fanny, enables us to form a tolerably clear picture of what happened.   But before I make any comment on it, it shall be supplemented by two letters written shortly after from within the Quaker fold at Balby.[1]

On January 8, 1736–7, Fanny writes as follows to her sister Nancy at Dam House (the letter reaching Byrom through his sister Phebe) :—

" My love and duty to my dearest sister forbid me being any longer silent.   Obedience and the love of my Creator and Redeemer makes all things sweet and easy, even the absence of my dearest relations, whom I love more dear than ever, in God and for Him, whose divine love adds to the number of my friends and makes the bonds of friendship strong and lasting ; absence cannot lessen but does increase mine.   I enjoy all things in content.   I meet with respect from all, in particular the kind friends with whom I reside, who send their true respects.   Be content, my dear, with the divine will ; I am truly so.

" The world, or even an husband to one of us, might have occasioned a separation in this life.   And shall we refuse, when God condescends to wed us to Himself ? Can we wish a better union, or be more happy in one another than in Him our Father, husband, and everlasting friend ? O let us love Him, and He'll never leave us, nor suffer His children to be overcome by the world or its allurements.

[1] A small village about a mile from Doncaster, which in the days of George Fox, who often lodged here, had been a great centre of Quakerism. In 1658 and 1660 general " Yearly Meetings " of Quakers were held here.

"I have much I could say, but a long letter may be tiresome at present. 'Twill be satisfaction, I doubt not, to tell my friends that my happiness increases daily in a tranquil and lasting peace in my soul and conscience. I hope my dearest uncle and aunt will accept my duty. I desire my love to cousin Sally and all enquiring friends.

"I am my dearest sister's truly affectionate sister,
                              "F. HENSHAW"

"My dear love to Dr. Byrom. I would write, if it would not be disagreeable, and also to Breretons. I shall be very glad to hear my dear friends in Lancashire are well.
          "Balby, 8th, 11th month."[1]

It is worthy of remark how interestingly this letter shows Fanny's feelings as a sensitive sister at strife with the cross she has taken up in adopting the "plain language" of the Quakers. She knows that the use of "thou" and "thy" would strike strangely on her sister's ear; and she has carefully framed her letter so as not to have to use either the "plain language" or the customary "you" and "your", which she had abandoned with her change of faith. Her new Quaker speech only comes out at the very end, in the date of the month.

It was at the house of an esteemed member of the Society, Thomas Smith of Balby, that Fanny Henshaw had found refuge for the time being. About a week later the following somewhat facetious letter was addressed by him to Miss Sally Haynes, the cousin in whose company Fanny had been visiting Doncaster :—

                    Balby, 15th, 11th mo, 1736.
"'Tis easy to believe a person of thy generous disposition can excuse this freedom in me, though my design in it

[1] *i.e.* January 8, 1737, according to the usual Quaker method of naming the months, at an epoch when the British calendar year began on March 25th. This letter and the one that here follows it will be found on pages 86-7 and 79-80 of Byrom's *Journal*, Vol. II, Part I.

is to chide thee for returning out of Yorkshire, before thou
had seen thy cousin ffanny arrived at that port which thou
knew she steered her course to. Had I been sure that
person I saw through my neighbour Crips's chamber
window one morning had been SALLY HAYNES (the
which I suspected but was not certain of it), I should not
have passed by without speaking to her. I know thou saw
me, am sorry thou would not use the freedom to speak to
me in this country ; I should have taken it kindly. The
omision I readily pass by, believing it was not through any
ill will thou bears me, but a little humour in thee at that
time. Let me ask thee, on second thoughts, whether thy
coming to Balby with thy cousin ffanny, before thou had
left the county, would not have been agreable to thy present
disposition and temper of mind ? as well as, I doubt not,
well pleasing to thy Uncle Sutton, if thou had done it.
She is now at my house, and I believe is satisfied and easy
in her own mind ; what lies in my power to add to the
continuance thereof shall never be wanting. It's a pity
any difference on the score of religious tenets should beget
a shyness in relations to each other, or break off that amiable
correspondence that has once subsisted betwixt you : I
hope it has not. Pious persons, desirous to do to others as
they would others should do to them, can never want a
charity (for others that may vary from them in opinion in
matters concerning the conscience) which the Author of
Christianity and His apostles have so much recommended.
I'm persuaded thou wilt excuse my freedom in addressing
thee after this manner, and pass a charitable censure upon
the liberty I've taken.

" Please to give my dutiful respects to thy uncle and
aunt Sutton, cousin Nancy Henshaw, and accept the same
for thyself from him who desires thine and thy welfare and
happiness here in this world and to endless futurity.

" THOS. SMITH " [1]

[1] In Byrom's Journal this letter is misplaced, owing to an editorial
confusion of January (11th mo.) with November.

If Thomas Smith expected to receive a reply to this epistle from his young correspondent, he was disappointed. It was Dr. Byrom, the authorized postal censor for the Sutton family, who penned the reply—we are ignorant of its contents, but the family sent a message that it was "according to their sentiments, just what they would have said."

Attentive readers of the above correspondence will be able to reconstruct the probable course of Fanny's adventures, although there are some elements in them which must remain a matter of conjecture. We notice how she had read and admired William Law's *Serious Call*, perhaps also his *Christian Perfection* ; she had read (possibly on Law's advice) the *Imitation of Christ*. She had even been ready at one time to accept Byrom's suggestion of seeing Law (presumably by travelling to London). But she changed her mind, a new plan was formed for her, and she agreed instead to consider Law's representations in the form of letters. Meanwhile she had been in touch with several members of the Quaker body. Two of them had tried to visit her at Dam House, where her uncle would not admit them to her. But she was in correspondence at least with Samuel Miller and his wife Lydia of Manchester and with a particularly fine and sensible representative of the Society in the person of Thomas Smith of Balby near Doncaster, whose letter we have just quoted. In the last-named town Fanny had an uncle and aunt of the name of Cripps, at whose house she had evidently been a visitor and there become acquainted with some of the local Quakers, and amongst them with Thomas Smith.[1] With him, we know from the conversation recorded between Abel Strethall and Dr. Byrom on October 15th, Fanny had been in

---

[1] Thomas Smith (1682–1747) came of a well-known Quaker family. He is described as a yeoman, "a man of intelligence, honour, and general esteem". He was married and had eight children, of whom the eldest son, Thomas, also much respected in later years, was at this date about twenty-four years of age.

correspondence (though under difficulties) from the Sutton's house. And from Fanny herself, or else from his Manchester friends, Thomas Smith heard of the constraint that was being put upon the young woman by her relatives. He accordingly wrote and despatched to her guardian, Lawyer Sutton, towards the end of October the letter which I have printed in the preceding chapter.

Byrom is himself quite silent on the point, but otherwise all the evidence we have goes to show that somewhere about this time Thomas Sutton's attitude to Fanny completely changed. Instead of authorizing her virtual imprisonment, he allowed her great liberty and even became an advocate for her, in the face, most probably, of her aunt, who still continued to intercept her correspondence and to use John Byrom as an instrument to work upon Fanny's feelings. In Fanny's words, " the searcher of hearts wrought upon my uncle in my favour, and made him plead my cause with them that strove against me." He even perhaps, at a somewhat later date, took up the cudgels for her with extraordinary vigour against a local clergyman, that is, if the tempting conjecture proffered on page 98 of this book be right.

Thomas Sutton's change of mind was no doubt mainly due to a growing conviction that his niece's desire was not the mere passing whim of a neurotic girl, who was liable to fits of religious depression, but a serious purpose rooted in genuine spiritual experience and founded on a not unreasonable interpretation of Christianity. Her earnest presentation of the matter in the " Case " or " writing ", which he had himself requested her to draw up, touched him no doubt considerably. Moreover, according to tradition, he was much influenced by the letter which Thomas Smith wrote to him.

It is a matter of some difficulty to reconstruct from Byrom's fragmentary references what exactly occurred in the next few weeks. To poor Fanny, at any rate, those weeks must have been a time of agonizing uncertainty.

Byrom says that " the Quakers had been to fetch her and been disappointed ", the reason being that " she came with me to my brother's, instead of going quite away with this Mr. Smith ". This was on November 22nd, the day before Byrom wrote to Law enclosing a " strange note " from Fanny, and begging him to start the correspondence which might save her from her false step.

It would appear that at this point Thomas Sutton removed his objections to Fanny taking up her abode, as she desired, with her Quaker friends, and that in consequence Thomas Smith, in company probably with some staid matron of the Society, went to Dam House to escort their new convert. We may imagine Mrs. Sutton getting wind some hours previously of the danger impending and in a state of desperation sending an urgent summons for Dr. Byrom, with whom her niece had ties of respect and gratitude. The Doctor arrives just before the Quaker inroad and persuades the half-distracted maiden to remove herself out of reach of her new friends by coming away with him on a visit to his brother Josiah's house.

Next day Thomas Smith and a Manchester Quaker of the name of Moss [1] called on Byrom to remonstrate with him for his interference. Byrom was told of their visit, hesitated whether to face them, but could not make up his mind to do so (whereat, he says, they were " exceedingly offended "), and relieved his perturbation by writing to William Law.

Fanny, on the other hand, soon repented that she had allowed her friend the Doctor to dissuade her from the fulfilment of her purpose. Though she evidently liked Byrom and recognized his goodwill, she felt him to be a most undesirable neighbour at the present time. Two or three weeks before she had formed the intention of taking advantage of an invitation to pay a visit once more to her uncle and aunt Cripps at Doncaster. A riding-habit had

---

[1] We know this to have been the name of a son-in-law of Smith's, who lived in Manchester.

been prepared, and thither one fine day about the beginning of December she started off on horseback with her cousin Sally Haynes for a companion.

Mr. and Mrs. Sutton must have been well aware that at Mr. Cripps' house their headstrong niece would be within a couple of miles of the redoubtable Thomas Smith and a Quaker household which was only too ready to receive her.   Nevertheless they appear to have encouraged Fanny to take the journey.   We wonder if they informed the Cripps of the situation and of the upheaval that was threatening their household.   For her aunt Mrs. Cripps was much opposed to Fanny's decision, and though Mr. Cripps acquiesced in it " for the peace of the family," nevertheless (if, as seems almost certain, it is to him that Fanny afterwards wrote the indignant epistle which I have printed on page 104) he at any rate expressed himself in very strong language about the sect who were gaining this new adherent.

Fanny meanwhile had been receiving William Law's epistles and had read the first three of them, which Byrom posted on to Doncaster. (The other two letters had not yet been forwarded from Manchester when the catastrophe occurred.)   How far these letters worked in a direction contrary to their writer's purpose, we do not know ; probably they were in any case too late, for Fanny had by this time cast off her hesitations.   The fact remains that within a few days she informed her relatives that she was going off to throw in her lot with the Balby Quakers, the Smiths having offered her a home in their house.   Mr. Cripps, as we have said, acquiesced, but he doubtless guessed that his niece would be no passive member of the Quaker flock, and that much unpleasant gossip would soon be heard, when she took to preaching.   So he induced her to agree to the condition that she would not stay at Balby more than a few days, but remove to her native place in Staffordshire, where distance would render her more or less harmless to them.   So the much distressed creature was at length

" arrived at that port which she steered her course to ".
How she made use of her hard-won freedom must be the
subject of another chapter.

Byrom's Journal and correspondence show us that the
good Doctor maintained his interest in the young Quakeress
(as she now was) for some time longer, an interest that was
doubtless made more easy by the friendly intercourse which
he had at this period of his life with quite a number of
members of the Society. We find him, for instance,
briefly referring to "the misfortune of F. H. ", and to an
expected visit to Manchester on her part, in the letter he
wrote to Law on March 4, 1736–7, about Law's contemplated publication of a treatise against Quakerism.[1]   Shortly
after this he made one of his periodic visits to London, and
we have (among other entertaining items) a long and interesting conversation between him and Dr. Butler, whose
famous *Analogy of Religion* had but recently appeared.

On April 13th Byrom, doubtless rather shy over his
failure with F. H., at last plucked up courage to visit Law
at Putney, on a " pleasant, windy, dusty " day.   " I called
at Fulham and had two Brentford rolls and a glass of wine,
5d., and a little after two I went to Mr. Gibbon's, where
the dinner was just going up."   After dinner with the
Gibbons, Mr. Law " asked me if I cared to walk out in
the afternoon, and we did, and when we were out he said,
' Well, have you made any more Quakers ? ' "   Poor
Byrom ! he must have smarted rather at the great man's
implied censure on his mismanagement of F. H.'s affairs,
and it was perhaps a bit unworthy of Law to suggest that
Byrom's share in the fruitless persuasions was more mis-
chievous than his own ! Law was in a controversial mood
(he had not as yet that almost perfect sweetness of temper
to which he attained in later years), and he must have made
Byrom still more unhappy by his strictures on his much-
revered Antoinette Bourignon, a religious enthusiast far
more unorthodox than any Quaker.

[1] See page 231 below.

K

At any rate Byrom was shyer than ever, when he next ventured to visit Law, on a Sunday afternoon about five weeks later, and kept walking in the lane, while his cousin, Will Chaddock, was sent in to sound Law, " and soon after they both came out and I came to them, and Mr. Law said, ' Nobody but one that was vapoured with drinking tea would not have come in,' and he talked about Madame Guyon and her forty books, though she talked of the power of quiet and silence, which he believed was a good thing, that indeed it was *all*, if one had it ; but that a person that was to reform the world could not be a great writer ; that the persons who were to reform the world had not appeared yet, that it would be reformed to be sure ; *that the writers against Quakerism were not proper persons, for they writ against the Spirit in effect, and gave the Quakers an advantage ;* [1] that the Quakers were a subtle, worldly-minded people, that they began with the contempt of learning, riches, etc., but now were a politic, worldly society, and strange people —which word he used for them after I had shown him Thos. Smith's letter to S. Haynes [2] and F. H.'s to Mary Sutton,[3] to which last, ' Well, and what is there in all this ? ' and when I said a little while after, that they would be glad to know in what manner to answer Smith's letter, or whether to take any notice of it, he said there was nothing in it worth notice, or that required answering if they had no mind ; I told him of Smith's leaving a copy of verses with her, and then it was that he said they were strange people. . . ."

This is the last record we have of anything passing between Law and Byrom with regard either to Fanny

---

[1] I have italicized these words, because they give (as Overton noticed) a most important clue to Law's attitude to Quakerism.

[2] This is probably the actual letter printed on p. 140 above, to which Byrom had been asked to write the reply, in place of " Sally."

[3] Compare page 104 above, where Fanny refers to a letter from her aunt Sutton to her. Byrom also says that it was reading these two letters the night before which made him think of visiting Mr. Law.

Henshaw or to Quakerism.[1]   As regards not meddling further with F. H. or her new friends, Byrom evidently followed Law's counsel : we find him a little later on telling his friend Mr. Walker that he had not written again to F. H.—" I had taken advice upon that matter and was very easy ".   Nevertheless during this month of April, 1737, Byrom's mind was evidently considerably engrossed with "the affair of F. H.", and the familiar initials keep cropping up in the very full records of his doings and conversations which we have at this period.   On the Sunday afternoon following Byrom's last-mentioned visit to Law, Byrom went to drink tea with a Mr. Garden, a Manchester grocer removed to London, and the talk turned much on Quakers.   (Mr. and Mrs. Garden appear to have left the Quakers for the Established Church.)   After some rather unkind remarks about Mrs. Drummond " having turned Quaker for a husband ", and concerning a certain " sturdy girl " who " was not willing to go into service and so turned preacher ", they fell to " reasoning against them ".

   " I told them ", Byrom writes, " something relating to F. H., that Mr. Hoole [2] had talked to her about Dell's book [3] : I mentioned some things that Mr. Law had writ, query, that particularly of circumcision, ' Nothing,' etc. ; that Christians were as much obliged surely to obey Jesus Christ and baptize, as the Jews were Moses to circumcise.[4]   I drank bohea tea, four dishes or five, very good, and falling to talk about Quakers, and about Mrs. Bourignon at last.   I stayed

---

[1] But after 1740 only a few fragments of Byrom's Journal survive, and not many letters written *by* him.

[2] The Rector of St. Anne's, Manchester.

[3] Probably William Dell's *Doctrine of Baptisms*, several times reprinted by the Society of Friends.   Some of Barclay's arguments against water-baptism had been previously used by Dell in a simpler and more effective way.   Dell was an Independent preacher to Cromwell's army, and later Master of Caius College, Cambridge.

[4] I can find no actual statement to this effect either in Law's published works or in his extant letters to F. H.   Byrom may be referring to one of the missing portions of those letters.

so long till they were going to supper, and then I made motion to go, but upon being asked to stay . . . I supped, and there was a large dish of asparagus. . . . I stayed after supper till it struck eleven. Mr. Garden said there was a servant that wanted to leave the Quakers, and wanted a plain book upon water-baptism, and I mentioned that of Mr. Leslie's ; [1] and from thence I think we fell into discourse about his [*i.e.* Garden's] uncle, who translated Mrs. Bourignon's books . . . and he (Mr. Garden) said that the Quakers were very fond of her works till the book against the Quakers came out,[2] and then they were not : he said that Madam Guion he thought was superior to her, and I said to take the good from all and leave the rest for what it was, seemed the best way."

Meanwhile the scandalous news had come from Manchester that " F. H." had already entered upon her career as a she-preacher—she " had held forth to the Quakers at Whitchurch ".[3] Four days later Byrom meets his sister Betty at cousin Chad's and hears " that a gentlewoman had seen F. H. at a meeting-house and had spoke to her, and that she had taken her by the hand and said ' Friend.' " [4]

[1] This refers to Charles Leslie's *Divine Institution of Baptism*, 1697, directed against the Quakers. Leslie was a leading Nonjuror, known probably to William Law.

[2] For Antoinette Bourignon (1616–1680) see Professor Alexander MacEwen's interesting volume (1910). John Wesley, with his usual talent for extracting truth from the most unpromising quarters, reprinted portions of her writings. Her hymn, " Come, Saviour Jesus, from above ", is still to be found in the Methodist hymn-book (No. 526). Madame Bourignon was annoyed at being classed as a Quaker, and so wrote a book against their doctrines.

[3] A Shropshire town within easy reach of Leek in Staffordshire, whither F. H. had migrated.

[4] This and the foregoing references (April 13 to 28, 1737) will be found in Byrom's *Journal*, pp. 104–136.

I cannot resist the temptation to mention here that, about a fortnight after this last entry, Byrom records " great doings at Putney at the christening of Mr. Gibbon's son." Mr. Gibbon was Law's ex-pupil, and the baby was the future historian of the Roman Empire, born April 27th, 1737. Law remained in the Putney household, within reach of Byrom, till 1739, when the old grandfather died.

This probably refers to Fanny's threatened visit to Manchester, mentioned by Byrom in his March letter to Law.

There is an interval of nearly two years before we have Byrom's next reference to " F. H.", which occurs in the following pleasant passage, part of Byrom's letter written from London to his wife on March 15, 1738–9 :—

" I had an evening last night more agreeable at Mr. Glover's, who asked me to come there to meet one Martin, a Quaker, that teaches his little girl to write, and comes often to this coffee-house and is a very honest sensible man, and entertained the company very agreeably, though they could not enter into his notions. There was Mr. Taylor White [1] and a gentleman of Gray's Inn, and they three against the *Quaker and me, whose main principles suited together and were opposed by them.* This Quaker gave me a little book to-day, *Directions to an Holy Life,* from the Archbishop of Cambray, a translation by himself ; he is a good scholar, which Quakers rarely are. He wants, Mr. Glover says, to talk with me about F. Hens[haw]. He has writ a book, I hear, for women's preaching.[2] I suppose I shall be more acquainted with him now, and I like the man hitherto. I say this is a relief, for I have none [of] that converse or care for certain matters that seem to me very momentous, and which the continual noise and hurry of the place [3] robs one from attending to."

What a transformation scene is indicated in the words I have italicized ! And this was not the only Quaker with whom Byrom discovered a spiritual kinship at this time. Jacob Boehme or Behmen was becoming in these years the prophet of prophets to Byrom as well as to his master Law, and it is therefore interesting to read the last

[1] A familiar friend of Byrom's, a F.R.S. and afterwards a judge. See note to page 112 above for the unhappy influence of his company on Byrom.

[2] For Josiah Martin and his books see Note Two at the end of this chapter.

[3] *i.e.* London.

portion of the following lively passage extracted from another letter of Byrom's to his wife Elisabeth in Manchester, "Gray's Inn, July 26, 1739."

"Trade seems to be sinking and war rising, though nothing of consequence in the news about such things. The world turns round like a wheel, now one spoke at top and then another. There is nothing but a thought *above it* that can bring true peace to its rightful throne, the human breast. I had writ out the verses which I promised Mr. Law from Mr. Lloyd's book in a letter to him, and hearing that he was come to town, I called and gave 'em him, but did not go in because he was going to supper, etc. I hear that May Drummond [1] is in town ; F. H., I find, did not come as expected. I was last night at Jos. Clutton's, a famous chemist, a Quaker,[2] great admirer of Jac[ob] Behmen, who lent me a manuscript about him, the same I fancy that Mr. J. Walker had—how does he do ? I got it to divert a tedious hour a little, because the writer was, I believe, a very honest, deep, good man." [3]

From an entry in the Journal for August 1, 1739, it appears that Joseph Clutton had been to see William Law. Incidentally the same entry includes Byrom's account of how (not for the first time) he suggested that Law might like to become his pupil at shorthand. "I took out my book and showed him the proposal, but he just looked at it and gave it me again, and seemed to say that, if he knew it, it would be no use to him, that he could write faster than he could think, that for them indeed that wanted to write down what others said, it might do. I said, ' Valeat quantum valere potest.' "

---

[1] This is one of four or five references to May Drummond in Byrom's Journal between 1736 and 1739. See the Note on her at the end of Chapter I above.

[2] For Joseph Clutton see note on page 237 below.

[3] This refers, as Byrom explains later, to Andreas Freher. See note on page 237.

One last reference to F. H., before she disappears from the records of her old friend—again in a letter to Mrs. Byrom, September 11, 1739 :—

> " I am really grieved at Fan[ny] H.'s report, poor creature ! I remember the man at Kersall [Manchester], where I could not help telling her that I did not fancy him above 'em all ; I hope it is not true. I thought her turning Quaker was an unhappy step, her preaching worse, but this seems to be worst of all ; but I must submit my judgment to wiser ones, though I can't help wishing her an helpmate of another nature." [1]

This evidently refers to a reported offer of marriage which the comely young Quakeress had had from one of her fellow-members. In this case Byrom's doubts as to the truth of the report were justified—we know that Fanny Henshaw remained single till the year 1745, when another Quaker, William Paxton of County Durham, " found her in the covenant of light and life ".

Before we close this portion of our story, the reader will be glad to know that the friendship between John Byrom and his " Master ", William Law, grew and ripened as the years went by, in spite of the infrequency of their personal intercourse. After Law had removed in the year 1740 to his retreat at Kingscliffe, near Peterborough, Byrom seems to have visited him only about once every three years, stopping with him as one stage on his way between Manchester and London. Nevertheless Byrom came to be much more at his ease in the presence of his revered saint, while from about the year 1752 Law's letters to Byrom show a marked increase in warmth and tenderness. Law died in full possession of his intellectual powers in April, 1761. A few months before this he told a visitor that Dr. Byrom was " a man after his own heart ". Byrom followed his friend in September, 1763 ; as far as we can judge from the fragments of his Journal and corre-

---

[1] For the foregoing quotations from the *Journal* during 1739, see Vol. II, Part I, pages 240–283, under dates named in my text.

spondence, he maintained almost to the last his customary interest in the religious and literary activities of the time.

Here we must take leave of the gentle, humorous, pliable, and withal very lovable John Byrom, to trace what we know of Frances Henshaw's subsequent history from the far severer records of eighteenth-century Quakerism, that is to say chiefly from her own writing, which, for all its testimony to the supremacy of the Spirit of God, is for the most part tinged with an atmosphere of asceticism, which is much nearer to William Law than to John Byrom.

NOTE ONE : ON JOHN BYROM'S POETRY

Byrom's two famous epigrams are not too easily found, and shall accordingly be given here. The first is a witty attempt to provide the adherent of the cause of James Stuart with a toast that was not necessarily disloyal to King George. It is described as " intended to allay the violence of party spirit " and runs as follows : —

God bless the King, I mean the Faith's Defender !
God bless—no harm in blessing—the Pretender !
But who Pretender is and who is King,
God bless us all, that's quite another thing !

The second epigram was an unlucky shot at guessing the relative worth of two musical composers of the day (1725). As it turned out, one of the men named has taken his place in the circle of the great, while the other is to-day almost forgotten. But the last two lines have become almost proverbial, and it is Byrom who appears to have originated the witticism. (The two key-words were applied in his day to two nearly similar notes on a fiddle.)

Some say, compar'd to Bononcini
That Mynheer Handel 's but a ninny ;
Others aver, that he to Handel
Is scarcely fit to hold a candle.
Strange all this difference should be
'Twixt Tweedledum and Tweedledee !

Some few of Byrom's religious poems are of a high order ; his free but delightful paraphrase of the twenty-third psalm, for instance. Besides " Christians, awake ", his mystical hymn " My spirit longs for thee " is still used for congregational singing. But much of his verse is more of the nature of religious philosophy couched in ingenious rhyme. I give two slight specimens on pages 113 and 323 of this book.[1] Here I would take the opportunity of printing a few lines which may be of practical help to some readers. They form part of a poem " On the Nature and Reason of all outward Law " (in Vol. II, Part II of the Chetham Society edition), and show that the *quondam* physician understood at least one important principle of the healing art and could apply it in a striking way to indicate one of the reasons for Christ's practice of healing the sick on the sabbath. I have not met with the idea elsewhere, but it is remarkably in line with the best modern psychology of spiritual healing.

> Whilst in the flesh, how oft did He reveal
> His saving will and godlike pow'r to heal !
> They whom defect, disease, or fiend possess'd,
> And pardon'd sinners by His word had rest ;
> He on the sabbath chose to heal and teach,
> And law-proud Jews to slay Him for its breach.
>
> The sabbath never so well kept before,
> May justify one observation more.
> Our Saviour heal'd, as pious authors say,
> So many sick upon the sabbath-day,
> To show that rest and quietness of soul
> Is best for one who wants to be made whole :—
>
> Not to indulge an eagerness too great
> Of outward hurry or of inward heat,
> But, with an humble temper and resign'd,
> To keep a sabbath in a hopeful mind,
> In peace and patience meekly to endure,
> Till the good Saviour's hour is come to cure.

[1] A selection of Byrom's verses will be found in the recently published *Oxford Book of Eighteenth Century Verse* (Clarendon Press).

NOTE TWO : ON JOSIAH MARTIN

(See page 149.)

Byrom had previously consulted this " Quaker writing-master " about some vellum and " Turkish paper " (May, 1736). Later on (April, 1739) we hear how Josiah Martin had become acquainted with Count Zinzendorf, the head of the United Brethren or Moravians, then on a visit to London. He took Byrom to meet the Count (" a good-natured, mild, loving-tempered man ", Byrom says) and to listen to an address by him, which Byrom transcribed in his shorthand.

For Josiah Martin's later acquaintance with Fanny Henshaw, see page 173. He was a Londoner, born in 1683, and he died unmarried at Holborn in 1747, leaving a library of some 4,000 volumes. James Gough, who thirty-five years after this was following in his footsteps by publishing editions of the quietist writers, mentions him (in 1772) as " one whose memory I esteem, as I believe generally do such as were acquainted with him, being a man of learning, humility, and fervent piety ".

There is preserved in the Society of Friends' Library a letter written by Josiah Martin in September, 1739, to a Quaker in Durham, which pays a warm tribute to the missionary work of the Moravians in America, and to the results of the preaching of the Wesleys, of George White-field, and of Benjamin Ingham (see page 242 below). With the last-named, who described to him his visit to the Moravian headquarters at Herrnhut, Josiah Martin was acquainted. He had also heard Charles Wesley preach at Gloucester. Martin ends the letter thus with apparent reference to both Moravians and Methodists :—" Thus we see what the Lord is doing by a people newly raised and prepared to go forth in their Master's name to convert the nations. ' May they be a means to provoke us to greater diligence,' saith my soul ; I am sure the day calls for it, and I am sure, if we make not haste to turn with zeal to the Lord, who has so often visited us, both immediately and instrumentally, He may remove our candlesticks and take our crowns and give them to others, which would be lamentable indeed ! "

Martin was evidently a good French scholar. In 1733 he published in French his *Lettre d'un Quaker à François de Voltaire* in reply to the great deist's friendly but misleading account of the Quakers contained in his *Lettres sur les Anglais*. Another book of his, to which Byrom refers here, is *A Vindication of Women's Preaching* (1717, 128 pages), a learned work, with long quotations ranging from Irenæus to John Locke.

But Josiah Martin's notable literary service was his introduction to Quaker readers and others of the personalities and works of the great French quietists, Fénelon, Archbishop of Cambray, and Jeanne Marie Guyon. In 1727 he brought out the tract on Madame Guyon, to which I have already referred (page 137). In 1735 appeared, from his pen, but anonymously, at Luke Hinde's, the Quaker bookshop, *The Archbishop of Cambray's Dissertation on Pure Love, with an Apologetic Preface, and an Account of the Life and Writings of the Lady Guyon*. This is a substantial book of 272 pages, more than half of which are occupied with the Preface dealing with the Lady Guyon. It went into a second edition in 1738 and a fourth in 1769.

The last of Martin's publications, the one he gave to Byrom, was entitled *Directions for a Holy Life and the attaining Christian Perfection, By the Archbishop of Cambray. Recommended to the serious perusal of the Lovers of Truth, and Professors of the Christian Name, of every Denomination.* It is a weighty little pamphlet of fourteen pages, instructing the reader in the art of inward " recollection ", in the practice of the presence of God under all the circumstances of life. It is said to be a translation of Chapter 7 of Fénelon's *Instructions et avis sur divers points de la morale et de la perfection chrétienne.* In his Preface Martin refers to the " rising heresy, which they call Quietism, a modern nickname for old Christianity ". The copy in the Friends' Library is a second edition, published in 1739 by Luke Hinde " at the Bible in George Yard, Lombard Street ". Another edition appeared at Bristol in 1747.

If the British Museum and the Bodleian Library are to be trusted, the productions of Josiah Martin are the only interpretations of Madame Guyon that were available in an English form up to the year 1770 ; with the sole exception of a curious tract published in 1698 (*i.e.* well within the lifetimes of the persons of whom it treated) entitled *Quakerism à la Mode or a History of Quietism, particularly that of the Lord Archbishop of Cambray and Madame Guyone.* (This is possibly the book to which Byrom refers on December 28, 1736, when he writes, " Have been reading the Bishop of Meaux (*i.e.* Bossuet) about M. Guion against Cambray "). Various works of Fénelon (1651–1715) were translated into English before 1739.

There is a fascinating study of the relationship of Quietism with eighteenth-century Quakerism in Chapters II and III of Rufus Jones' *Later Periods of Quakerism.* But the facts given above with regard to Josiah Martin's publications, together with the interesting statement made by Byrom in his letter to Law (see page 137) that " the Quakers pretend M. Guion to have been a Quaker ", etc., indicate that the *direct* influence of Fénelon and Guyon took effect from a considerably earlier date than that suggested by Dr. Rufus Jones.

CHAPTER IV

FANNY HENSHAW IN THE QUAKER FOLD

Fanny Henshaw has left us such a comparatively full account of the different crises through which she passed up to the time of writing out the reasons for her change of faith, that one looked forward to hearing her own version of the incidents which we have been considering through the good Byrom's spectacles. But, alas, our curiosity is not gratified. The following meagre summary covers the whole episode.

"After I had waded for about the space of two years, through unspeakable afflictions of body and mind, it pleased divine Providence to open my way and cause my relations to assent to my joining in society with the people called Quakers ; which I had not done above three or four months, ere my health was restored, to the surprise of all my acquaintance, and my mouth was opened in a powerful manner in a public testimony, to the praise of that almighty and all-sufficient arm, that had wrought my preservation and deliverance out of the manifold temptations and provocations I had had, through unfaithfulness, to pass through."

Two comments alone seem necessary. The first is that it is very much to Fanny's credit that neither here, nor in the earlier part of the narrative (where " opposition " is the strongest word she uses), does she utter a word of complaint or blame against her relatives, who put her under restraint, and, as Byrom himself admitted, treated her with various indignities ; nor is there any hint of resentment against the severity of William Law's strictures on her change of faith. The second point to notice is the pleasing circumstance that the disappearance of the repression of her spiritual life, and the opportunity accorded her to make use of her genuine gift of preaching, brought with it recovery of bodily health. In a rather similar way, some years later, as we shall see, another protracted season of bodily and mental depression was terminated by a happy marriage. Fanny's narrative proceeds as follows.

" I thus continued about six years, under the protection of God and obedience to the direction of His Holy Spirit, in a happy composure and tranquility of mind, growing daily in the experience of the things of the Kingdom and in the increase of the gift of the ministry committed to me. In this time I had been led to visit several counties in this nation, to the satisfaction of my friends and to my own peace, in receiving the answer of well done in my bosom ! But the opposer of all good, who secretly envies the growth of truth and would supplant the cause of righteousness by subtility and deceit, sought to exalt [me] and cause many to think of me more highly than they ought to think. I felt a storm threaten. And in the midst of popularity and applause [I] found my mind secretly called down to humility and retirement, and thereupon withdrew from Scarborough, where I was on a religious visit, as soon as the nature of my engagement there permitted ; nor do I know that I joined at all with the tempter, in his presentations in myself to lift me up, or took pleasure in hearing the satisfaction [that] friends and the great people expressed concerning my ministry. Yet I believe the boaster was not then so entirely slain in me, but there was the ground of temptation so far as to prove and work me much trouble, which indeed was the case ; for from a great degree of divine favour and approbation, a cloud was suffered to interpose betwixt me and my heavenly guide, and I seemed as one bereft of comfort and almost of hope. Great, exceeding great was my distress in this proving season ; but the Lord was with me, though I knew it not, and has delivered me and, I trust, will deliver me to the end, and bring me safely to His heavenly kingdom, where the wicked will cease from troubling and the wearied and tried soul will be at rest.

"In the course of this latter affliction I was brought very low, both in body and mind, and bewailed the loss of my Beloved day and night ; nor could I be consoled by any thing short of the return of His favour and life-giving presence ; it pleased Him at times to break in upon my mind, but He retired again, as a wayfaring man, that staid but for a night.[1] It pleased Divine Goodness never totally to take from me His Holy Spirit, nor my gift in the ministry, though I waded through such deep waters ; not, I believe, on my own account altogether, but that many through me might hear and fear and give glory to Him and Him only, who created the heavens and the earth, the seas and the fountains of water. Scarce ever was a time of more searching of heart amongst Friends, both young and old ; their tenderness and compassionate behaviour to me throughout the whole was worthy of the most grateful remembrance and record. Nay, what has often caused my admiration—in this situation, wherein I looked upon myself as one bereft of all comeliness, I was sought after by several of the chiefest persons in the Society as a companion for life. One [William Paxton], indued with every quali- fication I could desire, found me in the covenant of light and life, and steadfastly adhered to his fixed resolution to seek me therein, till [through much opposition arising] from a sense of my duty and the nature of his intentions, I was made his and he mine [in the unchangeable covenant of life]. The Lord was pleased to bless us together for the space of about eight years, [in which time I bore him four sons] ; and after being helped through many visitations of bodily afflictions, my dear and valuable husband resigned his precious life into the hands of Him who gave it."[2]

[1] Compare Jer. xiv. 8.
[2] The words between square brackets in the last two sentences were either added or replaced in the 1803 edition, probably by the son of the writer, who was her literary executor. (See page 76.)

AN EIGHTEENTH CENTURY FRIENDS' MEETING

This concludes the narrative of Fanny Henshaw (Frances Paxton she was when it was composed, Frances Dodshon when it was printed), with the exception of a few sentences, here omitted, of somewhat overdrawn praise of her husband's virtues, and of anticipations of the joys of heaven.

I now propose to go back to the point at which Fanny started the foregoing brief account of her experiences during the sixteen years or so following her escape from the remonstrances of John Byrom and William Law. For to quite a considerable extent are we able to supplement this account. Indeed I have found (in the Library of the Society of Friends) some record of her thoughts or activities during no less than twenty-six of the different years that elapsed between 1737 and 1781, by which time she had attained the ripe age of sixty-seven. Her career as a " Minister " will, I hope, throw considerable light on the characteristics of the Society of which she became a devoted member.

We have seen that according to the Byrom papers Fanny found her first refuge in the house of her friend Thomas Smith in the village of Balby near Doncaster, but that out of deference to her relatives she soon moved to her native place of Leek. Here she was probably entertained at first by the household of the two brothers Joshua and John Toft, who were doubtless the " Quakers for whom she had contracted an esteem ", mentioned in Byrom's letter to Law. Joshua Toft (c. 1690–1769) was a minister highly esteemed in the Society for his benevolence and sound judgement, and it is in the collection of letters which he left behind him that the most important of the documents relating to Fanny have been preserved.

The little town of Leek was at that time perhaps the chief centre for Quakers in Staffordshire. It was then and for long after a primitive place, the capital of a region of wild moors. In the next century a gifted writer of Quaker upbringing wrote of the Friends of Leek that they " had a cold, bleak, moorland character . . . they were neither good-mannered or affable ".[1]   If so the Toft family were a striking exception.

It was no doubt in her retreat at Leek that Fanny, as Byrom apprehended, made " her open entrance into outward Quakerism ". We cannot tell whether she had to go through the ordeal of a solemn interview with two appointed members of the Society, on whose report her recognition as a member would chiefly depend. (This procedure, which prevails at the present time in similar cases, was only introduced about this date.)   But in any case she began to be a regular attender at " meeting ", and, if she had not already done so, she now adopted the " plain dress ", the wearing of which was the distinguishing sign of those Friends who were prepared to emphasize their dedication to the service of Truth.   There were many members of the Society in those days who conformed to the vanities of the world, but a convert like Fanny would not be one of them.   We may picture her attired in a gown of some simple cut, which belonged to a fashion discarded by the ladies of the day, with a neat green apron and a hooded cap of some dark cloth or silk.[2]

Some weeks before this, as her letters testify, she had adopted the " plain language " of Quakerism.   If the

---

[1] Mary Howitt in her *Autobiography*, pp. 1 and 58.   Mrs. Howitt's family came from Apsford, near Leek.   I took this last quotation from the Journal of the Friends' Historical Society.   Since doing so, I have referred to the original, and by a curious chance find the further statement that one Friend alone formed an exception to this verdict, and his name was "Toft Chorley, who had a country dwelling in the moorlands near Leek ".   From other sources it appears that this Friend was grandson of Joshua Toft. There is preserved a letter in which he writes of seeing Fanny Henshaw's much admired May Drummond at Sheffield in 1769, and mentions her strong masculine Scotch features.

[2] The green aprons appear to have been customary between 1700 and 1750 at least, when the prevailing fashion was for *white* aprons.   (Mrs. May Drummond is described as wearing a green one in 1735).   The dress of the strict or " plain " Quakeress underwent a number of changes during the eighteenth century ; the general rule is said to have been conformity to some simple fashion *of a few years before*, which had become obsolete.

report which reached Byrom was correct [1] her first call to what most Quakers felt was the " awful engagement of the vocal ministry "—of breaking with her own voice the sacred silence of the meeting for worship—came to her almost at once after her admission, at Whitchurch, a small town not far from Leek. We have no evidence that this commencement of her ministry was accompanied by any special strain or tension : she seems to have had a natural gift for preaching, which responded easily to the movings of the Spirit. " Her health ", as we have already heard, " was restored, and her mouth opened in a powerful manner."

It must indeed have been quite exceptional for a young woman of only twenty-three, who had scarcely ever attended " Meeting " before her admission, to be launched at once, as Fanny was, into a career of regular public ministry. It appears that she started very soon on a series of journeys, visiting different meetings of Friends in the Midlands and North. In April, 1737, she was at Manchester, to the great distress, no doubt, of her Aunt Sutton. From there she soon after found her way to Kendal. A brief letter exists written by her from Leeds in December of the same year to James Wilson of Kendal,[2] expressing warm thanks for " the great kindness of my ffriends ", and " no small pleasure " at a visit which Thomas Smith had just paid her from Balby. Soon after she again returned to this hospitable village, and we have two affectionate notes to her from Friend Smith, who writes as if he looked upon Balby as her natural home. The following May she was visiting Manchester.

It appears that during this first year of her adherence to the Society she was duly recognized, presumably by the " Monthly Meeting " for the Leek district, as a " Minister ", i.e. as a person considered to possess pro-

---

[1] See page 148 above.
[2] James Wilson (1677–1769) was also a " convinced Friend ", and a Minister for over sixty years. John Wilson, mentioned on page 170 below, was his brother.

phetic insight, a gift of persuasive speech, and a convicting quality of life.

The years that follow were perhaps the happiest period of Fanny's life. She herself speaks, as we have seen, of continuing for about six years " in a happy composure and tranquillity of mind, growing daily in the experience of the things of the kingdom and in the increase of the gift of the ministry committed to me ".

We have, dating from September, 1738, the following account of one of her sermons preached at a private religious gathering at Balby, which she was again visiting in company with other "public Friends", as the Ministers were then called.

> " Fanny in a very persuasive and affectionate manner declared to us the necessity of an abstractedness from a too eager pursuit of the world and its joys. . . . Fanny's discourse was throughout an excellent comment on ' using the world as not abusing it ' ".[1]

Another enthusiastic estimate of her eloquence, by an admirer of a very different and, it may be, rather frivolous sort, probably belongs to this period of her life. (Taken from an old manuscript book, its authorship is irrecoverably lost.)

> When Henshaw speaks, behold the listening throng,
> Attention to the Music of her Tongue ;
> So pure her words and so refined her thought,
> She teaches now, what once the Apostle taught,
> No laboured nonsense of affected style,
> To puzzle half and make the rest to smile ;
> Her doctrine plain and easy understood,
> Who hears, must know, who follows, must be good.[2]

[1] This is an extract from a letter written by Thomas Smith, junior, of Balby (son of Fanny's old friend), then a young man of twenty-six, to her other friend, Joshua Toft of Leek.

[2] Taken from Volume 2410 in the Bevan Naish Library, Friends' Institute, Birmingham. The language and metre of these lines are remarkably similar to a rhymed appreciation of Fanny's admired Mrs. May

In the diary of a Quaker who lived on the Welsh border during the years 1739–42, we have records of Fanny Henshaw taking an active and leading part among other well-known " public Friends " at the so-called " Circular Yearly Meetings " held successively at Chester, Montgomery, and Bridgenorth. These meetings were great religious conferences which always included preaching gatherings, to which the public were invited. Thus at Evesham in 1771 a large booth was specially erected, and we hear of one woman Minister, who " stood for nearly two hours and with great clearness and ability explained the peculiar tenets of our Society, and a crowded audience paid a silent and so far respectful attention ".

Doubtless Fanny was during these years constantly " travelling in the ministry " in other parts of the country as well. Byrom wrote in 1739 that she was expected in London, and she was probably to be found as a rule at the regular Yearly Meeting held there in the early summer of each year.

We have now reached the second of the three prolonged periods of spiritual depression through which this intense servant of the Lord had to pass, in common with the majority of consecrated Quakers of the time. Rufus Jones has written how the journals of nearly all these itinerant ministers reveal that, like the other " quietist " mystics, they too " passed through periods of ' strippings ', of ' dryness ' and of ' desertion ', and they had to learn to be patient in ' dark seasons ', to rise above or be indifferent to ' states of feeling ', and to hold to the pure faith that God is

Drummond, which forms part of " Verses on several of the Quakers' teachers " appearing in the *London Magazine* for 1736. This contribution was apparently written by a sympathetic auditor, but it pours contempt upon some Quaker preachers, as much as it heaps praises upon May Drummond and others.

"But see where gentle *Drummond* next appears,
    With sense and judgment far above her years," etc.

In the Henshaw verses, lines 5 and 6 are quite a fair description of a not uncommon type of eighteenth-century Quaker preaching.

as near, as loving, and as operative in the ' dry season ' as in the times of ' fresh bubblings ' ".[1]

Fanny's " dry seasons " seem to have been peculiarly trying and persistent, probably bound up, as they were, with an over-emotional temperament and a delicate physique. It is to such an experience, and not to any ordinary bereavement, that she refers, when she writes, " I bewailed the loss of my beloved day and night ". There was naturally a good deal of self-reproach mixed in with her sorrow, and she admits that the popularity of her preaching, even among " great people ", had seduced her heart to some measure of exaltation and vanity, a serious sin in one who was taught to believe that the creature must be entirely emptied of self and become solely a mouthpiece of the Divine will.

The beginning of this spiritual crisis was at Scarborough, towards the end of 1742. We have, dating from the next few months, two letters addressed to Fanny by John Fothergill, one of the noblest spirits in the Society, then at the close of a life of service.[2] They are the letters of a tender and wise counsellor. As in both the writer sends his love to Thomas Smith, it would appear that Fanny was again residing at Balby.

In the first of these communications John Fothergill encourages her, in her " afflicting, winnowing, trying time ", to hope that she will soon be given comfort and peace, suggesting that there may be " some mixture of bodily indisposition ", which can be suitably relieved. " Thou may have [at] some time [i.e. in the work of the ministry] given more away than thou had certainly to spare, which, though we do it but in a mistake and not wilfully, yet some chastisement follows, to teach us more care and wisdom too " ; " thou can learn and gather good in divers respects out of this furnace ", and much else in brotherly love.

Some six weeks later Fothergill writes again, saying that

---

[1] *Later Periods of Quakerism*, ch. 3, p. 75.
[2] For John Fothergill the elder (1676–1744) see *Later Periods*, pp. 12–14.

he is sure God's love is nearer her than she thinks, and he hints that she is " teasing herself overmuch " with self-reproach. If only she can " be kept reasonably still and somewhat cheerful ", all will come right. He thinks that a visit to her friend Grace Chambers [1] may be of advantage to her health and spirits ; he begs of her " reverent stillness of mind ", and ends up on the confident note that he may live to see her cheerful.

This visit to Grace Chambers' home in the neighbour-hood of Kendal was a success, and it was there probably that the cloud began to disperse. But not all at once. The next summer we find her hostess writing to Joshua Toft while on a journey with Fanny, who " has been quite over-done in body and spirit ". And here is an undated letter, also to Joshua Toft, which evidently comes from the period of this companionship.

Esteemed Friend,

In remembrance of that love that in years past visited my soul and united it in pure fellowship with the faithfull, do I now in this my low and deeply exercised state salute thee and the rest of my kind Friends at Haregate,[2] humbly imploring that He in whom all power is may preserve and keep you all as in the hollow of His hand from falling into such affliction and anguish of mind as is permited still to attend me. And whether I may ever be favoured with redemption is yet unknown to me and must be left to the good pleasure of Him who alone can cure the wounds of my spirit, which is the cause of (and far exceeds) the bodily indisposition I labour under. Therefore to Him alone do I look, well knowing from former experience 'tis in vain to look to or expect help from any other ; and except He be

---

[1] Grace Chambers (or Chamber, born Hall, 1676-1762) was one of the finest among the women Ministers of the century. Besides being active in the ministry right up to the year of her death at the age of eighty-five, she was noted for her hospitality to poor and rich, her skill in surgery, and her devotion in tending the sick.

[2] Close to Leek, where the Toft brothers lived.

pleased again to appear, I can never expect comfort, nor hope that any endeavours will be attended with success. For out of Him the best outward helps and injoyments are without vertue and relish and can't afford the least relief. But for the satisfaction of my Friends (particularly my kind friend Grace), I think I ought as far as I can to take such measures as may be thought likely to contribute in any degree to my good, and leave the event to Providence, who can (if consistant with His good pleasure) bring good out of what to human nature seems an evil (or trial) hardly to be bore, the withdrawing of Divine comfort and support in the time of temptation and feirce assaults of the enemy, who then appears as he really is, a roaring lyon, out of whose mouth none is able to deliver, 'till the Redeemer come forth of Sion.

The continuance of thy assistance and care respecting my outward affairs is an act of great friendship and condescention ; and I never had more need of the help of my Friends, both in a spiritual and temporal capacity, than in this my present afflicted circumstance, in which the utmost I can do is to labour for patience and resignation, untill (if ever) it may please the Almighty to cause an alteration or work deliverance for my captive soul. I might enlarge, but the subject is more afflicting than edifying. I shall therefore drop it at present, and with remembrance of that love which is my only refuge in this stormy time conclude

Thy truly welwishing though deeply exercised Friend

FRANCES HENSHAW.

I was informed, by a letter I had lately from my Uncle Cripps, of the death of poor cousin Sally, who a few days before I left Balby came to see me and seemed well in health, but was soon after seized with a fever which in fiveteen days took her off. The last letter I had from my Brother gave me an account [that] my sister and two of the children were much out of order. Various afflictions are permited to be my lot, but all seems as nothing in comparison of the loss of Divine favour, which to regain I should not think anything

too much nor any time too long to suffer, though to the
utmost period of my time here I would endeavour to wait
it with patience."

The most interesting part to us of this sorrowful letter is
the postscript.   It implies that Fanny was still on friendly
terms with her relations—her sister whose illness had provoked such a crisis in her own life, her Doncaster uncle
from whose house she had fled six years before, and her
cousin who had ridden with her on the fateful journey from
Manchester.   In spite of the complete transformation her
life had undergone from that of a silent and subdued
attendant at her parish Church to one of the spiritual
leaders of a little Israel, she was not one to break altogether
with the ties of the past.   One would like to think too
that she retained in some measure her old friendship with
Dr. John Byrom.

About this time Fanny entered upon a friendship with
a kindred spirit, Abiah Darby (born Maude, 1716–1794),
wife of the second of the three Abraham Darbys of Coalbrookdale, whose names are famous for their discovery of
new processes of casting iron.[1]   It is a pity that Fanny
did not leave behind her a diary such as Abiah's.   Though
the mother of many children, the latter was a constant and
unwearying traveller in the ministry, and was moreover on
friendly terms with her near neighbour John Fletcher,
parson of Madely, faithful worker with John Wesley, who
regarded him as the most consecrated Christian he had ever
known.   Occasionally too she preached not unacceptably at
Methodist gatherings, a most rare activity for a Quaker.

Here are some jottings from Abiah Darby's manuscript
journal, dating from the year 1744.

" About this time Frances Henshaw was at Sedgwick
(near Kendal) at our worthy Friends, Robert and Grace

---

[1] Her son, the third of the name, erected across the Severn the first iron
bridge ever made.

Chambers, where I went at times and stayed some days—
and Fanny and I being both under great dejection of mind,
we contracted an intimacy in sorrowful retirement. . . .
Thus my time went on. F. H. went to Shrewsbury and I
stayed at Kendal, but we corresponded by letter in a mournful, moving stile." (What a splendid expression !) And
then Abiah Darby tells us how she doubted whether her
own heart was right in the sight of God, else she would be
favoured with His visitations—and much more in the same
strain as we have had from poor Fanny's pen. " Some time
after, I had freedom to accompany F. H. into the South.
I met her at Haregate in Staffs. at John and Joshua Toft's
about 30.2.1745." Here also she met her future husband
Abraham Darby. She then goes on to relate how F. H. and
she went up to Yearly Meeting in London, where she saw
more of Abraham, and thence to Norwich and elsewhere,
and on to Balby.

The years 1744 and 1745 were probably the most
exciting and eventful in Fanny's life, for they brought to
her the recovery of spiritual health along with the experience
of courtship and a happy marriage, they provoked her first
and only appearance in print (and any author knows the
excitement of this), and ended with something like an
excursion into politics on her part, incited by the irruption
into the neighbourhood of her home of the " rebel " army
of the Young Pretender.

In the first place, as she says in her narrative, at a time
when she regarded herself as " bereft of all comeliness ",
she was being sought after by several estimable persons as a
companion for life ! This was doubtless a great external
aid towards her emergence at length from the dark cloud of
desolation under which she had so long been buried. A
letter of hers exists, written from Salop (*i.e.* Shrewsbury) to
John Wilson, " merchant " at Kendal, in June, 1744, which
refers to one of these suitors. It is a very grateful tribute
to his friendship during her recent time of affliction, when,
she says, she was subject to much misrepresentation, and to

the value to her of his " cautionary hints ".   By this time,
she continues, help had come to her from the Lord.   Moreover a brother of her companion " S. A." (probably Susanna
Appleby—see below) had, she implies, asked her hand in
marriage.   As to whether he is a suitable partner, " time
must manifest and future contingencies ".

Fanny goes on to thank the Kendal merchant for his
attention to her " paper ", which he was proposing to read
" in a full meeting ".   She asks him, if he thinks proper,
to circulate it either in manuscript or print.   " In the
writing of it Kendal was in my view."

The " paper " here alluded to is a little eight-page
tract entitled *A Serious Call in tender Compassion to the
Sinners in Zion*.   The title is interesting.   For it would
inevitably suggest to most eighteenth-century readers
William Law's masterpiece (then in its fourth edition),
with which we know she was acquainted ; and it is thus
natural to suppose that its author was willing to allow
herself to be counted as a humble fellow-labourer with her
former antagonist.   The tract is dated Kendal, 2nd month,
1744.   It is an earnest appeal addressed partly to those
" in whom the love of pleasure is so prevalent that it is the
deity they bow to ", while they excuse themselves with the
" weak weapons of human reason " ; and partly to those
who, though they have some knowledge of " the truth as it
is in Jesus ", find it difficult to release themselves from the
chains of pleasure, so as to surrender themselves to Him.

The writer implies that she has herself been in this last
category ; and she also alludes to her subsequent experience
of the deep sorrow that accompanies the withdrawings of
the Spirit, with whose aid she had before been favoured—
" but the counsels of God are deep, and when the light,
which makes manifest, is withdrawn, we grope as persons
in the dark, and are utterly unable to understand the
mysteries of godliness, though we feel the mystery of
iniquity working in us."

I see no trace in this *Serious Call* (which is not a composition of any great interest) of any direct influence from the writings of the author of the great work of that name, though its warnings are very much on the same lines. As in her autobiography, Fanny Henshaw writes with the diffidence of a person who shrinks from the task of exposing her thoughts upon the printed page.[1]

The events of the twelve months following this episode of the Kendal tract have been already somewhat anticipated in my quotations from Abiah Darby's journal. We there left Fanny with her friends at Balby. The next entry somewhat abruptly states that Abiah " stayed at Balby till Fanny was married "—an event which must have taken place in the summer of 1745.

Of Fanny's husband, William Paxton, we unfortunately know almost nothing. But we have her own testimony that her marriage, in spite of her husband's " many visitations of bodily afflictions ", was a happy one. They lived at Durham, and four baby sons were born to them during the eight years of their married life. I have found during this period only one notice of Fanny's absence from home on religious visits, and we may therefore believe that she led for the most part a quiet life, looking after the needs of her growing family. It is pleasant, however, to discover that she and her husband assisted in March, 1745–6, at Abraham and Abiah Darby's wedding at Kendal. In 1751 Abiah was entertained by the Paxtons in their Durham home.

I must now revert briefly to the closing months of 1745, the year of Fanny's marriage. The " Young Pretender ", Prince Charles Edward, having defeated King George's army, had recently crossed the Scottish border ; and his troops had captured after a few days' siege the city of Carlisle, only some fifty miles from Fanny's home in Durham. That town was for the time defenceless, and the

---

[1] " [I have] in plainness and simplicity wrote my experiences " are the last words of this tract. It was printed originally at Kendal, reprinted apparently at both Dublin and Bristol in 1745, and again after Fanny's death in 1793.

alarm was great. It was during this crisis that the young wife felt inspired to write a letter to King George, urging him in Old Testament style to come forth on the side of social righteousness and in aid of the suppression of vice, " the oaths and drunkenness and other abominations " that abound in his kingdom ; then he may trust that the country's enemies will be scattered and the judgements that seemed impending dispersed.

More interesting than this rather conventionally prophetic epistle are two letters of Fanny's relating to it, more particularly as they are both addressed to Josiah Martin, the scholarly Quaker " writing-master " and author, who was the friend of John Byrom and the English editor of the French quietist writers.[1] To him on the 30th of November Fanny writes asking for assistance in securing the delivery of her letter to King George, after showing it to Friends, if he thinks fit ; otherwise she may have to come up to London to present it in person, from which service she would fain be excused. The rebels, she adds, were near the city of Durham, and there had been " great commotions ".[2]

There is a second note of Fanny's about a month later, expressing regret that the London " Morning Meeting " of the Society,[3] to which the letter (as was the usual practice in such a case) had been submitted, should have altered two of her sentences, and rather vaguely intimating that she may after all have to come and present it herself, if it cannot be delivered by them unaltered. This is all we know of the fate of her letter—we can only hope that Fanny was eased

[1] See page 155 above.

[2] Prince Charles' army had been expected to march along the East Coast route, and in consequence John Wesley, so we read in his Journal, travelled quickly up to Newcastle, where he had many adherents to shepherd. He records somewhat previously to the date of Fanny's letter that a thousand rebels were within seventeen miles of Newcastle. Probably they did not touch Durham either, as their army took the West coast road, via Penrith and Lancaster ; they entered Kendal on November 22nd and Manchester on December 2nd. Of their visit to Manchester John Byrom's daughter has left a most interesting record in diary form.

[3] See note on page 76.

of the spiritual burden under which she was prompted to write it.[1]

In the year 1753 Fanny lost the husband to whose virtues she afterwards bore emphatic testimony, and so was left in her fortieth year a widow with one or more young sons. Her bereavement seems to have been followed by renewed concern to take upon herself the cares of a travelling minister. Her principal companion, so far as we know, at this time was one Susanna Appleby, probably a younger woman than herself, as she lived on into the next century.[2] We have already, I think, come across her in Fanny's letter to John Wilson, and in 1751 Abiah Darby had met the two friends together at Bishop Auckland. And now we find that in November, 1753, that is within a few months of William Paxton's death, the two women were starting off on a preaching and visiting tour to Norwich, London, Bristol, and elsewhere.

It was and still is customary, when Friends have a " concern " for such religious visiting, for them to secure a " minute " from the Monthly Meeting of which they are members, expressing " unity " with them in their intentions. The two minutes which Frances Paxton and Susanna Appleby secured on this occasion still exist ; it is interesting to find among the names of the nineteen Friends of Durham Monthly Meeting, who signed Fanny's Certificate, that of William Dodshon, her future husband.[3]

[1] She appears to have written a second letter to the King just thirty years later, urging him to be lenient in dealing with his rebellious American subjects, and so " prevent the rending of a potent empire ". It was printed in the *Gentleman's Magazine* for 1775. The idea of approaching the reigning monarch in times of crisis with a solemn message somewhat after the example of the Old Testament prophets was a familiar one—too familiar, I should say, in the Society of Friends.

[2] We know very little of Susanna. She was a friend of Abiah Darby, and was living in Durham in 1775.

[3] For those who are unacquainted with the form of minute for religious service customary in the Society of Friends, the actual words of the certificate granted to Fanny Paxton may be of interest.

" Dear Friends, Our well-esteemed Friend Frances Paxton having acquainted us that a religious concern hath remained upon her mind to visit

Either on this or on some similar occasion a few years later, a Friend, who is believed to be Fanny's old acquaintance Joshua Toft, sent the two ministers the following document of counsel. It is a witness to the high value set upon spiritual intuition. Many of its wise precepts are worthy of application to ourselves.[1]

A few familiar hints to F. Pax. and S. Ap., in their journey for the service of Truth.

1. Make it a rule to speak of none, but those you can say something good of.

2. Be careful not to hear nor enquire the state of the Meeting till you have visited it.

3. Judge not of Friends by outward appearances, but wait to feel before you speak to them or of them.

4. Never take reports of persons when you can come to the knowledge of them.

5. Give way to each other's weight in Meetings and Families.

6. Take not too much notice of each other in publick—avoid contradiction and disputes.

7. Endeavour to hide and help each other's weakness.

8. Be careful to lay no burthens upon each other that you can avoid.

Finally—Travel together in peace and Love and may the God of order, peace, and Love be with you and help you in these and all other Christian duties, is the desire of one that travels for and with you in Spirit.

the several meetings of Friends in London, and to take meetings on her journey thither to the West by Bristol, and in her return by the city of Norwich and the meetings on the road, as she may be led in the wisdom of Truth, requesting our certificate; These may therefore certify you that we have very good unity with her both as a member and a minister, and with desire for the prosperity and promotion of the blessed Truth, in the love of which we remain your Friends and brethren, etc."

[1] With them we may compare the much more extensive "Advices for Ministers and Elders" drawn up officially in 1783. (*Later Periods*, pp. 128–130.)

After a brief record (in Abiah Darby's journal) of Fanny and her friend passing through Coalbrookdale in the summer of 1754, we come suddenly to a notice which provides another landmark in Fanny's career. It is taken from the *Gentleman's Magazine*, the leading literary periodical of the day, to which Dr. Johnson so often contributed. In the column allotted to marriages occurs the following entry (1755) : " Wm. Dodsham (*sic*) of Durham to Frances Paxton ; being of the people called Quakers ; the lady made a learned discourse upon the occasion."

As to the adjective " learned " doubts are permissible ; it probably means full of Scripture quotations. But anyone who has taken part in the solemn ceremony of a Quaker wedding will understand how it is possible for the bride to make a discourse without disturbing the meeting— though it must, I conceive, be a very rare event, even when the lady has a gift of ministry.

William Dodshon is unfortunately a still more shadowy individual than William Paxton. Even the spelling of his name is a most uncertain matter. His family were Quakers, well known in the county of Durham. From the letters (to which I shall presently refer) written to Fanny by her friend John Thorp, we know that he was living in 1780, and we are glad also to hear mention of his " kindness towards her and sympathy with her", and of his " bearing (according to his measure) a part of her burden ", when she was afflicted with depression and ill-health. Except for this and one other brief notice, to be mentioned shortly, we know nothing further at all about William Dodshon, not even the date of his death : nor do we hear of any children being born to Fanny by this marriage.

From a reference in a brief letter which Joshua Toft wrote to Fanny some two years after her marriage, it appears that the family removed to Bristol about this time. Of their stay in the West only one record remains, a letter signed by Frances Dodshon in company with two other

women Friends of Bristol and dated 30th, six month, 1766.[1]
It is headed " Women's Meeting " (that is, of Bristol
Friends) and is an appeal for more diligence in attending the
(probably fortnightly) gatherings, " as you tender [*i.e.* hold
dear] the welfare of the Society in general and the poor in
particular ".

Apart from this there now comes a period of over twelve
years during which the records are silent, with one exception—a series of notices in Abiah Darby's journal for the
year 1763 (the year, by the way, of Dr. Byrom's death).
Herein we read how, soon after Abiah had in her turn
become a widow, Frances Dodgtion (*sic*) and William
Dodgtion, " Fanny's husband ", arrived on a visit to the
Dale.   They took part, together with their hostess, in
religious meetings on several successive days.   At three of
these Fanny " had service ", at one she had " the chief
time ".

On her next visit to Abiah (in 1769) Fanny is accompanied by her son, presumably William Paxton junior.
He cannot have been more than twenty-three years old
at this time.   Abiah again records Fanny's acceptable
service at a " General Meeting ".   The occasion is of
some interest, as the good " Parson Fletcher " of Madely
was one of the gathering.

Very shortly after the entry just recorded Abiah Darby's
journal comes to an end—a real misfortune for our present
purpose, as we should have very much liked to hear the
diarist's impressions of her journey to Scotland in company
with Fanny, undertaken in 1774.   We have to content
ourselves with a brief notice appearing in the papers of
Edinburgh Yearly Meeting, to the effect that Abiah
Darby of Coalbrookdale and Frances Dodgson of Leek came
from Kelso to Edinburgh and returned through Berwick
and Alnwick, in which places they had large meetings with
the inhabitants.

[1] One of them, Hannah Fry, bears a well-known name still connected
with Bristol.

We have now arrived almost at the end of our fragmentary biography of William Law's fair correspondent. There is only one further notice to record of any travelling in the ministry on her part. It concerns a journey to Wales taken in 1777 or 1778. Martha Routh, to whom I shall allude again, informs us that Frances Dodshon accompanied her thither on a religious visit, wherein she, " my dear and esteemed companion, though in a very low and depressed state of mind, was often clothed, in her gospel mission, as with a King's royal apparel ".

During the last eighteen years of her long life, Fanny Dodshon's activities were evidently much hindered by poor health, as well as by intermittent returns of the intense religious depression from which she had suffered in her youth. These distressing visitations were doubtless largely due to her bodily ailments : but they were in some measure occasioned by deep sorrow over what seemed to her to be the godless condition of the nation, and, in her own Society, over " the obvious, painful prevalence of the nature and spirit of the world, the famine of that Word, whose entrance giveth life ". She grieved over her comparative uselessness as a minister for Christ " on the Church's account, wherein the number of upright labourers is small ". At times she even suffered, like her contemporary, the poet Cowper, from the awful doubt whether God had not, for the sins of unfaithfulness which she imputed to herself, abandoned her for ever.

This is the dark side of the picture. But evidently there were compensations. For some of these years she still had with her a husband who seems to have been loving and understanding. She had many affectionate friends, rich in Christian experience, who honoured her for her services to the Truth. And there were " seasons ", we are told, when " by the power of Divine love and light " she was raised above her depression of spirit, so that " when of ability to attend meetings, she was at times enabled to preach the gospel with life and power ".[1]

The following extract from one of her letters to her friend John Thorp (dating probably from about 1778) gives a vivid picture of a devoted Christian soul struggling with fierce temptations to doubt and despair.

" Dear and truly sympathising Friend,
            " I seem to myself guilty of ingratitude in being so long silent, after receiving so valuable and encouraging an epistle from thee, which I often read with close attention, and with humble and fervent desire to be helped to lay hold of some degree of that living faith and hope, thou so fully and feelingly expressest thyself to be favoured with on my behalf, and which I endeavour to encourage my drooping spirit in concluding would not be the case with thee, or my dear friend Sarah Taylor or any of the living in Israel, if I were really (as I am painfully tempted to fear) totally cast off or forsaken by the Father of Mercies.[2] Yet, although I consider things in the most favourable light my afflicted state will admit, and esteem it, as I justly ought to do, a favour which I cannot be too thankful for, to be thus under the notice, tender regard, and deep travel in spirit of many faithful souls, it is beyond expression what I yet suffer, for want of the evidence or revival of living faith and hope in my own mind, that the Lord will again return and show mercy to my disconsolate, imprisoned soul, which goes

[1] See the *Memoir* preceding the *Letters of John Thorp* (p. xxvi), from which the letter about to be quoted is also taken. This selection includes eight letters addressed to Frances Dodshon between 1775 and 1781, and one dated 1788. They overflow with sympathy and consolation, couched largely in the language of Scripture, and with very few personal or local references. The general tenor of the writer's remarks is similar to that of the two letters from John Fothergill, from which I have quoted earlier in this chapter.

[2] Compare with this and what follows Cowper (in a letter dated 1793) : " A consciousness that He exists, that He *once* favoured me, but that I have offended to the forfeiture of all such mercies, is ever present with me." But Cowper's obsessions were, of course, far more serious.

mourning all the day long and cannot be comforted, because the blessed Comforter, He who alone can deliver my soul, seems yet afar off : and the cruel accuser almost continually at hand, to bear down and frustrate my utmost endeavours to draw near to the Fountain of help and strength, to be enabled to lay hold of the hope and faith to resist the fiery darts of the wicked one.

"Oh ! my dear friend, could I but hope that I am of the number thou mentionest of the Lord's chosen ones, whose names are written in the Book of Life, I should esteem no baptism too deep, nor any suffering too long or too great to endure. But herein lies my great discouragement, that I seem in my own painful apprehension to suffer as an evil-doer, or one who through inattention or want of due circumspection has offended an all-gracious Being, and caused Him to withdraw His blessed presence, light, life, and Holy Spirit ; and oh ! what in this stripped, desolate state has the poor soul to cleave to or flee to for refuge or support ? As the experienced Psalmist says, ' If the foundations be destroyed, what can the righteous do ?' They have not another to go to, nor can expect preservation, comfort, or help, but from Him, who they experimentally know hath the word of eternal life and also the key of David, and alone can open their shut-up state and by His powerful voice say, even to the spiritually dead, ' Come forth !' Then, and not till then, can we feel our spirits quickened by Him, who is of a truth the resurrection and the life of every truly living soul, that lives to and in Him."

John Thorp (1742–1817) of Manchester, the young Minister with whom Fanny Dodshon corresponded during these years, was a fine representative of his class, and has moreover points of interest for the student of William Law's relationship to Quakerism. A farmer's son, he was a native of the country near Macclesfield, where Fanny

was residing in her old age.   While still in his teens he
had come over from the Established Church to the Society
in which she had made her home, and within its borders he
laboured for the Truth during the remainder of his life.
The little volume of seventy letters from his pen that has
come down to us breathes very much the same spirit as
do the letters of William Law, and is not altogether unworthy of being set on the shelf beside that precious Collection.   It is probable that John Thorp was acquainted with
Law's later writings.   Some of his expressions appear to
me to be reminiscent of the great quietist.   Law's spiritual
master, Jacob Behmen (Boehme), Thorp certainly knew
and admired, very possibly through the medium of the
English edition of 1764–1781, with which Law's name is
associated.   If I am not mistaken, John Thorp quotes
Behmen at least four times in his published Letters, the
first of these quotations being in his last letter to Fanny
Dodshon—" It is a great sin to despair of the mercy of
God : despair is the most powerful talon of the enemy ".[1]

This particular letter is full of expressions of hope that
the renewed attack (perhaps after some years' interval) of
Fanny's former affliction will be " wholly baffled."   It was
written when the aged Quakeress had some five more years
of earthly existence before her.   She died in 1793 at the
age of seventy-eight.   We too may hope that these were
years of comparative peace and light.   All we know, however, is that in this last phase she was again living in the
neighbourhood of her native place of Leek, at Macclesfield in Cheshire, with her son William Paxton and his
wife.   Four months before her death there is one brief
record of a " season of consolation " spent with her in the
manuscript diary of Deborah Darby, who writes of Fanny
as having had a " precious gift in the ministry."   Deborah
Darby (1754–1810) was daughter-in-law to Fanny's old

---

[1] The editor of Thorp's Letters, apparently being apprehensive of the
unorthodox flavour of the name, has substituted the words " a pious writer "
for " Jacob Behmen ", which is to be found in the original manuscript.

friend Abiah Darby, and herself exercised a very potent ministry of consolation for the last thirty years of her life.

On the 25th of 7th month, 1793, the most critical year of the French Revolution, Fanny Dodshon was smitten with a stroke depriving her of speech and activity. " Yet she appeared ", so runs the " testimony " of her Monthly Meeting, " to those about her to be quite sensible, and often in fervency of spirit with the Lord ; and, we have no doubt, was happily prepared to unite with those whom John the beloved disciple saw in the vision of light, who came out of great tribulation, and had washed their robes and made them white in the blood of the Lamb. On the 1st of the 8th month she quietly departed this life, and was decently interred in Friends' burying ground in Macclesfield, the 4th of the same ; after a large and solemn meeting, attended by divers Friends from distant parts, and many others not of our Society ; aged 78, a Minister about 56 years."

So much of Fanny's life, even in its broad outlines, lies hidden in obscurity, that it is difficult to form a judgement of its fruitfulness. There is little doubt that to her fellow ministers and elders in her religious Society she seemed a faithful disciple, whose purpose was set to handing on to others gleams of the Light entrusted to her. She enjoyed the friendship and respect of devoted Christian leaders like John Fothergill and Abiah Darby. The testimony from which I have just quoted sums up her life-work in the following words.

" Soon after she was united in membership with our Society she was called to the work of the ministry, for which service she was eminently qualified, by her Lord and Master, and laboured much in the exercise of her gift, whilst health and ability were afforded ; travelling into most parts of England, Scotland, and Wales ; her openings were clear in the doctrine and authority of the gospel, and communicated with lively zeal ; she was frequently led to speak to the states of individuals, and we have no doubt her labours have been blessed, to the spiritual help and edification of many."

More impressive than this somewhat official record is the following tribute from the pen of Martha Routh, a younger and gifted minister, who is selected by Rufus Jones as one of the typical leaders of eighteenth-century Quakerism.   In her Journal Martha Routh describes how for some fifteen years ending in her twenty-ninth year she was seeking the final call to become wholly dedicated to the work of the Gospel.

" Many times", she writes, " did the current of ministry [*i.e.* in the Friends' Meeting for Worship] so flow towards me in an encouraging manner, that my soul at times seemed melted within me ; and I think through no instrument, more evidently pointed or with more consolation, than through that worthy handmaid, Frances Dodshon.   How had she to proclaim, as on the housetop, the secret sentiments of my heart, in offering up for sacrifice all but the one thing required ! She was till then an entire stranger to me, but after-wards became a near and intimate friend." [1]

Fanny Henshaw's life had another side to it.   She was twice a wife, and the mother of at least four children.   She was living at the time of death with a married son and his wife.   We have no reason to think that she neglected her responsibilities towards husband and children, except in so far as her liability to religious depression may have made her a rather disconsolate member of the household.   The impression of her left upon our mind by the records to be found on the foregoing pages is undeniably a melancholy one.   But the framers and collectors of records among eighteenth-century Quakers had scarcely any interest in the brighter, sociable side of life, which was present in the lives of even the most intense ministers of the Society. Among a quantity of rather trivial unpublished letters

---

[1] *Memoir of Martha Routh* (1743–1817), pp. 29–30.   The date referred to appears to be about 1770, when Fanny was fifty-five.

written by William Law to his friend Miss Hester Gibbon
I picked out one which contained the following sentence :
" After I received Mrs. Hutcheson's letter, I ordered
cheesecakes to be made by way of rejoicing ".   From the
printed correspondence and works of the puritanic author
of the *Serious Call* we should never have guessed that he
was capable of indulging his childlike delight at some good
news in this very human way.   Similarly we may hope that
during the long pilgrimage of that " deeply tried servant "
of the Lord, Fanny Henshaw, there were many green
oases of cheerful social joys, which compensated somewhat
even in " this vale of tears " for the painfulness of her
wrestlings with the powers of evil.

CHAPTER V

SOME CHARACTERISTICS OF EIGHTEENTH CENTURY QUAKERISM

THIS is not the place for any comprehensive account of Quakerism—of the beliefs and practices of the Society of Friends. But those who are not familiar with the changing scenes of Quaker history will probably welcome at this point some further account of the denomination and the system of thought, with which William Law and John Byrom were brought into conflict, and which exercised so powerful an attraction over Fanny Henshaw. This is all the more desirable because, as will appear from succeeding chapters, it was towards an outlook closely akin to that of Quakerism that Law's own convictions began to move soon after the period of the Henshaw correspondence.

On reviewing the situation, it seemed to me unsatisfactory to attempt to fill this need with an essay of my own, when there already exist, imbedded in more extended and competent studies, several detailed accounts of eighteenth-century Quakerism, that are from different points of view admirable. I am therefore, with the author's permission, reprinting in this section the most relevant portions of Dr. Rufus M. Jones' *Later Periods of Quakerism*,[1] namely, those describing the characteristics of the company of "itinerant ministers", who moulded the thought of the Society and of whom Fanny Henshaw was a not unworthy example ; together with some account of the " quietism ", which was so large an element in their outlook, and which was in later years a link with Law's

[1] My quotations are all taken from Chapters I, II, III, and VII of this work. I have transposed a few passages, and made one or two purely verbal alterations to smooth out the connections, but I have endeavoured to avoid doing the slightest violence to the author's meaning.

thought, though in 1736 he had comparatively little sympathy with it. I think the reader will agree that the picture given in the following paragraphs is one of rare lucidity and charm ; the writer, moreover, had taken pains to master all the available material in a way achieved by very few other students of the period.[1] The biographical sketch given in the last chapter has already afforded many indications of what the Quaker body was like, and will, I hope, serve as a useful illustration to the generalized account that follows.

*   *   *   *   *

One of the most unique features of Quakerism in the eighteenth and early nineteenth centuries was its spontaneous and unorganized itinerant ministry. For more than a hundred years a continuous stream of travelling Ministers went forth from one end of the Society of Friends to the other. They were without question the makers and builders of the Society of the period under review. They formed a kind of " inner church " within the Church. What they called " the Truth ", which was their lofty phrase for Quakerism and its spiritual ideals, absorbed them body and soul as a patriot in the stress of his country's need is absorbed in preserving and promoting the national life.

It became a well-settled custom for these Quaker message-bearers to record their experiences in autobiographical narratives, which they called Journals. These Journals furnish the best material in existence for a study of the mental outlook of the Quaker leaders of the times,

[1] Other valuable estimates of eighteenth-century Quakerism are contained in *The Quakers : their Story and Message*, by A. Neave Brayshaw (of which a new edition has recently appeared) and *The Quaker Ministry*, by John W. Graham (Swarthmore Lecture, 1925). Neave Brayshaw's estimate is distinctly less favourable than that of Rufus Jones or J. W. Graham.

their religious ideals and aspirations, and the general condition of the Quaker meetings in the various sections of
the world.

It is obvious to one who has read the Journals and
Memoirs in bulk, that the itinerant Ministers were drawn
almost exclusively from one psychological type. They
were all persons of the class to which mystics and prophets
belong. They, as we have seen, were conscious of divine
intimations from early childhood ; their conversion and
call seemed to them the direct work of God wrought
immediately upon them ; their " mission " appeared to be
laid upon them as distinctly as upon the Hebrew prophets
of old ; they spoke only when they felt themselves *moved*,
and they delivered only what they believed was *given* to
them. They considered themselves the objects of peculiar
providential care and guidance. They were not surprised
when extraordinary deliverances came to them or when
ways were made where there seemed no way, for that had
always been God's method with His messengers. They
implicitly trusted interior impressions whose origin they
could not trace to any known source in consciousness,
and thus throughout this long period almost all Quaker
ministry was unmeditated and spontaneous, *i.e.* of the
prophetic type.

The remarkable thing about this ministry was, not that
the Ministers exhibited such implicit faith, but that it
worked, that it was actually constructive. In the language
of St. Paul it "edified". The men and women who were
called, it must be realized, were rare and unusual persons.
They often lacked the power, which comes with intellectual
development, to think problems through logically, but they
had for the most part striking native capacity, that indescrib-
able thing which is called *gift*, a certain quality of grace,
a kind of unerring accuracy of intuition, and withal a
covering of the divine presence which gave them power
far beyond the actual avoirdupois weight of their words.
They were, speaking generally, persons of radiant and

saintly life. They showed the fact of communion with God in their faces, and they succeeded, to an unusual degree, in refining and purifying their natures in the desire to be " stainless mirrors for their God ". These men and women are striking illustrations of the fact that *life* speaks louder than words. They often were unlettered. For the most part they knew little history and less literature. They had no training in theology, and no skill in homiletics. They spoke generally with a rhythmical intonation which would make their preaching seem odd and quaint, if not ridiculous, to us to-day. But in spite of all this they actually moved men when they spoke ; they convicted sinners and they aroused the careless and indifferent. They made God seem real, and Christ a mighty attractive power, and eternity an affair big with destiny to men like us. They went out with timorous humility as to their fitness for the great service, but they came back bringing large sheaves of harvest for their labour.

Their mission was a twofold one. Primarily, it was to build up and perfect the " Society ", which for them was the true Church of Christ, the precious and peculiar Israel of God ; and, secondarily, it was to proclaim their great gospel message to the wider world out beyond their fold. They saw, as the rank and file did not see, the real significance of the Quaker faith ; they understood through long meditation why the founders had suffered for their Truth ; they quietly felt themselves called out to live absolutely for the *cause* ; they were so impressed with the preciousness of the inheritance that they faced with joy any sacrifice whatever which was involved in carrying it on untarnished. They were quick to note in the membership signs of conformity to the world or to other forms of Christian faith, while they, on the contrary, kept the gaze steadily focused on the distinct and differentiated Quaker peculiarities, and on the spiritual ideals of their Society. Wherever they went they were the bearers of the ideal. They saw, like earlier prophets, the signs of the times, the ominous tendencies toward backsliding and degeneracy, the deviations from the days of the fathers, the subtle contaminations of the world, and the insidious lure of false lights. They stuck their finger on the place that was ailing, and they pleaded with intensity of passion for the preservation of the pure and glorious Truth which they believed God had especially opened, in a new dispensation of grace, to the fathers of Quakerism. Stern with themselves, they were also stern with their hearers. They would have nothing to do with compromise, they were determined to hew to the line, and, as we shall see, it was the itinerant Ministers who drew the lines which differentiated " Quakerism", and marked it off from other types of Christianity. They created its ideals, they keyed the body up to its task of keeping the discipline pure at all costs, and, finally, most important of all their services, they *discovered* and mustered out the young recruits who in turn became their spiritual successors in the work of ministry.

The second feature of their work as they travelled about was the presentation of their gospel—the " Truth ", as they called it—to those outside the " Society ". They represented, though with a marked slowing down of zeal, the continuation of that immense passion for propagation which characterized the Quakers in the early flush of their discovery. They frequently appointed public meetings in communities which they visited, especially in the unsettled regions of America, and in these meetings they gave a kind of laboratory exhibition of the Quaker method and the Quaker idea. These appointed meetings began, as all Quaker meetings began, without anything to appeal to eye or ear. The congregation was quietly told that this was an occasion for the discovery of the living God and for communion with Him, and that nothing would be spoken until the Teacher of His people and the Shepherd of souls should open something Himself in the minds of one of His messengers. Then a silence would fall over the company, often more impressive than the somewhat formal silences of the distinctly Quaker meetings, and the gathering would be prepared for the words, often tremendously powerful with their inspirational quality and their cadenced strain.   The effect of these meetings was to pick out and win over persons in the neighbourhood who were disposed toward mystical religion and who were ready for this type of Christianity which put the stress on direct relation with God and on individual responsibility.

One natural result of this extensive itinerancy was the eventual prevalence of a single type of Quakerism throughout the far-sundered communities that composed the Society.   It was as though a common pollen fertilized every spiritual flower in the entire garden.   There was no written creed, there were no fixed forms or ceremonies, nobody could quite *describe* what constituted the essential marks and characteristics of the Quaker " faith ", and yet wherever Friends maintained a group life—in Ireland, in Great Britain, in New England, in Pennsylvania, in the Southern States, in the " new " West, in the Islands of the Sea—there was among them a similarity in ideas, in phrases, in conscientious scruples, in emotional tones, in spiritual perspective and emphasis, in garb and manner, in facial expression and vocal modulation.   The members were persons, often of insistent individuality, maintaining at all costs their right to think, and act, and worship for themselves, and yet some subtle influence, without their knowledge, had transformed them all into one profoundly marked *genre*.

*   *   *   *   *

We have in the Quakerism of the eighteenth century, it must be said, an impressive exhibition of a Quietism that was corporate rather than individualistic.   Everywhere where we can find a clue that leads us back into the prevailing habits of the Quaker groups, we find in evidence a deep-seated fear of everything " man-made ", and we see a variety of methods in operation designed to suppress

" own-self " and to hamper or crucify the " creature ". Corporate silence—a silence prolonged unbroken sometimes for hours—came more and more, as the century progressed, to be exalted as the loftiest way of worship. The silence of all flesh, the suppression of all strain and effort, the slowing down of all the mechanism of action, the hushing of all the faculties of thought, were urged as the true preparation for receiving the divine Word.

The most insistent note of this Quietism is its distrust of human nature, its call for the annihilation of the self, and its expectation of the manifestation of a *divine work* when once the human powers have been humbled and laid low. The primary aspirations and the profoundest travail of soul of those who set forth on this spiritual pilgrimage are for the crucifixion of self and the death of the " creature ", and the goal of the pilgrimage is the attainment of a state of *pure* repose and contemplation, in which God flows in and takes the place of the crucified me, becomes the only inward reality, and inaugurates whatever action is acceptable to His perfect and holy will. The highest spiritual state, on whatever path the soul is travelling, is to the quietist always " pure ", *i.e.* it is a state uncontaminated by any definite mental content. The soul and God have met, and all of self is hushed as His presence flows in and bathes the soul with the fountains of life.

The natural psychological result of this intense aspiration to annihilate the " creature " and to become wholly free from " the lead of human reason " was an excessive tendency to be introspective, to watch with minute and painstaking observation " the inner flow of things ". The focus of attention was turned upon inner states, and the mind in its long periods of withdrawal from objective happenings was likely to be occupied with an eager examination of all the inner " states " passing before the footlights of consciousness, to discover which ones bore the mark and brand of own-self and which ones appeared to be from beyond the regions of self, and so divinely given. The face of the devoted saint was thus turned away from the tasks of the world and busied with a refined discrimination between those inner pointings which could be referred to a higher source and those feelings and willings and thoughts which were due to native faculties. His problems were in the main these inner problems, and not those that are concerned with the building of the city of God in the world of our complicated social relationships. He became an introspective expert, but he gathered little power to grapple with the massive tasks with which the human society of his day was crowded. Another difficulty was inherently involved in this desire to force the citadel of self completely to capitulate. It was an aspiration which threw profound suspicion and distrust upon those very God-given powers by which men are equipped to live the abundant life, and by which they are able to serve the world in which they are bound to work out their earthly destiny. If " the lead of human reason " is to be destroyed and all the faculties of mind and heart are to be annihilated, that means that *this* world has no mission in our spiritual training, and that no processes which expand our capacities of judgement, and which discipline our will, and which fashion our character are of any value. The very furnishings for our momentous voyage through " time and mutability " are to be jettisoned as soon as possible, and we are to sail only as we are blown by breezes which come wholly from another world. It is a situation which a rigid dualism of " worlds " forces upon one, and these Friends saw no way out of it. In that hard strait they accepted it with all its stern consequences and made their uttermost sacrifice out of sheer loyalty to their light—the highest and clearest their souls could see.

*   *   *   *   *

There are many evidences in the eighteenth-century Journals that the public Friends of the period were characteristically of the psychical, ecstatic type. They were for the most part solid, well-balanced persons, but they were at the same time persons who were predisposed to "invasions", to inward impulses whose origin they could not trace, and they were persons, too, who easily dropped into telepathic rapport with the groups in which they sat. It was no uncommon feat for these itinerant messengers to sit absolutely unmoved for hours and to be withdrawn not only from action but from concrete thinking as well, and still to be intensely alive and concentrated. It needs hardly to be said that most normal persons are incapable of this ! The mind, as we know too well, flies away from the mental task before it and is brought back only to shy off again on another tangent. To concentrate in this absorbed and distracted fashion in itself calls for a peculiar psychical type, and such in fact were many of these Ministers. And with that trait of mind and disposition, we know not how or why, goes also the telepathic power—the power to feel out states and conditions and unuttered desires in persons far or near. Some of the extraordinary successes which these Ministers thought they made in uncovering the minds of those to whom they spoke may be unconsciously coloured in the telling, but there can be no doubt at all that they sometimes made surprising revelations, and they apparently did do a real work in these speechless ministrations, which they called " travailing with the suffering seed." [1]

[1] The following quotation from the Journal of John Griffith (1713–1776), one of the most devout and devoted of the itinerant ministers of this period, illustrates the completeness of the Quaker reliance upon internal guidance, as opposed to outward reason. (The date of the entry is 1749. I have not observed that it has been quoted elsewhere.)

" From thence (*i.e.* Gloucestershire) to the quarterly meeting for Wiltshire ; being altogether unexpected by Friends there and a stranger, the close searching testimony given me to bear, especially relating to the state of some active members, might be better taken and might have more effect than if the same had come from one better acquainted with their states. I always coveted to be wholly unacquainted with the states of meetings by outward information in all my travels, and when, by the discourse of Friends previous to my attending them, there appeared any probability of their inadvertently opening in my hearing anything of that kind, I have generally either stopped them or walked away out of hearing. But in general Friends who entertain us in our travels have more prudence and

The quietistic temper tended among Friends, as has happened wherever that temper has been strongly in evidence, to exalt the marvellous and to emphasize the sphere of the supernatural. The Journals are for the most part sober, restrained narratives. The writers are almost always modest, humble-minded persons who also had a remarkably delicate sense for truth, so that one will look in vain here for oriental flights of imagination or for medieval luxury of saintly incidents. But nevertheless there is a pretty steady focus of attention on the supernatural. The things of most real importance to these men and women were events and " happenings " (though they never allowed that word) that could not be explained by any known processes. Ideas which " came " without any strain or effort of ratiocination, feelings and insights which burst upon them as unexpectedly as the " cape of cloud from the invisible air ", fields of labour which were " laid upon " them when the creaturely will was silent, seemed to them to belong in a different order of things from the ideas and feelings and proposals which could be accounted for in normal processes of experience. The ability to feel out " states ", to diagnose inward situations, to tell what was passing in somebody's mind, to read as in an open book the " condition " of individuals and meetings, were achievements attended with all the mystery of the direct finger of God ; and the importance of this " gift ", as has generally been the case with quietists, was made unduly great. They lived continually in the expectation of *providential* guidances and deliverances. The mist which saves their ship from pirates is a " providential mist " ; the delay of a coach which enabled them to make connections and hold a meeting is a " providential delay " ; the arrival of a letter which throws light on some perplexity of plan is a " providential

a better guard in these respects ; as indeed all ought, for it straightens and may give much uneasiness to right-spirited ministers, who have a sure infallible guide within, and therefore have no need of any outward guide or information in their services." (*John Griffith's Journal* (1779), p. 189.)

event ". A Friend feels, for instance, that one room in an inn is unsuitable and finds it impossible to feel " easy " until it is changed. Sitting in the room to which he has changed he observes a passer-by who impresses him, follows him and finds an opening for service. The entire concatenation seems a series of " providential arrangements " of a supernatural order. The Journals abound in incidents of this sort or of similar type, and there can be no question that the itinerant Ministers lived in a *climate of expectations* of supernatural help.

As always happens when the quietistic attitude makes wide conquest, the Friends of this type continually exhibited a fear of intellect and tended to narrow the sphere of reason. At first they insisted that prayer and ministry must be oracular, that is to say, must be the result of an immediate " moving ", the pure jet of a divine spring of life, but as the quietistic temper of mind progressed, it became not at all unusual for members of the Society to expect all important matters to be settled by heavenly openings. The affairs of meetings for business were transacted on this basis. Nothing, or at most as little as possible, was matured or prepared in advance. All subjects were approached in a frame of silence, and those who " spoke to business " were expected to speak " under guidance " and not " under the will or wisdom of the creature ".

The quietistic ideals, as they were gradually developed by the spiritual leaders in England and America, dwelt upon withdrawal from contact with the world and from responsibility for shaping the affairs of men and of nations —withdrawal even from an interest in politics. The conquests which best fitted these ideals of Quietism were conquests of the inner spirit. The world confronted them, stubborn and unmalleable. It seemed to be a realm of darkness and hostility to spiritual aims. Their business, as it appeared to them, was to bring every power of heart and mind and will into obedience to the Light of Christ which shone in their souls, to build an inner Kingdom where

Christ might absolutely reign, and to this conquest they devoted all their energies.

The Friends were " the quiet ones " in the world of their time. They had few learned men. They hardly knew what the great world around them was thinking. They had none of the usual marks of greatness or distinction. The descriptive content of their lives is not rich or varied. They were not heroic fighters with spiritual weapons, like the Quakers of the first generation, nor, with the exception of John Woolman, impressive workers for great social and humanitarian reforms, like their successors in the nineteenth century. They will interest our age, if at all, because they were sure of God and lived, in a world of rather sordid aims and increasing scepticism, with their sensitive souls opened inward toward eternal realities. They saw no way to remake the world or to establish the Kingdom of God in the earth on any great scale, but they went quietly on bearing their testimony to the living God, and were constantly refreshed and fortified by inward resources, which the world could neither give nor take away.

*　　　*　　　*　　　*　　　*

Dr. Rufus Jones' description which I have been quoting in the preceding paragraphs does not directly deal with the Quaker attitude to the sacraments of the Church. Something may well be added on this subject.

It was their intense conviction of the immediate contact of God with the soul, to be realized at all times and in all places, that led to the depreciation of sacramental rites by George Fox and the first Quakers. They believed that they had the substance ; the symbols were not needed and just dropped away.

"The claims of the inward light", writes the ablest historian of early Quakerism, " demanded a separation

from all that was outward in religion, and left no place
for a man-made ministry or for reliance on the external
features of baptism and the Lord's supper. But the
leaders showed conspicuous courage in so completely laying aside these venerable institutions, and relying instead
upon the inward spiritual provision of whose substance
they were only the shadows. The courage was theirs,
because it was rooted in experience, they knew the
Divine ordination, they were baptized with the washing
of regeneration and renewing of the Holy Ghost, they
had found their spiritual food and communion in Christ
Himself." [1]

Many Christians will feel that such a revolution in
Church tradition and practice was rashness rather than
courage ; nevertheless it is difficult for any one reading
the records of their lives to doubt that the early Friends
possessed the Spirit of Christ in abundant measure.

George Fox expresses the matter as follows :—

"This is a nearer and further advanced state, to
be with Christ in the fellowship of His death than only
to take bread and wine in remembrance of His death.
. . . For outward bread, wine, and water, are from
below, visible and temporal. . . . So the fellowship
that stands in the use of bread, wine, water, circumcision, outward temple, and things seen, will have an
end : but the fellowship which stands in the Gospel, the
power of God, which was before the devil was, and
which brings life and immortality to light, by which
people may see over the devil that has darkened them,
this fellowship is eternal and will stand. . . . The
apostle told the Corinthians, who were in disorder
about water, bread and wine, that he desired to know
nothing amongst them but Jesus Christ and Him
crucified." [2]

What George Fox failed, I think, to realize was the

[1] W. C. Braithwaite, *Beginnings of Quakerism*, pp. 137–38.
[2] *Journal*, p. 342 (1656). Compare also pages 48 and 106 above.

need of the ordinary man and woman, who are but beginners
in the school of the Holy Spirit, for some regular reminder
of the story of the incarnation and passion, that is so vital
to every one of us.

In order to justify the Quaker view, it was necessary
to explain away certain New Testament texts, and the
attempts of Barclay and others to do this were not conspicuously successful. It is easier to meet the appeal to
these texts to-day, when the best scholarship is divided as
to whether Jesus Christ during His earthly life founded or
contemplated the foundation of any institution or ordinance.
More important to the Quakers than any consideration of
texts was the instinctive conviction that the Jesus of the
Gospels could not possibly have meant to place two acts of
ritual at the centre of the religion of abundant life which
He brought to mankind ; a conviction which moreover
seemed in line with the interpretation of Jesus in the writings
of Paul, of whom it has been said that " there have been
hardly any religious leaders, if we except George Fox, who
have valued ceremonies so little ".[1]

And as against the apparent weight of evidence for the
indispensability of the sacraments provided by the experience of the vast majority of Christians, there must be set
the spectacle, more vividly distressing in the seventeenth
century than to our generation, of the bitter strife that
Christendom has waged over the meaning and the manner
of observance of those holy rites.

Barclay remarks that it has often been
"the policy of Satan to busy people and amuse them
with outward signs, shadows, and forms, making them
contend about that, while in the mean time the substance is neglected ; yea, and in contending for these
shadows he stirs them up to the practice of malice,
heat, revenge, and other vices, by which he establisheth
his kingdom of darkness among them, and ruins the
life of Christianity. For there have been more ani-

[1] Inge : *Christian Mysticism*, p. 70.

mosities and heats about this one particular [*i.e.* the Eucharist], and more bloodshed and contention, than about any other." [1]

This consideration is of course not an absolutely conclusive argument, but it carries much weight.

I will add just one more quotation, from one of the most devoted twentieth-century workers of the Society of Friends, to which I think the Quakers of earlier centuries would have fully subscribed.

"Friends hold that the Sacraments are real and spiritual, and not confined to certain rare and stated acts or rites. The marks of the Holy Spirit's Baptism are to be seen in the daily life of consecration, and His action is continuous, not once for all in childhood, but needed ever more and more, as the soul yearns for larger experience of the Divine cleansing and renewing.

"And in like manner, of the Communion it may be said, that Friends find in our Lord's teaching, not the institution of a rite, but the inculcation of that entire dependence on the Love of God, as manifested in Christ, which makes us aware that our very life is sustained, not by material food in itself, but by the power of the life within each one of us." [2]

Two remaining points may be considered briefly here.

The history of all Christian bodies indicates that a certain growth of the worldly, indifferent spirit was inevitable within the borders of the Society of Friends in the second or third generation. The declension set in, soon after 1685, with the end of persecution. Habits of industry, thrift, and honesty combined with this to lead to

---

[1] Barclay: *Apology*, Prop. XIII, Sect. IV.

[2] Joan M. Fry: *For Fellowship and Freedom*, 1908 (p. 4). For a very similar Anglican view, expressed in language remarkably like the above quotation, see the chapter on *The Necessity of a Church*, in *A Practical Faith*, by the Rev. Harold Anson (1925, with a Preface by the Rev. H. R. L. Sheppard).

material prosperity. By 1730 Quakers were generally being treated with respect. Under the Whig Government, which brought in the Hanoverian Kings, they were in considerable favour with politicians and even with some of the bishops, and secured important legislative concessions. Another powerful factor was the adoption of birthright membership,[1] which meant the transition from a " pure " Church of believers only to a " mixed " body including many who had but an inherited and therefore often nominal religion.

The worst consequence of the changed conditions was that many Quakers grew rich and that the habit of acquiring riches was fostered. And wealth was then, as it is now, the chief cause of corruption in the Society. The best Friends knew and grieved over what was going on. George Fox preached in his last messages against the love of riches. Spiritual indifference, habits of luxury and display, compromise with unchristian customs began to be prevalent. Some change was justifiable as a reaction against the exaggerated Puritan condemnation of innocent diversions and of art. But the mischief went further than this.

John Byrom, we have seen, was well aware of the worldliness of many of the Quakers. William Law was also aware of it, though with great restraint he never refers to it in his writings against them. Fanny did not apparently realize the fact till after she had attached herself to the Society ; then she must soon have become very painfully aware of it, and her tract addressed to *Sinners in Zion* was most probably addressed primarily to lax Quakers. She no doubt took part in the movement of revival and reform which was set going soon after the middle of the century by a number of the most earnest and gifted of the Elders and Ministers of the Society. Perhaps the two leading spirits in this movement were John Griffith, from

---

[1] Officially this measure was only introduced in the year 1737 (the year of Fanny Henshaw's convincement), but the action then taken ratified what had been custom for a good many years past.

whose Journal I have quoted above, and Samuel Fothergill, a son of the friend who wrote letters of consolation to Fanny in her times of depression. Too much reliance was placed by these reformers on the external weapon of tightening the rules of the " Discipline ", which was intended to control, in conjunction with the threat of possible " disownment ", the dress, habits, and activities of members. Nevertheless the historians inform us that the reform movement did much to arrest the growth of the spirit of worldliness and unbelief, and was the beginning of a better period for the Quaker body.

To turn to another question, one would like to know how far the quietist forms of belief which have been described in this chapter tended to check those humanitarian and practical activities which are the indispensable fruits of the Gospel. Overton, when defending very fairly both mystics and mysticism against the charge of neglect of good works, after appealing to the example of John Tauler, Madame Guyon, and others, remarks that " the sect in England, which has been most conspicuous for its mystic views, has also been most remarkable for its deeds of practical Christianity ".[1] But the last part of this statement was less true about the year 1736 than at almost any other time of the Society's existence. The reasons for this have been already suggested at the end of my quotations from Rufus Jones' history. On the other hand, as he says elsewhere, " some of the Friends, whose religion appears from their journals to be most inward and introspective, were nevertheless profoundly stirred by human suffering and were dedicated to the ministry of relief ".[2] The supreme example of this combination was John Woolman (1720–1772), to whose efforts the eventual abolition of negro slavery owes a very great debt, while his *Word of Remembrance and Caution to the Rich* has actually been printed to serve as a Socialist tract. Other examples are John

---

[1] *Life of William Law*, p. 211.
[2] *Later Periods*, vol. ii, p. 813.

Churchman (1705–1775), Thomas Shillitoe (1754–1835), and perhaps Dr. John Fothergill (1722–1780), another son of Fanny's friend, with John Bellers (1654–1725) at an earlier date.

Nevertheless it needed the impact upon the mysticism of the Society of the spiritual movement initiated by the Wesleys, with its rediscovery of the New Testament and its passion for liberating human souls, to produce the generation of reformers which in the succeeding century made the Quaker name honourable among those who are concerned for the righting of social wrongs.

PART II

WILLIAM LAW AND QUAKERISM

CHAPTER I

THE DRAFTS AGAINST QUAKERISM

INTRODUCTORY NOTE

IN this chapter will be found a reproduction of a number of manuscript drafts in Law's handwriting, now preserved in Dr. Williams' Library. They were presumably written not long after the Henshaw Letters of 1736. A discussion of their probable origin and destination will be found in the next chapter.

The fragmentary drafts fall naturally into three groups, which I call A, B, and C below. The order of those included under B and C is at times uncertain.

A. THE FOUNDATION OF QUAKERISM

Note.—The interesting connections of this fragment with one of Law's published works are fully dealt with in the next chapter. It is further the only one of the fragments of which the contents have any close similarity with Law's letters to Fanny Henshaw, *e.g.* in the emphasis on "to hear a woman preach", the way John iv. 24 is brought into relationship with Old Testament religion, and especially in the use made of the parable of the Pharisee and the Publican. The fine tribute to the Quakers for their upholding of the doctrine of the "inward light" should be compared with the somewhat similar passage quoted on pages 274 ff. below, which Law published in 1740 in his *Animadversions on Dr. Trapp*.

Here I must take notice of an error of another sort of adversaries to this holy sacrament, who, upon pretence of spiritualizing religion and embracing Christ in a more inward and nearer way than by outward ordinances, reject not only this sacrament, but all other outward institutions and appointments of Christ in the Church. And yet so inconsistent is this pretence with itself, that, though these people renounce the Church, priesthood, and sacraments, because they are outward and carnal things, yet their own outward communion, outward forms and ceremonies of their own invention are chosen by them, because they are outward and are as essential to them as a sect, as the institutions of Christ are to the Church. Did they reject the priesthood, because it was too carnal a thing to hear the outward word, and therefore had no preaching amongst themselves, they would be so far at least consistent ; but to reject the teachers, who are at least as certainly in the chair of the Apostles, as the Scribes and Pharisees were in the chair of Moses, when our Saviour said so of them, to reject these to hear a woman preach, whom the Apostle has forbid to speak in the Church (and has declared it a shame for a woman to speak in the Church), is surely very far from being a work of the Spirit.

I shall say nothing to this deluded people on their open disobedience to express laws and institutions of Christ, which they are as much obliged to observe, as the Jews were obliged to observe the law of Moses ; but shall only in a word or two consider their foundation, as they ground it upon a pretence of being too spiritual to observe outward ordinances.

God is a spirit and they who worship Him must worship Him in spirit and truth, is the foundation of Quakerism,[1] and yet this was as true and a truth of the same obligation,

---

[1] This is fully justified by Quaker writings. See, *e.g.*, Barclay's *Apology*, Prop. XI, Sect. XV, where these words from the fourth chapter of St. John are described as " the first, chiefest, and most ample testimony which Christ gives us of His Christian worship ".

when Moses gave the Law, as when our Saviour preached the Gospel.

And it was as much for the sake of this truth, that the service and worship of the temple was appointed in the Old Testament, as it was for the sake of this truth, that our Saviour taught His disciples an outward form of prayer. If therefore the spiritual Jew must have been looked upon as an apostate, had he said, he would have nothing to do with their sacrifices or the atonements of their high priest, for this reason, because *God was a spirit and must be worshipped in spirit and in truth*, it cannot be shewn that he is guilty of less apostacy, who for the same reason renounces the Church, sacrament[s], and priesthood of the Gospel. For as the Christian religion is an inward and spiritual thing, and wholly signifys the spiritual power and operation of Christ in the birth, life, and growth of our inward man, so the Jewish religion was of the same spiritual nature, seeking and intending nothing else by all its laws, sacrifices, institutions, and purifications, but the production of that same inward man or that which the Apostle calls Christ in us, and the spirit and power and life of Christ being revealed and manifested in us. And as the Quaker may justly say that the Gospel is not a religion of outward ordinances, so the same may and is as justly said of the Law, that it was not a religion of outward ordinances ; for the Apostle expressly says, that *he is not a Jew which is one outwardly*, therefore their religion did not consist in outward ordinances ; but that *he is a Jew which is one inwardly*, and therefore their religion was inward.[1] No one therefore upon pretence of the spirituality of the Gospel can have any better reason to renounce the priesthood and institutions of the Gospel than a Jew had to renounce the whole Law of Moses.

Besides, the Quakers by acting thus, on the pretence

[1] See Rom. ii. 28. This line of argument is used more than once in Law's *Demonstration* for a somewhat different purpose. Thus, on page 38, Law quotes the same verse from Romans, asserting that " Christ was the substance, the heart, and true meaning of all their (*i.e.* the Jewish) ordinances ". Compare also page 19 of the same work.

[of] spirituality, fall into the very error that they condemn and set up a religion of outward ordinances. For to make it a great matter or a mark of true spirituality to renounce outward ordinances, is exactly the very individual error of placing the perfection of religion in the bare observance of outward ordinances. So that the Quaker and the Pharisee seem to be very near akin and to have both of them their measure and rule of perfection from outward ordinances. The one thinks he is spiritual and perfect because he is wholly seperated from outward ordinances, the other thinks he is perfect because he is wholly intent upon them. The one places as much merit in outwardly forsaking them, as the other does in outwardly observing them, so that they both seem to be taken up with outward perfection and to have both of them a religion of outward ordinances. The Pharisee, when he prays according to the principles of his sect, prays thus, " God I thank thee, that I am not as other men are, extortioners, adulterers, or even as this publican ; I fast twice in the week, I pay tithes of all that I possess, etc." [1]   The Quaker, if he prays according to the principles of his sect, as the Pharisee did, must pray thus, " God I thank thee, that I am not as other men are, not even as thy Apostles or Saints and Martyrs of all ages were ; I practise no water baptism or outward supper of the Lord, as they did ; I pay no tithes, I own no bishops, priests, or deacons, I keep no Church feasts or fasts, etc." Here you see the Quaker and the Pharisee both praying according to the principles of their sect ; both agree in the same carnal confidence in and boast of outward works, only with this difference, that the Pharisee places his merit and confidence in having *done* outward good works, the Quaker places his merit and confidence in having *refused to do* outward good works. Therefore both of them have a religion and perfection of outward works and ordinances.[2]

---

[1] Luke xviii. 11, 12.

[2] It is interesting to compare the use Law makes here of the parable of the Pharisee and the Publican with his use of it in the second letter to

When our Saviour said to the man that was born blind, " Go and wash in the pool of Siloam," [1] had he not gone, he had given you a plain instance of the Quaker's obedience to our Lord's command for water baptism and the supper of the Lord. And had he refused to go, for this reason, because it was going so far from Christ and seeking that by the means of outward water and local pools, which was in Christ alone and to be had from Him alone, he had been a plain example of the Quaker's nearer way to Christ than by outward ordinances.

If anyone should conclude from what has here been said, that he may justly despise this sect of people and reproach all their other doctrines and practices, and more especially that continual inspiration and guidance of the Holy Spirit and the reality and benefit of that inward and divine Light, concerning which they have made such full and open declarations, he will very much abuse what I have said to his own great hurt. Had I any contempt for them

Fanny Henshaw (page 41 above). The verbal differences in the two passages seem to indicate that he had the latter passage in his mind, but not before his eyes, at the moment when he penned this draft. Notice how he has toned down here his condemnation of the Quaker. In the letter the Quaker is described as *worse* than the Pharisee, because he trusts in *bad* works instead of in good works. Here the two are " very near akin ", the Quaker's trust being in *negations*. I think that most modern Friends would acknowledge that the whole of this paragraph of Law's forms a salutary criticism of the kind of sins of negation into which their Society has been too apt to fall in the past.

To the Methodist and Evangelical of his day Law himself appeared to be teaching a doctrine of justification by works (of devotion and charity) instead of by faith in Christ alone. This is John Wesley's chief charge against him in his first letter to Law at the time of their breach in the year 1739. To some extent Law admitted the charge. He insists that we are saved or justified by works as well as faith, as the Gospels, he thinks, clearly teach, but only so far as both faith and works are regarded not as our own but as gifts of Christ. " But add Christ to faith and Christ to works, and then they are but one and the same power of God to salvation, and all difference between faith and works is lost." (*Of Justification by Faith and Works. A Dialogue between a Methodist and a Churchman*, 1760, p. 221.) In this tract Law refers again (pp. 219, 220) to the parable of Luke xviii., imagining the Pharisee as boasting *in his faith*, instead of in his works.

[1] John ix. 7.

or was anything I have said the effect of it, I should be in a worse state than those that neglect outward ordinances. Had I stood by the blind man refusing to go and wash in the pool of Siloam, I would have said all that I could to persuade him to go and would have borne him on my back thither.   This is the contempt that I have for the Quakers. And had I not been able to persuade him to go, I would not have ridiculed his opinion of Christ's being the true only good or his belief that all power and virtue was in Him alone, but only have shown him that from the greatest and best of truths he drew a wrong consequence, and exceeding hurtful to himself.

But this by the by : I now return to my subject.   You have seen that the holy sacrament is a solemn recognition of our redemption by Jesus Christ, and that it consists of two great and essential parts, the one in acknowledging, believing, and pleading the body and blood of Christ as the true and great atonement for our sins ; the other in eating and partaking of His body and blood, as our act of faith, that He is a principle of life to us.

Now here it may be proper for you to observe, that whatever . . . [1]

[1] For the explanation of these concluding sentences, see page 227 below.

*   *   *   *   *

B. The Spirituality of the Gospel and the Lord's Supper

(i)

Note.—This closely-reasoned and eloquent passage is directed against one of the principal contentions of the Quakers, namely, that Christ came to turn men away from all outward ceremonies and ordinances, such as were those of Judaism, to a purely spiritual type of religion. Thus Barclay writes :—

" If the use of water, and bread and wine, were that wherein the very seals of the new covenant stood, and did pertain to the chief sacraments of the gospel and evangelical ordinances (so-called), then would not the gospel differ from the law or be preferable to it." [1]

I can, however, see no indication that Law in this fragment has in mind any of Barclay's specific arguments in relation to worship or the Lord's supper (as he has when dealing with the subject of baptism). Possibly he had been reading some other Quaker treatise.

---

[1] See Barclay's *Apology*, Proposition XIII, Section IX. Robert Barclay (1648–1690) was the son of a distinguished Scotch soldier, afterwards Laird of Ury near Aberdeen. Educated in Paris under Roman Catholic influence, he became at an early date widely read in theology and Church history. In 1667, following his father, he joined the persecuted sect of the Quakers, and soon began to apply his keen intellect to a reasoned defence of his new and deeply cherished faith. In 1676–8 he produced, first in Latin and then in English, *The Apology for the true Christian Divinity, as the same is set forth and preached by the people called in scorn Quakers.* This remarkable book became at once the recognized standard exposition of the Quaker creed and, passing through many editions, has retained its position of authority till quite modern times.

The spirituality of the Gospel above the Law consists in this, that the Gospel preaches Jesus as come in the flesh, as plainly revealed, who and what He is, and what manner of salvation He has wrought for us.   The Law by various types and figures preached Jesus Christ as coming, and only by outward signs and ordinances pointed at His nature and characters.   So that the most spiritual Jew could only by an obscure faith trust in God for an unknown Messiah, and their faith was only an exspectation of having Him revealed unto them.

But the Christian is delivered from this obscure faith and exspectation of a Messiah, only made known by signs and prefigurations ; he has seen Him revealed and therefore sees plainly all that the types and figures of the Law pointed at.   Thus the Apostle says, " Without controversie, great is the mystery of godliness, God was manifest in the flesh, justified in the spirit, seen of angels, preached unto the Gentiles, believed on in the word, received up into glory." [1]

The spirituality of the Gospel above the Law consists in this mystery of godliness, Jesus Christ was hid under the letter of the Law ; the Gospel has revealed that which was hid under the letter of the Law, and therefore it is more spiritual than the Law or is the very spirit of the Law, because it has revealed that which the letter of the Law pointed at.   So that the difference between the spiritual Jew and Christian is this : the former only waited for a Messiah, signified to him by types and figures, the Christian has this Messiah openly revealed.[2]

It is the open and outward manifestation of the incarnation, birth, life, death, resurrection, and ascension of Jesus Christ, that constitutes the spirituality of the Gospel.   But if it is the outward manifestation of these things that con-

---

[1] 1 Tim. iii. 16.

[2] It will be noticed that the three last paragraphs cover much the same ground as the first part (pp. 46–49) of Law's fifth letter to Fanny Henshaw, though there are no close verbal parallels.   They are also closely related to the first three paragraphs of page 62 of his *Demonstration*.

stitutes the spirituality of the Gospel, then surely the spirituality of the Gospel cannot consist in having no outward ordinances. For is not the body and blood of Christ upon the cross as much an outward thing or outward ordinance as the body and blood of Christ upon the altar or communion table?

And is not the death of His outward body upon the cross as much an outward means of salvation as the reception of His body and blood in the sacrament? Is it a carnal thing to respect sacraments that consist of outward perishable things? And is it not equally carnal to respect a body of such outward flesh and blood as the Jews could nail to the cross and kill? The Apostle saith, " We are sanctified through the offering of the body of Christ " (Heb. x. 10), that is, the body of Christ on the cross. Is not this as carnal as to say we are sanctified through the offering and pleading and eating the body of Christ in the sacrament? Is not one the same appeal to an outward thing or ordinance as the other? If the body offered on the cross can assist our salvation, why not the body offered in the sacrament?

Again, the Apostle saith, " If Christ be not raised, your faith is vain, ye are yet in your sins." [1] Now if the forgiveness of our sins depends upon the outward resurrection of that outward body that the Jews killed, is not this as carnal as to make the forgiveness of our sins depend upon baptism and the sacrament of the Lord's supper?

Therefore the Quakers' spirituality of religion is a gross fiction of their own, a subtle evasion of the Gospel and a total apostasy from it. For the incarnation of Christ, the death of Christ, the resurrection of Christ, and the ascension of Christ are so many plain outward ordinances of salvation ; and he that rejects outward and elementary means from the Gospel salvation, necessarily rejects the whole of the Gospel. For that body of flesh and blood that was born of the Virgin Mary, that was crucified, that was buried, that rose again,

[1] 1 Cor. xv. 17.

that ascended into heaven, was as truly outward and elementary, as the things of which the two sacraments consist
are outward and elementary. And therefore the outward
institutions of the Gospel and an outward Christ must
stand and fall together. If you will not own an outward
means of salvation, you cannot own an outward Christ ;
and if you will not own an outward Christ, who has saved
you by an outward elementary body, by an outward death
and resurrection and ascension, you are yet in your sins and
unredeemed.

Christ was received spiritually before He came in the
outward flesh. But if such spiritual receivers of Christ
had refused to own Him in the Gospel, rejecting an outward
body of elementary flesh and blood, rejecting an outward
death, an outward resurrection and ascension of such a
Christ as had been killed by the Jews, had they chose to
abide by a spiritual Christ, calling that the substance,
rejecting an outward incarnation in the flesh, calling [it] a
carnal, elementary shadow [1]—had they been thus spiritual,
they had been exactly of the Quakers' religion, who are too
spiritual to receive Christ under any outward, elementary
manifestations. So plain is it that the Quakers deny an
outward Christ as insignificant, by every argument they use
against the outward sacraments.

Again, to imagine that the Gospel can have no outward
institutions, because it is a spiritual religion, is the same
absurdity as to say that a spiritual religion can contain no
outward rules of life, nor enjoin any outward obedience, nor
need to be outwardly proffessed. For outward institutions
are no more contrary to the spirituality of religion, than
outward obedience.[2] If Abraham did not become a carnal
man by obeying the command of God to leave his country

[1] These three words were commonly used by Quaker writers about the
sacraments, etc., especially the word *carnal*, which they borrowed from the
Epistles of St. Paul.

[2] Compare the second letter to Fanny Henshaw (page 37), where Law
asserts that the outward Scriptures and the outward sacraments " are equally
carnal and equally spiritual ".

and kindred ; if Moses did not become carnal by pulling
off his shoes at the command of God ; if our Saviour did
not cease to be a spiritual man, when He said it became Him
for the sake of righteousness to be baptized by John ; if
St. Paul did not become a carnal man, when he obeyed the
voice from heaven by an act of outward obedience and by
suffering human hands to be laid upon him ; if our Saviour
did not act contrary to the spirituality of religion when He
breathed upon His Apostles, and said, Receive ye the Holy
Ghost ; if He did not become a carnal man, when He made
clay and spittle and anointed the eyes of the blind ; if He
did not reward a carnal faith, when virtue went out of Him
to the woman, who said within herself, " If I may but touch
the hem of His garment, I shall be whole " ; if the Apostles
did not become carnal men by obeying the command of
Jesus to tarry at Jerusalem and wait there for the promise of
the Father, then we have the utmost assurance that the
observance of baptism and the supper of the Lord has no
inconsistency with a spiritual religion.

For I defy anyone to shew, that it is more carnal to be
baptized than to stay at Jerusalem, or more carnal to eat
bread and wine as the body and blood of Christ, than to
suffer Christ to breathe the Holy Spirit upon His disciples.

*   *   *   *   *

He that thinks or holds that outward exercises of religion
hurt or are too low for his degree of spirituality, shews
plainly that his spirituality is only in idea ; that it is something that is in him only as a speculation, or as something
that is in his head and not in his heart.

The truly spiritual man is he that sees God in all things,
that sees all things in God,[1] that receives all things as from
Him, that ascribes all things to Him, that loves and adores
Him in and for all things, in all things absolutely resigned
unto Him, doing them for Him from a principle of pure and

---

[1] These words seem to be a reminiscence of Law's study of Malebranche
" omnia videmus in Deo ".   See page 113 above,

perfect love of Him.   There is no spiritual person but this.
Every outward thing has the nature of a sacrament to him ;
as to the pure all things are pure, so to the spiritual man
every thing is spiritual.

*   *   *   *   *

There is no spiritual person but this, and to such a one
the outward institutions of religion are ten times more dear
and valuable than to those that are less spiritual.   As the
truly charitable man loves to meet outward objects of
charity, the truly humble man loves to meet outward
occasions of being abased, so the truly spiritual man loves
all outward objects and institutions that can exercise the
religion of his heart.

And to think that the spirituality of religion is hurt by
the observance of outward institutions of religion is as
absurd as to think that the inward spirit of charity is hurt
by the observance of outward acts of charity, or the spiritual
joy of the heart destroyed by singing an outward hymn, as
our Saviour and His Apostles did.

*   *   *   *   *

And I defy any man, though he has never so much
assistance from the Jesuits, to show that the outward word
or outward prayers and outward psalmody [and] outward
teaching is consistent with a religion that is too spiritual to
admit of outward institutions.[1]

(ii)

Note.—The following two fragments are closely
connected in thought with the preceding passage.

The first one represents a constantly recurring theme
in Law's mystical creed.   It is a doctrine familiar to

---

[1] The last five short paragraphs were originally written as unplaced
fragments, but are in a line of thought similar to the preceding argument.
We may compare with them the maxim attributed to the German mystic
Suso—a favourite author with William Law : " He who finds the inward
in the outward goes deeper than he who only finds the inward in the inward ".

the Quakers, though not, of course, applied by them as Law applies it.   Thus Barclay also quotes 1 Cor. x. 3 and 4, to show that the " spiritual body of Christ . . . was the saving food of the righteous both before the Law and under the Law ".[1]

Other fragments exist, which repeat almost verbatim, but in a less connected and finished form, portions of the passage just printed.   They probably represent a first draft of it.

As to an inward Christ, that was the Light of all men that come into the world, and in a certain respect the Saviour of all men, in respect of this spiritual Saviour, the Law was as spiritual as the Gospel. He stood then at the door of every man's heart, just as He does now.[2]   And the Apostle says that their fathers " did all eat of that same spiritual meat, and did all drink of that same spiritual drink (for they drank of the spiritual rock that followed them, and that rock was Christ)." (1 Cor. x.)   Therefore an inward Christ was as present to the Jew as to the Christian [3] and therefore the Gospel was not carnal, because . . .

*   *   *   *   *

To support this spirituality of religion, the Quaker hath invented spiritual sacraments—I say invented, for they are nothing else but a meer fiction of his own.   For it

[1] *Apology*, Prop. XIII, Sect. II, *ad fin.*

[2] Compare " Thus He [Jesus Christ] stood at the door of Adam's heart, as near as He stood to the Apostles' : and thus He stands and will stand knocking at the door of every man's heart, till time shall be no more ". (*Demonstration*, p. 61.)

[3] An exactly similar use of the text (1 Cor. x. 3–4) is made in one of Law's latest works.   " Are we not here told expressly by the Spirit of God that very same thing of the patriarchal generations, which the Christ of God said to those that believed in Him, that by eating His flesh and drinking His blood, they have eternal life ? " (*Confutation of Warburton*, p. 61.)

is as certain that there is but one outward baptism and one outward sacrament of the Lord's supper as that there is but one outward Christ.

Jesus Christ has instituted but one baptism and that of water, and but one sacrament of His supper, and that of outward bread and wine ; this is as certain and plain in the Scripture, as that Christ was but once incarnate and but once died upon the cross.

C. The Baptism of Water and the Baptism of the Spirit

Note.—The third group of fragments deals with the Quaker view of baptism. It is evidently based on a fairly careful reading of the whole or parts of the lengthy Proposition XII of Barclay's *Apology*—" Concerning Baptism ". Thus Law has copied out about a page from one of the most fundamental parts of Barclay's argument (Sect. III of Prop. XII), and has done so with substantial accuracy. Generally speaking he treats fairly the arguments of Barclay with which he deals ; only in one place does his indignation lead him to accuse the Quaker of " all the low trick and deceit and falseness that can well be put together ". The treatment of the subject is naturally controversial, but there is at times a beauty and dignity about the language, and to most of those who disregard the doubts cast upon the received words of Matthew xxviii. 19 the arguments will probably appear convincing.

Law has put, as we should expect, this command to baptize in the place of emphasis, and then, assuming it as a point of departure, he has prepared no less than four methods of meeting Barclay's challenge for a proof that *water*-baptism is meant. Three of these are printed below (the fourth is largely redundant), and I have (to make them begin intelligibly) repeated in each case the starting-point of the argument.

The last fragment given justifies the retention of water-baptism against the plea that it should be swept away with the other rites of the " old " dispensation. Some other fragments I have omitted as being either in the nature of repetitions or otherwise of little interest.

The continuity and order of the paragraphs is admittedly problematic in some cases, as Law wrote them down on odd and unnumbered sheets of paper, at times just filling up blank gaps on sheets already partially used.   But though in some cases a more satisfactory arrangement than mine might be discovered, I am fairly confident that I have done no serious injury to the meaning of the writer.

Law's fellow nonjuror, Charles Leslie, wrote a number of controversial writings against the Quakers, and more particularly *A Discourse proving the Divine Institution of Water Baptism* (see page 148 above). There are some indications in these fragments that Law (like Byrom) was acquainted with this book of Leslie's, which deals with Barclay's arguments in a manner not very dissimilar from his own.   But I have not noticed in the fragments any clear case of borrowing from Leslie.   Law hardly ever borrows, even from his master Behmen.

(i)

Thus says R. Barclay, " There is but one baptism—and this baptism is a pure and spiritual thing, to wit the baptism of the Spirit and fire—of which the baptism of John was a figure." [1]

All this is the grossest of all fictions, founded upon nothing but mere sophistry and evasion.

* * * * *

For pray observe, the matter in question is, what you are to understand by our Saviour's commanding His Apostles and their successors to baptize all nations in the name of the Father and the Son and the Holy Ghost. This is the one baptism in question.

[1] See the summary prefixed to Barclay's Proposition XII on Baptism.

(ii)

Our Saviour, when He was risen from the dead, when all power was given unto Him in heaven and on earth, instituted baptism [and] commanded His disciples, " Go ye and teach all nations, baptizing them in the name of the Father, the Son, and the Holy Ghost." [1]

He [Barclay] asks, how do I know that *water*-baptism is meant ? [2] Just as I know that by " teaching all nations " the *outward preaching* of the Gospel is meant. Baptism has as determinate a meaning in Scripture as teaching has.

I know there is a baptism of fire, there is a baptism of affliction, there is a baptism, which only means thus much, that the fire or spirit and affliction are sometimes spoken of with allusion to baptism. And had not baptism in itself a plain and known meaning, there could be no ground for these allusions.

Our Saviour at the institution of the sacrament took bread. Now here is just the same uncertainty what we are to mean by the bread He took, as by [the] baptism He appointed. For there is in Scripture a bread of life, a bread of tears, a bread of affliction, and there is a bread that came down from heaven. Therefore the Church has no proof that it was outward material bread made of grain, that was there spoken of.[3]

---

[1] For the great mystical importance which Law attributed to the use here of the name of the Holy Trinity, see the quotation from the *Regeneration* on page 38 above.

I am also inclined to think that Law revered this text because it is the earlier portion of a saying of the Lord, which concludes with the words " And lo, I am with you alway, even unto the end of the world "—words much beloved by Law, as giving assurance of the indwelling Christ. Thus they are quoted at least three times in his *Address to the Clergy*, where they form the concluding sentence summing up the message of that book, the last sentence that Law ever wrote. Compare also *Remarks on the Fable of the Bees*, p. 31, where the words are quoted with the command to baptize.

[2] See Sect. VII of Prop. XII of the *Apology*.

[3] In another very similar draft, which I have not printed, Law varies the argument as follows : " First he [*i.e.* Barclay] says, here are two different baptisms ; which is all false. For John speaks of no baptism but that which

And the contrary may be demonstrated by the Quaker's argument. Thus : the bread that our Saviour took in the sacrament, He said was His body ; but He said of Himself that He was that bread that came down from heaven, therefore the bread, which He said, was not material bread of this world's grain, but bread from heaven.

Thus the Quaker proves that our Saviour did not institute water-baptism, when He bid them to go and teach all nations, baptizing them in the name of the Father, the Son, and the Holy Ghost, because a little before His ascension He told them that they should be baptized with fire not many days hence.[1]   And yet how could our Saviour more certainly shew them, that what He here said of their baptism had no manner of relation to His command for baptizing all nations ?

For His command to teach and baptize all nations was a baptism that the Apostles and all their successors to the end of the world were to practise ; for our Saviour promised to be with them in that teaching and baptizing to the end of the world.   But the baptism He here spoke of was not real baptism, but only an allusion to it, it was not a baptism that they were to practise, but to receive, it was not to be baptism common to all Christians, but to be received by them not many days hence.

Now that the baptism of the Holy Ghost and of fire spoken of by St. John was strictly to be understood of the miraculous descent of the Holy Ghost, is further plain ; first from our Saviour's own words to His Apostles just before His ascension, *John indeed baptized with water, but*

---

he practised, and takes occasion only to speak of Christ with an allusion to his own baptism.   When the Psalmist speaks of the bread of tears [*i.e.* Psa. lxxx. 5], he does not speak of a bread different from that which is made of grain, but he only speaks of sorrow, with an allusion to bread.   Thus the Baptist speaks not of another baptism, different from that which is with water, but he only speaks of the Holy Spirit with an allusion to baptism."

[1] See the passage cited in the last note but one, and Sect. III of Prop. XII.   The reference is to Acts i. 5, where however " fire " is not mentioned.

ye shall be baptized with the Holy Ghost not many days hence,
plainly limiting this baptism to a baptism they were to
receive and not to a baptism they were to perform, plainly
limiting it to a certain time, the day of Pentecost, by these
words, *not many days hence.*

Secondly, this is further plain from the words of St.
Peter, who [said that], when he visited Cornelius and spoke
to him of Jesus Christ, " the Holy Ghost fell on them as on
us at the beginning " ; and then he adds, " then remembered
I the word of the Lord, how that He said, *John baptized
indeed with water, but ye shall be baptized with the Holy
Ghost,*" plainly shewing that this baptism of the Holy
Ghost was to be limited to and understood of the miraculous
descent of the Holy Ghost.   And that this baptism was in
its whole nature and end entirely different from the baptism
that they were to perform as their own action, is plain from
hence, that after having received this baptism of the Holy
Ghost, Peter immediately adds, " Can any man forbid
water, that these should not be baptized, who have received
the Holy Ghost as well as we ? "

(iii)

Our Saviour, when He was risen from the dead, when
all power was given unto Him in heaven and on earth,
instituted baptism [and] commanded His disciples, " Go
ye and teach all nations, baptizing them in the name of the
Father, the Son, and the Holy Ghost."

Now the Quaker says this cannot be *water*-baptism,
because, if it was, it will only be John's baptism.[1]   Just as
absurd as to say that Christ is John !   Or that, if Christ
gather disciples to Him, He is then doing no more than
John did, because he had disciples.

The water-baptism of John was a profession of society
with John, of submitting to him, in order to stand in his
state with regard to the Messiah.   The water-baptism of

[1] Sect. III of Prop. XII.

Jesus Christ is a profession of being joined to Christ, of entering into His state of sonship and acceptance with God.

This man wants to know the difference between John's baptism and Christ's, if they are both by water, or how one can be more valuable than the other.[1] The difference is that of earth and heaven, though both of them are baptisms by water.[2] Might he not better ask, how it can be more beneficial to believe in Christ, than to believe in John the Baptist, or how an act of obedience and society with Christ can be better than an act of obedience and society with John ?

And as he, that should have refused the baptism of John and the terms of it, should have had no benefit from John nor his state of penitence and preparation, so he that refuses that water-baptism, which is as truly our profession of Christ and seeking to be in society with Him, as water-baptism was the means of being received by John—so he that refuses this water-baptism, refuses all the riches and treasures and blessings of the Gospel, he refuses to own Christ as his Redeemer and Head and Lord, to make profession of his having the Father for his God, the Son for his Redeemer, and the Holy Ghost for his sanctifier. He refuses that water-baptism, which stands as the appointed sign and profession . . .

(iv)

Our Saviour when He was risen from the dead, when all power was given unto Him in heaven and in earth, instituted baptism [and] commanded His disciples, " Go ye and teach all nations, baptizing them in the Name of the Father, the Son, and the Holy Ghost."

R. Barclay calls for proof that water is meant in the baptism instituted by our Saviour.[3] When our Saviour said to His Apostles not to depart from Jerusalem, but to

---

[1] Sect. VIII of Prop. XII.
[2] Compare Letter 5 to Fanny Henshaw, page 52 above.
[3] The reference is to Sect. VII of Prop. XII.

wait there for the promise from the Father, does there need any proof that by Jerusalem He meant that city which was inhabited by the Jews and called so by them ?

Now I defy anyone to shew any more true reason for uncertainty in one case more than in the other. For baptism has as truly one fixed and determinate signification in Scripture as Jerusalem has.

(v)

The Apostle saith of the service of the tabernacle, that it stood only in diverse [washings].[1] Whence R. Barclay thus argues : " If then the ' time of reformation ' be come, or the dispensation of the Gospel which puts an end to the ' shadows,' then such baptisms and ' carnal ordinances ' are no more to be imposed. For how baptism with water comes now to be a spiritual ordinance, more than before in the Law, doth not appear, seeing it is but water still." [2]

If you read but the Apostle in the place quoted, you will find Barclay's doctrine expressly confuted by the Apostle in this very discourse, and whilst he was [on] the same subject. For he says, " having an high priest over the house of God " ; and here, after having rejected the ordinances of the tabernacle, he asserts the necessity of water-baptism, joins it with purity of conscience.[3]

But he [Barclay] wants to know, how water, which can only wash the body now as it did under the Law, can be a more spiritual ordinance now than it was before.

This question is grounded upon a gross ignorance, for it supposes that water-baptism must have only that degree of good in it, or benefit to the person baptized, that water of itself can give him. . . .

---

[1] See Heb. ix. 10 : " the first tabernacle . . . which stood only in meats and drinks and divers washings and carnal ordinances, imposed on them until the time of reformation ". But Barclay quotes " baptisms " for " washings ". (Law's manuscript omits the word by oversight.)

[2] Correctly quoted from Sect. VI of Prop. XII.

[3] See Heb. x. 21 and 22, " having our hearts sprinkled from an evil conscience and our bodies washed with pure water ".

P

Now if there were any sense in this question, a Jew might for the same reason ask, how his religious baptism, in obedience to the command of God, could be a more spiritual thing or do him a more spiritual good, than if he had fallen into the water by chance ; for the water would be the same and be equally a washing of his body in either case.   But if baptism commanded has its good or its nature, not from the nature of water but from the command of God and our obedience to that command, then the nature or benefit of Christian baptism cannot without great folly be sought for in the nature and quality of water, or stated according to it.   If a Jew had bid the blind man to go to the pool of Siloam and wash, or [if] he [i.e. the blind man] had gone himself or fallen into it, before Christ commanded him to go and wash in it, he had only washed his body ; but when he went into the water in obedience to Christ, he received his sight by washing in the water.[1]

Let it be supposed that some prince should make an offer to some captives, whose lives were in his hands, that if they would accept of such articles of labour and slavery under him and profess this by baptizing their bodies into water, they should have their lives secured under him upon such terms.   Let it be supposed that afterwards he proposes to adopt them as his sons, upon condition they would gratefully acknowledge him to be their merciful father and promise a filial obedience to him, and profess this by baptism in water, would it not be egregious folly for a disputant to tell these people that water-baptism was only a washing in water, and that this second baptism could be of no more benefit to them than . . . [the first ?] ?   Yet this is all the sense that the Quaker shews upon the subject of baptism.

[1] John ix. 7.   Compare the similar reference in fragment A, page 209 above.

CHAPTER II

THE ORIGIN AND DESTINATION OF THE DRAFTS

THE most striking and the most carefully written of the fragments printed in the last chapter is undoubtedly that which I have placed first under the title of *The Foundation of Quakerism*. Moreover it contains within itself good evidence of the circumstances under which it was written.

The reader will have noticed that Law begins by referring to the Quakers as " another sort of adversaries to this holy sacrament ", and that at the end of his strictures on the Quakers, after the words " But this by the by : I now return to my subject ", he sums up the signification of the Lord's supper as setting forth Christ as (1) the atonement for our sins, and (2) a principle of life to us. The draft then concludes abruptly with the words,

Now here it may be proper for you to observe, that whatever . . .

These particulars indicate pretty clearly that the whole fragment was written by Law as a digression in some treatise, dealing with a person or persons, not Quakers, considered by him as responsible for false teaching with regard to the Lord's supper, in which he sets out what he regards as the true doctrine of that sacrament.

Now the work of Law entitled, " A Demonstration of the Gross and Fundamental Errors of a late Book, called *A Plain Account of the Nature and End of the Sacrament of the Lord's Supper, etc.*",[1] is precisely such a treatise, and

---

[1] The full title, like many eighteenth-century titles, is much longer, having the following words in addition : " Wherein also the Nature and Extent of the Redemption of all Mankind by JESUS CHRIST is stated and explained ; and the Pretences of the *Deists*, for a Religion of *Natural Reason*

moreover it was published in April, 1737, not long after Law was writing the Henshaw Letters.   On turning over the pages of that treatise, I discovered that pages 39–53 were primarily devoted to Law's proof that the sacrament reveals Christ as (1) the atonement for our sins, and (2) a principle of life to us.   And near the bottom of page 53 there appears the following beautiful passage :—

" As you can receive or believe nothing higher of our Saviour, than that He is the atonement for our sins and a real principle of life to us, so every height and depth of devotion, faith, love, and adoration, which is due to God as your Creator, is due to God as your Redeemer.

" Jacob's ladder that reached from earth to heaven and was filled with angels ascending and descending between heaven and earth, is but a small signification of that communion between God and man, which this holy sacrament is the means and instrument of.

" *Now here it may be proper for you to observe, that whatever* names or titles this institution is signified to you by, whether it be called a sacrifice propitiatory or commemorative, whether it be called an holy oblation, the Eucharist, the Sacrament of the Body and Blood of Christ, the Sacrament of the Lord's Supper, the heavenly banquet, the food of immortality, or the Holy Communion and the like, matters not much."   (And then Law proceeds to explain how each of these names shows just one aspect of Christ in the sacrament.)

The words which I have italicized in this passage [1] are

instead of it, are examined to the Bottom.   The whole humbly, earnestly, and affectionately addressed to all Orders of Men, and more especially to all the Younger Clergy."   By William Law, M.A.   London, 1737.

[1] Since writing the above I have noticed that by a curious coincidence it is precisely this passage, somewhat edited, that Overton selects to show Law's high estimate of the holy communion (Overton's *Life of Law*, p. 288) ; and that G. Moreton also quotes part of it as one of two typical passages in his Preface to the *Demonstration* in the 1893 edition of Law's works. To have inserted the digression on Quakerism here would have been a real artistic loss to the book, and Law was doubtless influenced by this consideration.

the exact words with which our fragment ends, and they form just one complete line of the original (1737) printed text ! Moreover the last paragraph of the fragment admirably sums up the preceding fifteen pages of the *Demonstration*. It therefore seems as clear as daylight, that our fragment was written primarily as a digression on the Quaker " adversaries to the holy sacrament ", to be inserted at this point of page 53 of the *Demonstration* ; and (with less certainty) that it was written between November, 1736, when Byrom first drew Law's attention to the subject of Quakerism, and say the end of the March following. By that date the *Demonstration* would be ready for final printing, and then, after all, this digression was withdrawn and the book printed without it.[1]

Before we turn to consider some evidence of Byrom's bearing on the question before us, a few words are desirable in relation to the *Demonstration* and the " adversary " with whom it was concerned.

Benjamin Hoadley (1676–1761) was one of the central figures in the ecclesiastical history of the time. An enlightened though not brilliant advocate of justice and liberty—he was foremost in urging a completer toleration for dissenters—he was not a man of any deep religious fervour and he was inclined to be rationalistic in his theology as well as " worldly " in his way of living. In 1717, when Bishop of Bangor, he provoked what is known as the Bangorian controversy by his frank abandonment of the claim of the Anglican Church to any sacred privileges over and above the dissenting bodies. It was thus he who occasioned

---

[1] An alternative supposition would be that Law wrote this fragment at some later date, intending it for insertion (not however carried out) in a subsequent edition. There was a third edition of the *Demonstration* in 1752, and a second edition at some time between 1737 and that date. But in view of Byrom's evidence given below and the gradual change in Law's attitude to Quakerism and in his emphasis (after 1740) on the outward sacraments, it appears far more probable that it was written in 1736-7, when his opposition to Quakerism and his interest in the sacraments was at its height.

Law's first adventure in print, the famous *Three Letters to the Bishop of Bangor*, wherein Law defends with rare wit and vigour the apostolical succession and the whole high-church position.

In June, 1735, there appeared anonymously a book entitled *A Plain Account of the Nature and End of the Sacrament of the Lord's Supper*, of which the central theme was that the supper was never intended as anything beyond a simple commemorative rite. Though the authorship was not acknowledged by Hoadley, who had by that time been advanced to the important bishopric of Winchester, there is no reasonable doubt that he wrote the book.[1] Its appearance caused great excitement in Church circles during the years 1735 to 1737, many books and pamphlets being published both for and against the position advocated by it. It was therefore natural that Law, who would be specially interested in the publication through its reputed connection with his old antagonist, should be preparing an answer during the winter of 1736–7. It was just then that through Byrom his attention was drawn to the Quaker views of the sacraments, and the two subjects fitted in well together.

We have seen how Law asked Byrom that "no transcripts" should be made of his letters to Fanny Henshaw, and asked him also to "date" and "take care of" the manuscript of her *apologia*—her "Case", as they called it : and how Byrom in his letter of December 21st expressed the belief that Law's letters to Fanny "may be useful to others", and the hope that the writer would finish and expand them. It is pretty evident that Law replied to this that he was intending to write forthwith something against

---

[1] Byrom was on visiting terms with Bishop Hoadley and his son, Dr. Hoadley. In November, 1733, the latter told Byrom that his father was preparing to publish something about the sacrament.

Dr. Hoadley on one occasion told Byrom that he "had a country house at Stockwell, where his neighbours were Quakers, who said to him, *Friend*, and he said to them, *Friend* ; and that he had not got their *thee* and *thou* yet, but would ; that if they used that language they must expect to hear it, that he did it not out of disrespect ! "

Quakerism. At any rate, we have the following letter, written to him by Byrom a few weeks later ; the first sentence evidently refers to the letters to Fanny which Law wished returned for reference.[1]

To
   The Revd. Mr. Law
      to be left at the 3 Nuns next
         to the Admiralty by Charing
            Cross, London.

                Manchester, March 4, 1736/7.
Revd. Sir,
    I have, according to your order, sent up all your letters by the carrier to Mr. Chaddocke,[2] whom I shall desire to convey them to the 3 Nuns, as you direct.

    I know not whether I did right in bringing the work upon you, but I cannot be sorry that it is become the occasion of your writing upon the subject which you mention, because I hope assuredly that[3] it will be blest with a good effect.

    It has been my secret wish that you might publish something with regard to Quakerism, especially since the misfortune of F. H.   I believe Socinus [4] is the first man that ever reasoned away the common sence of the texts relating to baptism, as the Quakers do.

     [1] The original, hitherto unpublished, is in Dr. Williams' Library.

     [2] No doubt Byrom's hospitable relative in the City, familiarly styled " Coz Chad " in the *Journal*. It was he who accompanied Byrom to visit Law at Putney on April 30, 1737. (See page 146 above.)

     [3] After " that " Byrom had written " the publication of ", and then crossed the words out.

     [4] Socinus (1539–1604), an Italian who took refuge from persecution in Poland, is usually regarded as the founder of modern Unitarianism.   I do not think there is any evidence that his views influenced George Fox and the first Quakers, who differed from him in fundamentals.   Shortly before the time of Socinus, Caspar Schwenkfeld of Silesia, one of the finest of Luther's contemporaries, taught the disuse of outward sacraments ; and he may be regarded as a worthy forerunner of the Quaker movement.

I hear that F. H. is to come shortly to be at a Quaker's in this town.   Your not mentioning the letter, wherein I sent you a copy of hers from Balby, to me, makes me uncertain whether it came to your hands or miscarried. The carrier that has your letters will be in London on Thursday next.

I am, Your ob[edient], h[umble] s[ervan]t,

J. B.

This newly-discovered letter fits in admirably with the *Journal*, wherein we find Byrom recording under Monday, March 7th : " Writ last night to William Chaddock that I had sent Mr. Law's letters in a box wherein some linen was gone up for me."

Turning over the pages of the *Journal* to April 22, 1737, we read that Byrom was informed by his friend Charles Rivington,[1] the well-known bookseller, that " Mr. Law had written a book against Bishop Hoadley's account of the sacraments, that would come out, he thought, next week, and [there] was a very remarkable title-page, that he thought would make it sell, but he could not remember it (this morning I found it in the *Daily Post*) ".[2]

Mr. Law's new book (*i.e.* the *Demonstration*) apparently did appear, as anticipated, during the next week.   Ten days later Byrom bought it for " 4s.", and on May 20th he records, " This morning I read at breakfast out of Mr. Law's new book, and thought it very plain and good, but could not have thought, unless he had said it, that there was any stricture *against* the Quakers ".

Now in the *Demonstration*, as we have it and as Byrom read it, there is no stricture on or reference to the Quakers.[3]

[1] See footnote on page 241 below.

[2] See note to page 227 above ;   evidently in those days booksellers approved of long titles.

[3] There may possibly be just one indirect stricture on page 50, where Law writes, " to say, *as some do*, that our Saviour could not speak of that in St. John, which is intended by the sacrament, because the sacrament was not then instituted, is very weak and unreasonable ".

Revd S.^r   Manchester March 4. 1736.

     I have according to y.^r Order sent up
all y.^r Letters by the Carrier to Mr Chaddocke
whom I shall desire to convey them to the 3 Nuns,
as you direct.

     I know not whether I did write right
in bringing the Work upon you, but I cannot be
sorry that it is become the Occasion of y.^r Writing
upon the Subject wch you mention, because I hope,
assuredly, that the Publication of it will be
blest with a good Effect.

     It has been my Secret Wish that you
might publish something with Regard to Quakism
Especially since the Misfortune of F.H. I believe
Socinus is the first Man that ever reason'd away
the Common Sence of the Texts relating to Baptism
as the Q.^{rs} do.

     I hear that F.H. is to come shortly
to be at a Quakers in this Town, y.^r not mentioning
the Letter wherein I sent you a Copy of hers from
Balby to me makes me uncertain whether it came
to y.^r Hands or miscarried. The Carrier that has y.^r Letters
will be in Lond: on Thursday next. I am y.^r Ob. H. S.^r

DR. BYROM'S LETTER TO WILLIAM LAW [See pages 231–2]

But the discovery of this manuscript fragment surely explains Byrom's remark extremely well. Shortly after writing this fragment, with the intention of inserting it as a digression in the appropriate place, Law, we may presume, informed Byrom of his proposed " stricture ", and then at the last moment, perhaps after reading it in proof, decided not to print it.   We may suppose that he withdrew it from the pages of the *Demonstration*, because he wished to deal at the same time with other heresies of Quakerism besides the denial of the sacrament of the Lord's supper.   This would have been beyond the scope of the *Demonstration*, though it may be noticed that that book contains (on pages 80–109) a very long and important digression upon the inadequacy of the natural reason in contrast to the inward Light, ending up, like our fragment, with the words " I now return to my subject ".   In his correspondence with Wesley in 1739 Law invokes the book to show the scriptural character of his teaching in regard to faith in Christ.   The work thus appealed to persons as diverse as the Quaker Roger Shackleton [1] and the high-churchman Samuel Wesley, who, writing to his brother Charles in November, 1737, says, " I never (elsewhere) saw Hoadley so thoroughly proved an atheist ".

So much for the first of the fragments that we are now considering.   As to the origin of the remainder (that is, of those included in Groups B and C of the last chapter), there is good ground for assuming that Law began writing them not long after this period and that he was thus feeling his way towards carrying out Byrom's wishes in the matter, by publishing a separate work dealing with the errors of Quakerism.

These other drafts (which are similar in form to the first) are written on the front and back of eleven loose unnumbered sheets.   Five of them are on the reverse side of what appears to be an early and in the main discarded draft of the *Demonstration*, dealing partly with points which Law may have

[1] See the next chapter.

omitted afterwards as savouring rather too much of personal controversy with the author of *A Plain Account, etc.* One of the sheets has the following words spaced out as on a title-page :—

A DEMONSTRATION OF CERTAIN FUNDAMENTAL ERRORS

in a late Treatise entitled *A*

Plain Account of the Sacrament, etc., humbly

earnestly and affectionately addressed to all

sincere enquirers into the Nature, End, and effects

of the Holy Sacrament, and more especially

to the younger Clergy of this Kingdom.

This is no doubt an early draft of the actual title, which I have already quoted.

Here we have an external connection between the composition of the *Demonstration* and the writing of the manuscripts which suggests that they were written not long after the publication of that work in the spring of 1737. In any case they remained mere incomplete drafts, dealing principally, as has been seen, with the sacrament of baptism. As I hope to show in the next chapter, the fact that they were not worked up into a publication is probably connected with the changing emphasis of Law's teaching in the years following and with his desire to avoid controversy with a body, some at least of whose members he could not fail to recognize as true disciples of Jesus.

CHAPTER III

WILLIAM LAW'S CONTACT WITH CONTEMPORARY QUAKERISM

THE Nonjurors, I think it is fair to say, were in general the most exclusive and the most sacramentarian branch of the Anglican Church.   And one of the most distinguished men in their ranks was Charles Leslie (1650–1722), author of *The Snake in the Grass, or Satan transformed into an Angel of Light*, and other anti-Quaker writings.   Leslie is indeed perhaps the ablest and most effective of all the writers against Quakerism.   In his preface to the *Snake* he wrote as follows :—

> " The great design of the Devil is, and always has been, to beat down the priesthood and outward ordinances ; knowing that religion must needs fall with them, and men be left senseless and open, to steer without compass, guided only by the winds of enthusiasm.   In this cause he has armed the Atheists and Deists to join with the more plausible Enthusiasts and Latitudinarians.   These all cry out upon priestcraft." [1]

Enthusiasm, that bugbear of eighteenth-century divines, Leslie defines as " a false pretence to Revelation ", and he holds Quakers to be the most dangerous of enthusiasts.

For Leslie, Law as a Nonjuror, and possibly also as a personal acquaintance, would be likely to have a profound respect, and we are not surprised to find that in his first treatise, the *Letters to the Bishop of Bangor*, he echoes to some extent the views of Leslie, and regards the latitudinarian Bishop as the natural ally of Deists and Quakers.

I find that in the pages of the *Bangorian Letters* (to which I shall revert in the next chapter) the Quakers are mentioned at least sixteen times, and they are nearly always

[1] *Op. cit.*, Preface, Sect. II (3rd edition, 1698).

in very poor company. Law brackets Quakers with Muggletonians, Socinians (the spiritual ancestors of the Unitarians), Deists, Infidels, Jews, and Turks. And it is only rarely that they are in company so respectable as that of Presbyterians or Independents. In fact they are the typical fanatic,[1] and one would imagine that Law hardly regarded them as Christians. It is evident that their denial of the outward sacraments is their prime heresy in his eyes.

After this first work of our author there comes a great change. In the course of the next twenty-two years Law published his *Serious Call* and seven other remarkable books. And in all of these there is, I believe, only one single reference to the Quakers,[2] and none at all to any other English dissenting sect. Moreover at the end of this period (*i.e.* by 1740), owing to the influence of Boehme's mysticism upon Law, the tables were turned upon him with a vengeance. The consequence is that in almost all of his remaining eight publications, beginning with the *Animadversions* on Dr. Trapp in 1740, we find Law defending himself, either specifically or in effect, against the charge of " Quakerism " or " enthusiasm " brought against him by his Anglican opponents, and defending himself without ever taking the opportunity of saying anything damaging in regard to the Quakers.

If we ask why in the middle period to which I have alluded (1718–1739) Law avoids in his publications references to Quakers and other Dissenters, the answer is simple enough. It is just that (in spite of the Henshaw Letters) his main interest has shifted, once and for all, away from ecclesiastical and ceremonial differences on to the great ethical and devotional requirements of the Gospel, and he

---

[1] I do not think that in this first work of his Law uses *enthusiasm* or *enthusiast* in either a good or a bad sense.

[2] *Christian Perfection*, ch. v, p. 63, where he speaks ironically of the Quakers as " enlightened " enough " to find themselves at liberty from the use of the sacraments " ; but the emphasis here is on the sin of the average Christian in making the acquisition of wealth one of his aims.

deliberately avoids anything which will lead his readers astray from these supreme issues. I hope in the next section to illustrate this point and also to indicate another influence which between the years 1735 and 1740 may have led Law to retrace his steps somewhat and again to put more emphasis on the outward sacraments, though from a far more spiritual standpoint than in the *Bangorian Letters*. The controversy with Quakerism which Byrom thrust upon him in 1736–7 was a powerful co-operating factor in this temporary tendency, as it necessarily brought the question of the sacraments into the foreground. By 1740 the tides of his thought were beginning to move in a different direction, as we shall see from his two replies to Dr. Trapp.

It was in the year preceding the publication of these little books that Law made the only two personal contacts with Quakers of which any trace remains. To the first of these we have unfortunately only one obscure reference. It appears that Joseph Clutton, a well-known Quaker chemist,[1] was a "great admirer of Jacob Behmen", and possessed a manuscript of Andreas Freher,[2] an interpreter of Boehme,

---

[1] Joseph Clutton is only known as the author of several extant medical pamphlets and of a writing about tithes. There is also preserved a letter of his, full of affection and humility, written (in 1724) to Fanny Henshaw's friend, Joshua Toft, wherein he calls his own epoch "a crooked generation", as compared with former "generations of love and light".

Jacob Boehme, as appears particularly in his book, the *Signatura Rerum*, had certain intuitive theories on the healing properties of minerals and vegetables. Christopher Walton even claims him as the forerunner of the homœopathic system of Hahnemann, based on the principle, *similia similibus curantur*. He also claims (but on very slender evidence) that Law foresaw the same development of medical science, and suggests that this was in part due to his study of Freher's elucidations of Boehme. (*Notes and Materials*, pp. 555–9.) Now Joseph Clutton's principal publication is a long pamphlet, dated 1729, entitled *A short and certain Method of curing continued Fevers*, treating of particular "febrifuges". I therefore offer the guess that the Quaker chemist's admiration for Boehme and Freher was partly at least owing to their common interest in the healing art.

[2] Andreas Freher (1649–1728), a native of Nuremberg, who resided in London for over thirty years preceding his death. Many manuscripts

some of whose commentaries were carefully copied out by Law in the years following this date. This manuscript Clutton lent to Byrom, and probably also to Law. For Byrom briefly records (in August, 1739) within a week of his seeing Clutton, that Law told him, *inter alia*, that Mr. Clutton had been with him also. We wish we knew more, but at any rate Law had established a link with one Quaker, through their common reverence for the Teutonic seer : and it is conceivable that it was through this friend that he secured the loan of most of the Freher manuscripts, which are said to have had a great influence upon the shaping of his mystical system.

Law's second link with Quakerism has happily left a far more impressive record. Among the collection of letters addressed to him now in Dr. Williams' Library, the following from a north-country Quaker is one of the most interesting.[1]

of his writings in German and English, some made by William Law, lie still unpublished in Dr. Williams' Library and the British Museum. See Walton, *op. cit.*, pp. 678–88 and *passim*.

[1] The favourable impression given by the letter that follows here is confirmed by what is otherwise known about Roger Shackleton, its writer. Born of Quaker parentage in 1691, he was an elder brother to Abraham Shackleton, who migrated to Ireland, founded the famous Friends' boarding school at Ballitore, County Kildare, and was the ancestor of a long line of Quaker Shackletons. Roger, on the other hand, remained at York. He died in 1766. He is described as " a person of solid sense, great worth, and benevolence, much esteemed within and without the pale of his own Society ". In 1733, being a man of substance, he is said to have been appointed to serve as Sheriff of York, probably out of a malicious intention to extract money from him. For being unable as a Quaker to take the oath of allegiance and the Church sacrament, he could not serve and was required to pay a fine amounting to £150. We are informed that he had great influence with one at least of the Archbishops of York of his time, who " valued his character and was pleased with his conversation ". Some other letters of his (to his brother Abraham) on very varied topics survive, and show the same sympathetic touch and sound judgement which characterize the letter printed here. [See *The Shackleton Letters* (1726–1763), in Vol. IX of the Journal of the County Kildare Archæological Society (1918), by Margaret F. Young ; *Memoirs of Richard Shackleton* (1823), pp. 59–64 ; and *The Barringtons, A Family History* (1917), p. 234.]

To William Law,
  at the 3 Nuns near Whitehall,
    Westminster in London.

York, the 20th, 11th mo., 1739.[1]

Worthy Friend,

Thy very acceptable letter of 15th November last I in due course received and I rejoyce much at the state and frame of mind which it expresses ; and I doubt not but thou art inwardly thankfull on that account to the God of mercies, the authour of so good and gracious a work. I pray God to shew the knowledge of His salvation in Christ the divine seed unto all men, that their prejudices and great darkness may be removed thereby ; for He is only adequate thereto, and to His glorious name belongs the power and the glory for ever.

I can't but hint the just sence thou hast of human learning and of its subordinate usefullness and it tallies with what hath ever been the sence of our Friends on that point, although some may have perverted the meaning of some unguarded expressions, perhaps occasioned by others attributing too much to it, as making it the key indeed to unlock divine mysteries and a sufficient qualification to the ministry, and so thereby undervaluing and disesteeming the divine Spirit, which only knows and reveals the deep things of God and the deceitfulness and abyss of the carnal mind or heart of man, and is also the foundation of all true ministry. 'Tis a pity and my heart laments for the great loss of the Church in departing from this living fountain of Christ's Spirit and hewing to themselves broken cisterns (a carnal ministry), which can hold or afford no living waters.

But I hope thou, if abidest [2] faithfull and stedfast to the gifts bestowed on thee, mayst by thy writings call some

---

[1] *i.e.* January 20, 1740. Up to and including 1751, the British Calendar year began on March 25th.

[2] The pronoun " thou " is understood here and elsewhere in this letter.

home to a sense of the greatness of man's fall and of the universal redemption by Christ. I see how thy soul swells with ardour and intense affection in the bowels of Christ, when the depths of these two great truths are before thee,[1] that mankind might be reasoned into a persuasion and beliefe thereof and fly to their only helper and Saviour, who is come so near them as to be Redeemer at hand, present in them, offering them grace and divine assistance, on condition they turn to and receive Him by faith, which is also the gift of the operation of the Holy Spirit ; so that nothing is of man, nor to be ascribed to him, but of God, that worketh in us to will and do according to His own good pleasure—His holy name be praised therefore !

I have lately revised [2] the back part of thy *Answer to the Plain Account* [3] and can't but take notice how excellently thou hast displayed the use and abuse of reason. Without reciting the method and force of thy reasoning, in short I say I have perfect unity with it and rejoyce it is so justly and clearly demonstrated (which every prudent person must allow of), and I hope it will avail with some sober Deists, if that epithete may be allowed of. We have had two Friends who writt and acquitted them selves . . . hear . . . ay against . . . self-sufficiency of man . . . infidels . . . rather the preference.[4]

---

[1] Compare Law's *Christian Regeneration*, p. 161, " The whole nature of the Christian Religion stands upon these two great pillars, namely the greatness of our fall, and the greatness of our redemption."

[2] *i.e.* " looked at again ".

[3] This refers to Law's *Demonstration*, published 1737, as to which see the last chapter. It is remarkable that a Quaker should refer to this book so favourably, without commenting on the fact that its main subject is the exaltation of the sacrament of the Lord's supper. A large portion of it, which deals (pp. 80–109) with " the use and abuse of reason " and the inward light of Christ, is however detachable from the rest. It was much admired, and Law was pressed to republish it separately from the remainder of the book.

[4] Two lines of the original letter have here been almost destroyed. Hence the gaps.

I have read again and again thy *Grounds and Reasons* [1] and have spoke of it to many Friends and others. One bookseller hath had 25 and sold all but 2 and will have the like number at twice [2] and make a bargain, if he at first takes but 12, that he may have the quartern book [3] when he sends for the other 12. C. Rivington [4] bargains and buys them for him and the other bookseller hath sold what he had ; they chiefly go amongst our Friends, but they will lend them for the sake of doing good, which I am satisfied is thy motive in writing.

I see a letter from J. Belcher, [5] Governour of New England, to a Friend. The letter was of a genteel and religious turn, and the Friend who received it intends to send him William Penn's *No Cross No Crown* (a good title and a good book) and thy *Christian Perfection*, [6] which is a serviceable treatise to the cause of religion.

I hope thou will not take it amiss, that I desire thou would read George Fox' *Journal* and William Sewell's *History of the Quakers*—it is purely that all straightness and

---

[1] *The Grounds and Reasons of Christian Regeneration or the New Birth, offered to the consideration of Christians and Deists ;* first edition published at 1s. in 1739. Wesley was reading it in October of that year.

[2] Twice over, *i.e.* in two instalments.

[3] This was an extra book given free to the purchaser of a quarter of a hundred (25). See *Oxford Dictionary*.

[4] Charles Rivington (1688–1742) was at this time perhaps the leading theological bookseller and publisher, doing business in St. Paul's Churchyard, London. He was a personal friend of Byrom's (see page 232), and it was at his shop that Byrom bought his copy of the *Serious Call*. He published Samuel Richardson's famous novel of *Pamela*.

Charles Rivington was the ancestor of the head of the present firm of publishers of the same name. This firm has been conspicuous in the publishing world from his time to the present, almost without a break. (See *The Publishing Family of Rivington*, by Septimus Rivington, 1919.)

[5] Jonathan Belcher held the governorship of Massachusetts from 1731 to 1741. He was connected by marriage with English Quakers and proved himself a good friend to the members of the body residing in his jurisdiction, granting them relief as regards the payment of tithes and in other ways. (Susan Reed, *Church and State in Massachusetts*.)

[6] *A Practical Treatise on Christian Perfection* (1726).

shyness may wear off, because of differing sentiments and practices in some exteriour parts of religion—which we desire none to lay aside, but through plain discoveries and conviction. By applying to a Friend of ours, if knows any, they may be sent thee. Or if writes me, I will order thee them by a Friend to be lent and brought thee. And I hope in perusing them thou will have to acknowledge, that they were witnesses for God in their time and were full of the Holy Spirit and love of God to mankind, and that the former approved himself a faithfull labourer and able minister of Jesus Christ, though unskilled in humane literature. I doubt not but hast read R. Barclay's *Apology*.

I hear Friend Ingham,[1] who is beloved of the Methodists so called and a preacher, borrowed the *Grounds and Reasons*, *etc.*, which I sent them, and he liked and recommended it to them and remembered his love to me, to whom I have given an invitation to make my house his home when he comes hither. If he is so free, I shall have some discourse with him and impart it to thee, if he make any remarks on thy books. He is esteemed an ingenious man.

I hear he read and spoke well of the books recommended to thee. I know all who partake of the Holy Spirit are widened in their breast to mankind and it must be thy state to be loving and affectionate to all. Yet good men may have reserves in their love and esteem to others for want of conversation and fully knowing their principles and

---

[1] Benjamin Ingham (1712–1772) was for some years one of John Wesley's most intimate fellow-workers. His preaching helped to lay the foundations of Methodist Christianity in Yorkshire: but in 1742 he severed his connection with the Wesleys and became first a Moravian pastor and then an independent evangelist. It is possible that Ingham's reading of Law's books may have had something to do with his separation from Wesley. Ingham has already been mentioned as an acquaintance of Byrom's Quaker friend, Josiah Martin.

In view of the prospect which Roger Shackleton holds out here of Ingham " making my house his home," it is highly interesting to find that in 1734 Ingham had written to his mentor, John Wesley, to ask whether it was " lawful for a Christian to dwell with a Quaker, when under no necessity " ! (Tyerman, *Oxford Methodists*, p. 60.)

frame of spirit. The Apostles Paul and Peter afford a notable instance, and [for] this reason I have made the aforesaid recommendation, for there is great comfort in love and unity.

I am truly glad that the Truth is published by thee and that hast it so much at heart to proceed in that good work, as it shall please God to draw and incline thee. I hope He will add His blessing thereto and make many to be the receivers and publishers of it, to the weakening Satan's kingdom in mankind.

Now, dear Friend, I much desire that all who have come to the living knowledge of the Truth may abide and walk in the same in constancy and stedfastness ; as the Apostle Paul advised Timothy, Continue thou in the things thou hast learned and hast been assured of, knowing of whom hast received them. I am in much Christian affection,

Thy faithfull loving Friend,

Roger Shackleton.

I shall at any time be glad of a letter from thee.

How we wish we could recover Law's " very acceptable letter " to which this is a reply, and know whether the correspondence was continued ! In default of this we can only draw some probable inferences from Shackleton's letter.

First of all, it betokens an admirably and indeed surprisingly enlightened religious attitude on the part of the excellent Quaker, such as would have done credit to John Woolman himself. He was able to ignore the differences which separated them, the emphasis on the outward sacraments so marked in Law's *Demonstration* and to be found in a few passages of the *Regeneration*, both of which he praises, and to concentrate upon Law's fundamental teachings, which were so near to the Quaker view of Christianity.

Secondly we have here unexpected but quite definite evidence that Law's first important and characteristic mystical work the *Regeneration* was from the first months of its publication welcomed and read in Quaker circles. We may infer that a similar welcome awaited the still more congenially quietist writings of Law that followed it.

The remarkable appreciation of his writings revealed by this letter was probably not without its influence upon Law's estimate of the Quakers. From Shackleton's opening words we infer that Law had previously written to him in most friendly terms. Perhaps he was enabled by his contact with Clutton and Shackleton to modify the judgement he had expressed to Byrom two and a half years earlier, that the Quakers had lost their primitive " contempt of learning, riches, etc." and had become a " subtle, worldly-minded people ".[1]

It is at any rate noticeable that in the second tract against the Rev. Dr. Trapp, published in the same year (new style) as the last, Law refers to George Fox with studious respect : though we observe with regret that he had not taken advantage of Shackleton's offer to enable him to read Fox's Journal without the expense of purchasing it. Law's opponent had accused him of writing, in one of his profound mystical passages, as bad divinity and as bad sense as George Fox. " What degree of sense, or divinity ", Law replies, " George Fox was possessed of, I cannot pretend to say, having never read any of his writings ; but if he has said any good and divine truths, I should be as well pleased in seeing them in his books as in any of the Fathers of the primitive Church." [2] If the reader turn to the whole of the splendid passage, which this attack of Dr. Trapp's called forth,[3] he will notice two further references to Fox and one to the Quakers. And I think he will agree that, though guarded, they are decidedly friendly, implying that

---

[1] April 17, 1737 (page 146 above).
[2] *Some Animadversions*, p. 182.
[3] See Chapter VII below.

all Christians should be grateful to Fox and the Quakers, whatever their errors, for asserting so emphatically " the sufficiency of the Divine Light, the necessity of seeking only the guidance and inspiration of the Holy Spirit ".[1]

In the earlier conversation with Byrom from which we have just quoted, Law had said " that the writers against Quakerism were not proper persons, for they writ against the Spirit in effect, and gave the Quakers an advantage ". And in the light of these references in the *Animadversions* on Dr. Trapp, we may, I think, assume that we have in this remark the principal reason why Law did not proceed to the completion of his treatise on Quakerism, which, as we have seen, he had probably begun in 1737. He felt that such a controversy would even in his case be misunderstood as " a writing against the Spirit ", and he had from his personal contacts with them been now enabled to see that some Quakers at least revealed in their lives as well as in their writings the gifts of the Spirit better than many of the members of his own Church.

Moreover it was Law's settled principle not to engage in controversy with any man, who, whatever his doctrinal errors, appeared to be zealous for the leading of souls to Christ. It is true that once or twice in later life he sinned against these principles in regard to John Wesley and his followers, when under sore provocation from Wesley's violent attack upon him. But his proper antagonists were sceptics and deists, and advocates for compromise with the " world ", including ecclesiastics of the type of Hoadley, Trapp, and Warburton, whom he could not regard as anything better than deists. In the case of other Christian opponents his practice would be in harmony with the

[1] In an earlier passage of the same tract (p. 163) he brackets Quakers and infidels together ; but that is only because he is quoting from his opponent, to whom they appear to have been equally abhorrent. I find Dr. Trapp (in his *Discourse on the Sin of being Righteous Overmuch*) describing the Quakers as " one of the most pestilent sects that ever infested the Christian Church ". I wonder whether their persistent refusal to pay tithes to the clergy was their greatest sin in his eyes ?

advice he gave to a friend in 1756, " not to enter into disputes ", but to " wish him God speed in everything that is good ".[1]

These, one can have little doubt, were the uppermost feelings in Law's heart, when he put aside for good and all those sheets of controversy with the Quakers, which have been reserved for a Quaker editor to bring to the light of day. A strong contributing influence towards Law's decision would be his growing absorption in the teaching of Boehme, whose doctrine of the inner light was not far removed from that proclaimed by George Fox and his followers.

The years 1740 to 1749 were for Law a period of silence in the sphere of literature. During this time we have the record of Byrom's first visit to Law in his rural retreat at Kingscliffe, with notes of their conversation, rambling over a wide range of topics, in which the following curious passage occurs. " He (Mr. Law) had writ to Sir James Edwards against the Quakers, against printing Frere, that Frere himself had owned that he writ only historically." [2] " Frere " is no doubt the error of the transcriber of Byrom's shorthand for " Freher ",[3] a writer who, Law considered (as he did in the case of other difficult mystics), was preferably read in manuscript only by the select few. The first part of the sentence quoted seems therefore to stand as an isolated remark, on which no light is available : I have been unable to discover anything about Sir James Edwards, sufficient to furnish us with a clue to Law's meaning.[4] In any case it is unlikely that we have here

---

[1] Compare also his tender words in the *Answer to Dr. Trapp*, p. 3.

[2] Byrom's *Remains*, Vol. II, Part II, May 30, 1743.

[3] See page 237 above.

[4] A baronet of this name (related to a Lord Mayor of London of the same name) was at the time a resident at Walton-on-Thames, and may possibly have been on visiting terms with Mr. Gibbon, with whom Law had recently been living at Putney. A friend has suggested that this passage may mean that Law had written to Sir James Edwards to oppose the proposal of certain Quakers to have the manuscripts of Freher printed. If

any reference to a treatise against Quakerism : on the face of it we might presume an application to a magistrate against the customary refusal of some local Quakers to pay tithes, did we not remember that Law was an unbeneficed clergyman, and shrink moreover from associating his gentle character with such demands !

The last and ripest phase of Law's career as a teacher began in 1749. In all the remainder of his published works he scrupulously refrains from references to Quakers as such. It was customary at this time, as we have suggested, for Law's opponents to stigmatize his doctrine of the Christ within as Quakerism or " gross enthusiasm ". Two or three times Law refers to this charge of Quakerism, but without any comment on the term, which he does not repel with any vehemence. In his last work *An Address to the Clergy* (1761) Law for the first time in his life speaks out clearly as regards the attitude of the Christian to oaths and war. He makes no mention of any conscientious objectors to war-service, but in the passage on oaths he praises the " piety " of those who refuse to take any oath, adding the earnest wish that " it may come to be the piety of all the three estates of this kingdom ".[1] This may be taken as a reference to Quakers and Moravians, at this time the only considerable bodies of Christians in Great Britain who had a conscientious objection to oaths.

From the letters and conversations which passed between Law and Thomas Langcake (his most intimate friend in these years), we have evidence that Law was reading Quaker literature with enjoyment in the years preceding his death in 1761. Here is a definite expression of opinion on the founder of Quakerism, dated December 3, 1759.

---

this is correct, Joseph Clutton, who had been lending out these manuscripts, may well have been one of the Quakers in question. But, as there was no censorship of the press in force at this date, I cannot guess why Law should write to this baronet about the matter. There may be some omission or defect in the transcription of Byrom's Journal at this point.

[1] *Op. cit.*, pp. 79–82.

" I thank friend Hinde for his offer of *George Fox*, but have no leisure for folio reading : though the man that wrote it has enough of my esteem." [1]

" Friend Hinde " is almost certainly Luke Hinde, at that time the chief Quaker bookseller in London, also referred to in the next extract.   Doubtless Law had found his shop stocked with some of the old mystical books which he loved to buy.

Some two years before he wrote the last letter, Law was reading Isaac Penington, whose gentle spirit would naturally be more akin to him than that of most other early Friend writers—we wish he could have known his own contemporary John Woolman.   This from a letter dated April 9, 1758.

" I liked the spirit of Pennington in that book that you have sent me, which made me write for his works, as fit to be added to my spiritual library.   If you send them, I would have them bound, but leave it to you, either to send them or stay for a perfect book. . . . [Then follows a request for a volume of Swedenborg.] . . . Also from the Quaker's shop, the *Godly Life of Luterman*, if it be in High Dutch [*i.e.* German]." [2]

We have two further references to Penington in letters

---

[1] This and the extracts that follow are taken from original letters of Law and transcripts of Thos. Langcake's letters, which are in Dr. Williams' Library.   They are printed in Walton's *Notes and Materials* (pp. 600, 592, 593 and 596), embedded in his huge footnote on Law.

[2] I cannot discover any book with this precise title.   After some searching, I hazard the guess that Law is referring here to a German biography of Dr. Joachim Lütkemann (1608–1655), by Pastor J. Rehtmeyer, published between the years 1737 and 1748.   Lütkemann was a Lutheran pastor and theological professor at the university town of Rostock on the Baltic, who had to endure some persecution, and is described as being as devout in his life as he was learned in his writings.   If this conjecture is right, I am unable to say why Law, who was at this period strongly antipathetic to academic theologians, should have been attracted by the biography of this good man.

For Luke Hinde and " the Quaker's shop ", see page 157 above on Martin's books.

THE ENTRANCE TO WILLIAM LAW'S LIBRARY AT
KING'S CLIFFE

which passed between Langcake and the mystically-minded Henry Brooke [1] a few years after Law's death.

" The primitive Quakers and their writings Mr. Law had a regard for, but as to Isaac Pennington I do not recollect to have had any converse about him : though after Mr. Law's death I was myself satisfied he had read him with great approbation."

" Mr. Law said to me that Jacob Behmen was the first in excellency, *Hiel* [2] the next, and in the third place the Quakers—I believe he alluded in particular to Isaac Pennington, though I should think the deep mystic writers of the Romish Church surpassed them in their exceeding love of God and divine wisdom."

The degrees of excellence referred to in the second extract doubtless have regard to Protestant writers only ; at any rate it is not to be supposed that Law would have placed any of the Quakers above such Catholic mystics as Tauler, Fénelon, or the author of the *Theologia Germanica*.

[1] Henry Brooke of Dublin, nephew of the writer of the same name, author of a remarkable mystical romance, *The Fool of Quality*.

[2] *Hiel* is the name assumed by the author of a number of mystical books and tracts that were first printed and published at Leyden about the year 1580 in both French and Low Dutch. In 1687–90 they were republished in German at Amsterdam. The most important and influential of *Hiel's* writings seems to have been *The Book of the Testimonies Concerning the Treasure hid in the Field*. The author himself is said by Gottfrid Arnold to have been a simple, almost illiterate craftsman, named Hendrik Janson, who lived in the Netherlands about the year 1550.

This information is taken from the monumental work of the German pietist, Gottfrid Arnold, *Kirchen- und Ketzer-Historie* (1700), which reproduces long extracts from *Hiel's* works. William Law may have possessed a copy of this great book, which has never been translated into English. As far as I can discover, the only English book in which there is any reference to *Hiel's* writings is a small volume of selections from them " englished from the High Dutch " and published in 1781 by Law's Moravian disciple, Francis Okely.

The high value which William Law is said to have set upon this author raises the wish that some student might make himself master of his works and open out their treasures to us. Copies of *Hiel* are, I should imagine, very rare in this country. William Law's German edition still, however, reposes on the shelf of his library.

We can only guess just what writings of the early Friends are referred to by Langcake : it may well be that it was only Penington with whom Law was acquainted.[1]

In the remains of Law's library, which still lie on their original shelves in the Kingscliffe schoolroom, there is one Quaker book only. It is not Isaac Penington, nor any of the " early " Quaker writings ; but it has a large share of their spirit, the author, Hugh Turford, belonging to a generation which he regards as sadly fallen away from the stronger faith of their fathers.

Turford was a Quaker schoolmaster and published his book in 1702.[2] It became after Barclay's *Apology* perhaps the most constantly reprinted of Quaker books, having passed through no less than twenty-eight British editions. Law's edition is the sixth, published in 1758, so that he probably acquired it soon after he had bought Penington's works. It is a modest little volume containing several essays, of which the leading one is styled *The Grounds of a Holy Life, or the Way by which many who were Heathen came to be renowned Christians . . . by little Preaching*. Rufus Jones calls it " a worthy contribution, though humble and simple, to mystical literature ", and it is just the sort of book that would be after Law's heart, a straightforward, earnest plea for living out Christ and accepting Him in the heart, rather than merely professing and practising any denominational religion : an appeal for men to turn from attention to preaching and religious books to the Christ within, " the candle of the Lord that shines in our souls ", and to bring forth those fruits of the Spirit which are set before us in the Sermon on the Mount : a book with no trace of sectarian controversy in it, no attacks upon the outward sacraments, and of which the Quaker origin is not immediately obvious, though clear enough to any one reading between the lines. It is not surprising that Law placed this volume

[1] For one remaining reference to Quakerism in a private letter of 1759 to Langcake, see page 306 below.

[2] Nothing is otherwise known about his life. He died at Bristol in 1713.

in that section of his Library which consisted of *Books of Piety to be lent to any Persons of this or the neighbouring Towns.*[1]

So much for Law's contacts with the little world of outward Quakerism—with the members of the Society of Friends and their literature. It indicates that Law practised in private a more generous mode of Christian fellowship than he confessed to in public, even in his latest writings. In these he failed to do justice to the Christianity of the English Dissenters, as he did not scruple to do to the Lutheran Boehme and the saints of the Roman Church. It must be remembered that Law was himself, as a Nonjuror, technically a Nonconformist. He was able, it is true, to attend religious services which, apart from the prayers for the reigning dynasty, were substantially those of his own body. But he was cut off, by legal enactment and by his isolated position, from acting as minister or priest for such services, and was thus himself in some measure suffering persecution for conscience' sake. This doubtless helped to make him sensible of the evils and folly of persecution.[2]

On the other hand the Nonjurors regarded themselves as the true representatives of the Anglican branch of the Catholic Church and as quite distinct from ordinary Dissenters. It would therefore be natural that a certain strain of subconscious pride in Law's nature and a shrinking from giving still more reason to his adversaries to identify him with the " enthusiasts " of Dissent should cause Law to keep himself more aloof publicly from other bodies outside the Established Church than his loving nature and his

---

[1] For an article on Law's Library at Kingscliffe, near Peterborough, see *The Friend* for December 11, 1925, p. 1086.

[2] For the Nonjurors see note to page 111 above. Law held, partly owing to his isolation in a small village, a somewhat detached position. In 1731 he wrote, " The Nonjurors have no foundation to consider their Communion as a distinct Church from the Established, or in a state of greater purity ". (*Letters to a Lady on Romanism*, p. 228.)

principles disposed him to do in private life [1]—such principles of Church membership as are enunciated so powerfully in the extracts from his later writings, which will be found in the concluding chapters of this volume.

[1] An Anglican friend, who has read this, makes the following suggestion here : " May it not have been a genuine, though no longer controversially articulate conviction of the necessity of maintaining the fabric of institutional religion ? "   If so, compare what Law says in his *Letter on Church Membership*, " I join therefore in the public assemblies," etc. (page 304 below).

NOTE ON JOHN WEBB

The following curious letter, dating from 1754, is preserved in the Law correspondence, in the same bundle with the Shackleton letter quoted in the foregoing chapter. The writer was an unsettled type of Quaker, with something of an axe to grind, and it is not likely that William Law's mind was materially affected by his letter or the pamphlet sent with it. I have therefore not inserted it in the text of this chapter, but reproduce it as a note, as it adds something to our knowledge of a man who was for some time one of John Wesley's preachers, being mentioned in his Journal and in that of his brother Charles. He is described as a " strong Calvinistic, predestinarian preacher ", and in 1744 he had faced, in Charles Wesley's company, the violence of the Walsall and Wednesbury mobs. (Jackson's *Life of Charles Wesley*, vol. i, pp. 363, 366, 583, 587.) On January 1, 1746, John Wesley wrote in his Journal of dining in London with " poor John Webb, now thoroughly poisoned by Robert Barclay's *Apology*." The pamphlet mentioned in the following letter was printed in 1753 or 1754, and is partly a vindication of Quaker doctrine against Wesley and partly a protest against the worldliness of certain Quakers and the scant courtesy with which the writer says that he was treated by the monthly and quarterly meetings of the Society. In 1756 John Webb published a second pamphlet, containing a continuation of his former appeal, entitled *The Suffering Case of John Littell*, being an entreaty to the Yearly Meeting of Friends to take up the case of a poor man, who, he alleged, had been nearly ten years in prison for refusal to pay tithes. It seems probable that John Webb ceased to be a member of the Society about the time of the publication of these pamphlets. I can find no trace of his subsequent history.

Esteemed Friend,
       William Law,
              In time past I have had much pleasure in reading
some of thy books, particularly *The Serious Call, etc.*—And
being willing to make some small return, therefore have sent
thee the inclosed *Appeal unto the Honest and Sincere-hearted
among the People called Methodists and Quakers,* which I think
it is my duty to publish after this manner.

What will be the consequence of this publication ?   I
know not ; having had many a gloomy prospect concerning
it, the sight of which hath oftentimes caused my flesh to start
back at the very appearance of that which hath been pre-
sented before the view of my mind.

However it may be best to leave the determination of
that until another day, and if any good should arise from it
meanwhile, it will be a matter of rejoicing unto him, who
is with due respects

                    Thy loving Friend unknown
                         JOHN WEBB,
                              in the Steelyard, London.
March 21st, 1754.

P.S.—I should be glad to know this comes safe to
thy hand.

CHAPTER IV

WILLIAM LAW'S CHURCHMANSHIP—THE FIRST PHASE

THE reader will have noticed that William Law, in his controversy with Quakerism, is careful to restrict himself to a somewhat narrowly defined sphere of religious practice. In fact he only censures the Quakers for their rejection of the ordination of the clergy, of liturgical worship, and of the two sacraments recognized by his Church, as well as for the way in which they used their belief in immediate inspiration to pervert Church discipline, particularly in the sanction given to the preaching of women.

He never attacks them, as most of their antagonists did, either for disloyalty to the fundamental articles of the Christian creed and to the divinity of Christ, or in respect of their peculiar testimony against military service and other social usages.[1] The chief reason for this limited censure was that in many of their tenets, other than those that I have first mentioned, he was in a large measure of agreement with them. This must have been the case when he wrote the Henshaw Letters, and it became more and more so, as his mystical creed developed.

It would be possible to fill the remainder of this volume with notable passages from Law's writings, which prove the wideness of the field in which Quaker conceptions came to dominate his thought. But inasmuch as the area of discussion has so far been restricted to questions relating to sacraments and the ministry, to Church-worship and

[1] If we compare Charles Leslie's anti-Quaker treatise *The Snake in the Grass* (to which I referred in the last chapter), we marvel at Law's restraint; and Law had very probably seen that book. *The Snake* overflows with every kind of accusation and scandalous story against the morals and faith of the Quakers, who are represented in particular as denying the Trinity and the divinity of Jesus Christ.

Church-membership, I propose to confine myself for the most part to the task of showing how Law's views on these four closely interrelated subjects developed in the course of his career as a teacher.   The other matters, equally or still more important, in which he never expresses dissent from the Quaker position, must for want of space be left over for a brief treatment in my last chapter, so far as they have not naturally emerged in earlier extracts from his works.

In order to avoid misconception, and at the same time in a measure to disarm criticism, I will beg of the reader to remember the following fact.   Whatever the changes may have been in his religious outlook, Law never, so far as we know, departed from being a loyal attender at the sacramental and other services of the Church of England right up to the end of his long life.   Himself debarred as a Nonjuror from conducting those services, he might easily, like many other Nonjurors, have allowed his allegiance to the pre-revolution establishment to keep him away from church.   But he did not do this.   There is every reason for supposing that, during the last twenty years of his life in his Northamptonshire country home, he attended every possible service at the parish church : that is to say that he was in church every Wednesday and Friday and twice on Sundays, and received the sacrament of the Lord's supper at the hands of the Rector of Kingscliffe once a month at the least.   How this devotion to the services of his Church harmonized with his settled views will appear from the quotations I shall make from his own later writings.   Meanwhile we have to consider Law in the earliest phase of his life as an author.

In 1717, at the age of thirty, William Law, then an obscure and unbeneficed clergyman, made a meteoric appearance in current ecclesiastical controversy by his *Three Letters to the Bishop of Bangor.*   The adversary with whom he crossed swords was Dr. Benjamin Hoadley, the same broad-churchman whose later teachings on the

The Reverend
Mr. Benjamin Hoadly B.D.
Rector of S. Peter Poor. LONDON.

G. Vertue Sculp

WILLIAM LAW'S PRINCIPAL ANTAGONIST, AFTERWARDS
BISHOP OF BANGOR

sacrament he afterwards attacked.[1]   In these *Letters* Law is emphatically the high-churchman, the Anglo-Catholic of his day, and he at once earned the admiration and grati-- tude of the high-church party for his brilliant presentation of their case.   Not only so, but in our own generation the *Letters* have been re-published by Anglo-Catholic editors under the title of *William Law's Defence of Church Principles* [2] with the suggestion that Law's great contribution in this work to sound ecclesiastical doctrine, together with his subsequent insistence on a life of holiness, may enable Churchmen to overlook the errors of his later " universalistic mysticism ".

The *Bangorian Letters* insist throughout on the prime necessity of an outward privileged Church, " the absolute necessity of a strict succession of authorized ordainers from the apostolical times in order to constitute a Christian priest " : and without such a priest there can be no true or availing sacraments.   This doctrine is expanded by Law with all the force which his ready command of subtle reasoning and incisive irony supplied to him.   He seems to place acceptance of the dogmas of institutional religion on as high a footing as the great Christian virtues.   " Charity and chastity ", he says, " do not make a Church."   On the other hand there is no setting out here of the profound significance, the rich mystical contents of the holy sacraments.   Only once, in an exceptional passage on the need of fervency in prayer, does Law anticipate a little in these sorely controversial *Letters* the devotional fire of his later writings.

The following passage is, I think, representative of the central position taken up in the *Letters*. (It forms the climax of Law's reply to a quotation from his opponent, wherein the Bishop asserts that the authoritative benedictions and absolutions of the clergy are " trifles and niceties ",

[1] See page 229 above.
[2] Edited by J. O. Nash and Charles Gore (afterwards Bishop of Oxford), 1893.

R

because we ought not to " expect the grace of God from any hands but His own ".)

"It is in this sense, my Lord, that the people are said to be *authoritatively* blessed by the regular clergy ; because they are *God's clergy* and act by His commission ; because by their hands the people receive the graces and benefits of God's ordinances ; which they have no more reason to expect from other ministers of their own election, or, if the word may be used in an abusive sense, of their own *consecration*, than to receive grace from sacraments of their own appointment. The Scriptures teach us that the Holy Ghost has instituted an order of clergy. We say a priesthood, so authorized, can no more be changed by us than we can change the Scriptures or make new sacraments : because they are all founded on the same authority, without any power of a dispensation delegated to us in one case more than another. If therefore we have a mind to continue in the covenant of Christ and receive the grace and benefits of His ordinances, we must receive them through such hands as He has authorized for the purpose, to the end we may be qualified to partake of the blessings of them. For as a *true* priest cannot benefit us by administering a *false* sacrament, so a *true* sacrament is nothing when it is administered by a *false uncommissioned minister*. Besides this benediction which attends the ordinances of God, when they are thus performed by authorized hands, there is a benediction of prayer, which we may rightly think very effectual, when pronounced or dispensed by the same hands.

"Thus, when the Bishop or priest intercedes for the congregation or pronounces the apostolical benediction upon them, we do not consider this barely as an act of charity and humanity, of one Christian praying for another, but as the work of a person who is commissioned by God to *bless in His name* and be effectually ministerial in the conveyance of His graces ; or as the prayer of one who is left with us in Christ's stead, to carry on His great design of saving us ; and whose benedictions are ever ratified by Heaven, but [*i.e.* except] when we render ourselves in one respect or another incapable of them." [1]

In devoting so little space to the one work of William Law which takes the Catholic and high-church view of ecclesiastical order and discipline, I am laying myself open to obvious criticism.   It is difficult to find in these *Letters* passages of moderate length, which do adequate justice to Law's standpoint and method : the argument is too " continuous ", too controversial for satisfactory quotation by extract.   And I am unable to discover any organic connection between Law's conception of the Church in these *Letters* and his very different conception of it in his later works.[2]   Above all there is a harshness, an intolerance, an artificiality about this extremely clever book, which grates upon the lover of the William Law of the *Serious Call* and the *Spirit of Prayer*.   I must therefore content myself with asking those, who have the desire and the opportunity to test the matter further, to do so by reading the *Bangorian Letters* for themselves.   If they gain nothing else they will certainly be entertained at the exceeding discomfiture which appears to have overtaken the latitudinarian Bishop against whom Law's shafts were aimed.

[1] *Three Letters to the Bishop of Bangor*, p. 44.   I have referred in the last chapter to the attacks in this book upon the Quakers and other Nonconformists.

[2] It is worth noting that while Law often refers his readers back for their instruction to passages in other volumes of his works, he only once (in 1740), and then in an indirect and noncommittal manner, ever refers to the *Bangorian Letters*. (*Answer to Dr. Trapp*, p. 51.)

CHAPTER V

THE PERIOD OF THE *SERIOUS CALL*

SOME nine years after Law had written in the strain that I have just described, he set down the following words (in relation to the attendance of Christian folk at licentious stage performances) :—

> "The sacraments have nothing valuable in their own nature ; they are only useful to Christians, and to be treated with reverence, because Christ has appointed them as a means of holiness. But purity and chastity of heart is an essential and internal excellence, that by its own nature perfects the soul, and renders it more acceptable to God. To abhor therefore a jest upon the sacraments and yet divert ourselves with impure rant and lewd songs, is being like those who abhor idols and yet commit sacrilege." [1]

How are we to account for this remarkable change of emphasis, which, as I have previously suggested, pervades all the powerful books that Law produced during the twenty years or so following his first essay in print ? The simple answer is that Law underwent something of the nature of a conversion, which impressed upon him the tremendous fact that the religion of Christ has primarily to do, not with rites and ceremonies, but with the way we fulfil " the common duties of our ordinary life, which are commended upon every page of the Gospel ".[2] As to exactly how this conversion took place, we know nothing. Law scarcely ever records anything as to his own life and ex-periences. An acquaintance once told Byrom that Mr. Law, after leading a comparatively gay life, "had made his great change in the year 1720 ". There we must leave the matter.

[1] *The Absolute Unlawfulness of Stage-Entertainments* (1726), p. 164.
[2] *Serious Call*, p. 11.

As to the results of this conversion, Law's writings leave us in no manner of doubt. True, they are not distinctly observable in his next work, the *Remarks upon the Fable of the Bees* (1723), for the subject of that controversial book was the origin of the moral sense, and the obligations of present-day Christians do not come up for discussion therein. But it is significant that he chose an ethical theme, albeit a somewhat remote one, for his second field of controversy.

In the two tremendous books that followed Law comes to close grips with the daily and hourly life of the professing Christian of his time. The tract on the stage, from which I have quoted, became just one chapter of his *Practical Treatise upon Christian Perfection* (1726) ; and the lessons of that book were driven home with much greater power and precision in *A Serious Call to a Devout and Holy Life, adapted to the state and condition of all orders of Christians* (1729)—to give Law's masterpiece its full and expressive title. Few books have had such a marvellous effect upon a nation as these two volumes. I will only quote two of the many witnesses that might be called to vouch for this. Two of Wesley's most trusted fellow-workers, in the biography that they wrote of their leader about a year after his death, asserted that " by his excellent pen " Mr. Law was " the great fore-runner of the [Methodist] revival which followed, and did more to promote it . . . perhaps, than the rest of the nation collectively taken ".[1]

Now I think it is fair to select the following passage, to be found among the early pages of the *Serious Call*, as summing up the principal message which runs through all the chapters of both that book and the *Christian Perfection* ; if only we explain that it implies the expenditure of a considerable portion of the daily round in private prayer and communion with God. " Devotion ", Law tells us elsewhere, " signifies both ' a life devoted to God ' and ' a regular method of daily prayer '." (The sentence to be

[1] Coke and Moore, *Life of Wesley*, p. 7.

quoted first is perhaps overstated and was, like other passages in the book, particularly objectionable to John Wesley, greatly as he valued the work as a whole.)

"It is very observable, that there is not one command in all the Gospel for public worship ; and perhaps it is a duty that is least insisted upon in Scripture of any other. The frequent attendance at it is never so much as mentioned in all the New Testament. Whereas that religion or devotion which is to govern the ordinary actions of our life is to be found in almost every verse of Scripture. Our blessed Saviour and His apostles are wholly taken up in doctrines that relate to common life. They call us to renounce the world and differ in every temper and way of life from the spirit and the way of the world : to renounce all its goods, to fear none of its evils, to reject its joys and have no value for its happiness ; to be as new-born babes, that are born into a new state of things : to live as pilgrims in spiritual watching, in holy fear, and heavenly aspiring after another life : to take up our daily cross, to deny ourselves, to profess the blessedness of mourning, to seek the blessedness of poverty of spirit : to forsake the pride and vanity of riches, to take no thought for the morrow, to live in the profoundest state of humility, to rejoice in worldly sufferings : to reject the lust of the flesh, the lust of the eyes, and the pride of life : to bear injuries, to forgive and bless our enemies, and to love mankind as God loveth them : to give up our whole hearts and affections to God, and strive to enter through the strait gate into a life of eternal glory.

"This is the common devotion, which our blessed Saviour taught, in order to make it the common life of all Christians. . . . If we are to follow Christ, it must be in our common way of spending every day. . . . If our common life is not a common course of humility, self-denial, renunciation of the world, poverty of spirit, and heavenly affection, we do not live the lives of Christians." [1]

Now it must first be made clear that the intention of this passage was not the depreciation of the services and sacraments of the Church of England. In Law's day conformity was the fashion, and he was addressing himself primarily to persons who observed the outward forms of religion. But it is notwithstanding, I think, most remarkable how the emphasis throughout these books is completely removed from all that goes on within the consecrated walls of a church. Putting on one side a number of somewhat inconclusive references to church-going in the sketches of imaginary characters, I am only able to find in the two volumes taken together about seven distinct references to the sacraments or the services of the Church : and in all or nearly all of them the existence of these Christian institutions is mentioned in order to drive home the need of a life entirely consecrated to Christ and His teachings. "The bare eating of bread and drinking wine in the holy sacrament . . . are mere outward ceremonies and useless actions, unless they are performed in the spirit of religion." "He is the religious man who . . . worships God in every place by a purity of behaviour . . . who is as wise and heavenly at home or in the field as in the house of God." [2] There is no attempt anywhere to explain the peculiar and sacred benefits imparted through the rites of baptism and the Lord's supper.

While there is insistence on the great value of prayers, both public and private, yet "they are certainly but a very slender part of devotion, when compared to a devout life". "He that dares not say an ill-natur'd word, or do an unreasonable thing, because he considers God as everywhere present, performs a better devotion than he that dares not miss the church." [3]

---

[1] *Serious Call*, pp. 10–12.
[2] *Christian Perfection*, pp. 33 and 145.
[3] *Serious Call*, p. 85.

The only trace of anything that we can call ritual is the choice of the " canonical hours " of the Catholic Church as the most suitable times for the practice of private devotions. And Law expressly defends himself against the charge that such a method of prayer is " only fit for monasteries and nunneries ", saying that it is recommended as " the most perfect way of life " and " not pressed upon any sort of people as absolutely necessary ". Moreover it is instructive to consider the particular subjects of devotion which he recommends for the different hours of the day. They may be summarized as follows :—

6 a.m. Praise and thanksgiving.	3 p.m. Resignation to the will of God.
9 a.m. Humility.	6 p.m. Confession and penitence.
12 a.m. Universal love with intercessions for others.	9 p.m. The certainty of death.

Here we see how supremely ethical in the best sense of the word Law's devotional activities were : and he practised what he preached. With the exception of the last subject (which can scarcely be approved as part of the regular daily routine) all is concentrated on the increase of one's love, uprightness, and trust in God.

It is impossible, I think, to find in these books, in marked contrast to the *Bangorian Letters*, any emphasis on the exercise by the clergy of peculiar priestly functions, as ministers of the sacraments of the Church ; all we have, once or twice only, in this direction are references to the necessity that a priest attending at the " altar " should be pious and unworldly. One of the best known and most beautiful of the numerous characters sketched with consummate art in the *Serious Call* and the *Christian Perfection* is that of *Ouranius*, Law's ideal of the country parson. And yet throughout the description of his activities, there is no single mention of sacraments or of the Church services, other than that of preaching—itself relegated to quite a secondary place. The emphasis is all upon *Ouranius'* friendship with his flock, his daily visiting and watching over them, his forethought for their material needs, his example to them of a " holy temper ", and above all his continual private intercessions for them individually, good and bad, rich and poor.

I do not mean to say that Law, when he wrote these books, had any doubts as to the clergy possessing the rightful and peculiar function of officiating in the liturgy and sacraments. But his almost complete ignoring of this side of their Christian duties indicates both where his heart now lay and the general tendency of his teaching. *Eusebia* and *Miranda*, the ideal woman characters of the *Serious Call*, exercise the priestly office as effectively as *Ouranius* himself.

In the course of the two years following the publication of the *Serious Call* Law wrote the *Case of Reason* (1731) in reply to an exposition of the " natural religion " of reason by one of the ablest of the Deist writers. His thought here moves, as might be expected, in a region foreign to the question of sacraments and Church-membership. Only in one place is it assumed, without any explanation and as an illustration of the deficiencies of human reason, that God has revealed to man a particular method or methods of divine worship.

CHAPTER VI

THE DEFENDER OF THE HOLY SACRAMENTS

WILLIAM LAW's next published work was *A Demonstration of the Errors of a Plain Account, etc.*, printed in 1737. It was followed two years later by *The Grounds and Reasons of Christian Regeneration*, and in 1740 by *An Appeal to all that Doubt or Disbelieve the Truths of the Gospel*, together with two long tracts, the *Answer* and the *Animadversions*, both in reply to attacks made on Law's books by a certain Dr. Joseph Trapp, Oxford Professor of Poetry and popular London Rector.

Now here, in all but the two works named last, we find Law dealing emphatically with the God-ordained character of the sacraments as channels by which the divine nature may be communicated to the soul. The first-named book is primarily designed to prove that the Lord's supper has peculiar spiritual blessings attached to it, making it very much more than a bare " act of memory ", which was all that Bishop Hoadley asserted it was. The *Christian Regeneration* and the *Appeal*, while they are in themselves comprehensive statements of Law's newly thought-out mystical system, yet contain impressive descriptions of the supreme virtues to be found in baptism and the supper respectively.

Here we apparently have another great shifting of emphasis in Law's thought, a reversion at first sight to his original position in the *Bangorian Letters*, and yet only partially so, for there it was the " validity " of the sacraments, the question as to what body of men should administer them, and the like topics, that he was discussing : here he leaves all that on one side, assumes a valid administration, and sets out to interpret the deep significance of these divine mysteries.[1] If we want to understand the evolution of thought and belief through which Law passed in the course of his long life, we are justified in asking how this second change came about.

Now in the first place it is reasonable to believe that what happened was simply this. Law, as he partook of the sacrament in his parish month by month, or possibly week by week, was himself experiencing in these middle years of his life, how in " the great mystery " of the sacrament " all the blessings of our redemption and new life in Christ are centred ". For many such an explanation will be enough: and Law would never have written as he did, without an ample measure of personal experience.

Yet, inasmuch as it was only for a few years that the sacraments held such a comparatively central place in his thoughts, it is permissible to enquire whether there were any human influences which were used of Providence to this result. For I cannot myself doubt that there was a guiding Providence that led Law on, in spite of minor mystical vagaries, from one phase of thought to another.

We may, I think, point to two important features of Law's life which contributed to his esteem for the sacraments of the Church. The first is the incidence of the controversies into which he was drawn at this time. Reference has already been made to these on previous pages of this book. There was first, in 1731 and 1732, his correspondence with the lady inclined to join the Roman Communion, wherein his thought was bound to dwell somewhat on the supreme means of grace which forms the centre of Catholic devotion.[2] There followed in 1735 the general excitement caused by the publication of the volume in which his old antagonist Bishop Hoadley of the *Bangorian Letters* attacked the significance of the sacrament. And in this attack Law

---

[1] For this reason Law's *Demonstration* could appeal to the Presbyterian Alexander Whyte as one of " the two best books by far I have ever read on the Lord's supper ".

[2] See page 23 above.

thought he saw the marks of a man who was casting doubts
on the divinity of Jesus Christ.   Hardly had he decided to
throw himself into this controversy, when his friend Byrom
induced him to undertake the task of exposing the errors of
the Quakers, wherein again the question of the sacraments
was thrust into the foreground, if only because in their
teaching on the Inner Light and their insistence on the
Sermon on the Mount he had already arrived at a large
measure of agreement with them.

Here then was one series of events which caused Law's
thoughts to dwell on the sacraments of the Church.

But a much greater event in Law's life than any of these
was, I believe, contributing in the same direction.

Law had been for many years a diligent reader of the
mystic writers from Dionysius the Areopagite to Madame
Guyon.   But somewhere about his fiftieth year his attention
was called to the writings of Jacob Boehme (then known as
" Behmen " in England), the shoemaker-mystic of Silesia.
He was thrilled and fascinated at once, and became thereafter a life-long student and disciple of Behmen, though it
was only very gradually, as he mastered the different portions
of his profound and obscure teachings, that he set them
forth in his own works.

It is impossible to say how soon after the publication of
the *Case of Reason* Law began to absorb Boehme.   I am
inclined myself to think it cannot have been earlier than
1736.   Law was writing towards the close of that year both
the *Henshaw Letters* and the *Demonstration*.   It is only in
isolated passages in the *Letters* that one can trace Boehme's
influence ; in certain of these, when Law is referring, for
instance, to the function of the Holy Spirit, to the Light
within, and the need of stillness, the new quietistic note is
unmistakable.[1]   Over the pages of the *Demonstration*
there is spread a kind of infusion of Behmenism, that,
quite apart from questions of Church and sacrament, has

[1] The passages to which I refer occur on the following pages : 32, 43,
44, 66, and 67.

not yet absorbed some of Law's more legalistic methods of explaining the ways of God with men.

Contrast this with the simple and yet comprehensive, consistent mysticism of the *Christian Regeneration* and the *Answer to Dr. Trapp* in 1739 and 1740, and it is difficult to suppose that Law can have been reading Boehme for many months before he wrote his letters to Fanny Henshaw.

It is impossible here even to touch the fringe of Boehme's mystic creed. Shorn of its more imaginative and abstruse features it had much in common with eighteenth-century Quakerism.[1] But Boehme, unlike the Quakers and unlike Law up to this time, was essentially a nature-symbolist, a poet who found in every natural object a sacramental meaning. " The outward world ", in Law's words, was to Boehme " but a glass or representation of the inward." God had written a mystic " signature " on every material object. So to Boehme the sacraments, as he knew them in his own Lutheran Church, had an absolute value : although his teaching is neither clear nor consistent as to how far they are just symbols or rather actual channels (" mediums ") of the divine life. I do not think that the emphasis on the outward sacraments is to be found in any but a few of his voluminous and confused works : but close upon the end of his life (in 1624) Boehme wrote his *Treatise of Christ's Testaments—Baptism and the Supper*, and there are striking sections on these ordinances to be found in his *Books of the Threefold Life* and *of the Three Principles*, for both of which works we know Law had a special admiration. These books could be readily purchased by Law in the admirable English translations made by John Sparrow about the year 1650.

Now I am inclined to think that Boehme's interpreta-

[1] See chapters ix to xii of Rufus Jones' *Spiritual Reformers* for a study of Boehme from the Quaker standpoint. The early Quaker objection to Boehme, so far as it is recorded, was chiefly on the ground of his retention of the two sacraments. But of course there were other great differences.

tion of baptism and the supper made a great impression on Law, and that this accounts somewhat for the part they play in his early mystical works. This is not the place to set out the parallels that may be found between the teachings of the two thinkers in this field, but the passages to which I shall refer in the last four paragraphs of this chapter are very largely in line with Boehme's doctrines. Law never merely reproduces Boehme. He absorbs and re-interprets him, and often, without ever acknowledging it, modifies him in a subtle and yet most significant and profound way. (These important modifications have never yet, as far as I know, been noticed in print, all Law's interpreters having hitherto agreed to ignore the differences between him and Boehme.) Boehme was a Lutheran and deeply distressed at the disastrous strife that had broken out in the Reformed Churches on the subject of the Lord's supper. (Rufus Jones calls it " the supreme internal tragedy of the Reformation ".) One of his noblest passages is an appeal to all Christians to remember that " this ordinance is only a member-like bond of love ".[1]

To these facts we may, I think, attribute in part Law's complete avoidance at this time of all questions as to the " validity " of the sacraments—as to the manner of their administration and the qualifications of the ministrants. He is ready to allow that the sacraments, as administered, for instance, in the Lutheran communion to which Jacob Boehme belonged, may be equally the channels of God's grace as they are in his own Church.[2]

[1] " gliederliche Liebe-verhaeltniss " (*Testaments*, Pt. 2, ch. 3, sec. 33).

[2] In the three private letters written in 1731 and 1732 to " a Lady inclined to enter into the Communion of the Church of Rome ", Law had touched upon this question of *validity*. (See pages 23–4 above.) But it seems preferable not to bring these letters into the discussion, partly because they were never intended for publication, and partly because Law's language is so guarded and obscure that it is impossible to be sure which of the different Protestant Churches he would recognize as having within them " the means of Christian salvation ". There are portions of those letters which anticipate to some extent the truly Catholic passages, which are quoted in

While one cannot fail to be impressed with the significance of what Law has to say in regard to the sacraments in
the works with which I am dealing, it is easy to exaggerate
the place they have in these books.   Law's arguments in the
Demonstration for a mystical interpretation of our Lord's
words at the institution of the Eucharist are very convincing
and sometimes very beautiful : but many readers of that
book, including the Quaker Roger Shackleton,[1] and it
would seem Law himself in after years,[2] have found its
central message rather in the long digression, which maintains the divinity of Jesus and the supremacy over human
reason of His Light in the soul.

Again, the exquisite little book of the *Regeneration* is
throughout an essentially mystical and " super-denomina-
tional " treatise, and the three short passages in it which
relate to the rite of baptism appear to be easily detachable
from the rest, and to have been introduced chiefly because
the baptismal formula furnishes additional proof that our
supreme need is to obtain such a new birth " as may make
us again a living, real image of the Father, Son, and Holy
Ghost "—this expression representing almost the central
truth in Law's and Boehme's system.   It is significant that,
as Roger Shackleton informs us, the book found from the
first a ready sale among Quaker readers.

The four brief references to the sacrament of baptism

the chapter following this one.   But in these latter passages ambiguity is
in my opinion avoided by the way, for instance, in which the names of
George Fox and John Bunyan are introduced.   Overton deals at some length
with the Letters on Romanism in Chapter IX of his *Life*, remarking that the
position taken up in them may by some be considered to err in the direction
of " too Broad " rather than " too High Church ".   An illustration of
this would be the remarkable passage (on p. 227) suggesting that the divided
state of the Churches may be " overruled " by Providence, so as to " continually present unto God a greater number of souls justified by faith and
good works in Jesus Christ ".

[1] On page 240 above.

[2] See the emphatic references and quotations in the *Spirit of Prayer*,
Part II, p. 125 ; *Way to Divine Knowledge*, pp. 226–230 ; and *Address to
Clergy*, pp. 33–36.

in the *Appeal*, perhaps Law's greatest mystical work, are all on exactly the same footing as those in the *Regeneration* ; and Law here seems to rise into a sublime region in which Church rites and ceremonies are left far behind.   Nevertheless his interpretation of the atonement of Christ leads up naturally and grandly to a culminating passage at the end of the book which gives us in effect (as Overton says) a form of the Catholic doctrine of the " real presence " in the bread and wine on the altar.   It is true that Law never says that the reception in the holy sacrament is the *only* way in which we can partake of " the flesh and blood of eternal life which we lost in Adam ".[1]   But there is no question of the intensity of the conviction that shines forth from this great mystical passage.

On earlier pages of this book I have quoted some of the most beautiful sentences about the sacraments that have come to us from this period of Law's life.[2]   I will add here just one more characteristic paragraph.   (He is speaking of the words " Do this in remembrance of me ", in which Jesus instituted the Eucharist.)

" For when our Saviour says, ' Do this ', it is the same thing as if He had said, ' Do these two things appointed in the sacrament as your act of faith, that I am both the atonement for your sins and a principle of life to you.   Don't say bare and empty outward words, when you say, " This is my body which is given for you, and this my blood which is shed for the remission of sins ", but let *faith* say them and acknowledge the truth of them : When you eat my body and drink my blood, don't let your mouth only eat or perform the outward action ; but let faith, which is the true mouth of the inward man, believe that it really partakes of me, and that I enter in by faith ; and when you thus by faith perform these two essential parts of the sacrament, then, and then only, may what you do be said to be done in

[1] *Appeal*, p. 154.
[2] See pages 37–8 and 228 above.

remembrance of me, and of what I am to you.   For nothing remembers me but faith, nothing acknowledges me but faith, nothing finds me, nothing knows me but faith.' " [1]

[1] *Demonstration*, p. 41.   Cp. *Regeneration*, p. 168, Sect. 35 ; and *Answer to Dr. Trapp*, p. 25.

CHAPTER VII

THE PERILS OF RELIGIOUS CONTROVERSY

BEFORE I proceed to deal with Law's attitude to liturgies and sacraments in the concluding phase of his life, I want to introduce my readers to some magnificent passages in a work published in the same year as the *Appeal*. In the two portions of his reply to Dr. Trapp (*An Earnest and Serious Answer* and *Some Animadversions*) Law deals at length with the duties of the clergy. There are rather more references here than in the *Serious Call* to the administration of the sacraments, but the emphasis is again laid throughout on the need of a " peculiar holiness of life " and of a continual walking by God's Spirit in all actions, to the attainment of which ideal the Church sacraments and services are in the nature of " ministerial helps ". I need not quote further on this subject, but will at once proceed to a transcription of the pages in the *Animadversions* wherein Law deals with the question of religious controversy. I have already referred to them as being of special interest owing to the references they contain to George Fox and the Quakers.

Law begins by quoting a passage of his first reply to Dr. Trapp, to which that reverend gentleman had taken vehement objection. I will set it down here, because of the close parallel to it that can be found in Quaker writings.[1]

" But to turn to another matter : I had said, that ' Salvation wholly consists in the incarnation of the Son of God in the soul or life of man : that that which was done and born in the Virgin Mary, must be done and born in us : as our sin and death is Adam in us, so our life and salvation is Christ in us—as we are earthly, corrupt

---

[1] With this passage of Law's compare the quotations from the American Quaker, Job Scott (1751–1793), given by Rufus Jones on p. 290 of *Later Periods*.

men by having the nature and life of Adam the first
propagated in us, so we must become new and heavenly
men, by having the life and nature of Adam the second
regenerated in us.   But, if we are to be like Him in
nature, as we are like Adam in nature, then there is an
absolute necessity that that, which was done and born
in the Virgin Mary, be also by the same power of the
Holy Ghost done and born in us.   The mystery of
Christ's birth must be the mystery of our birth, we
cannot be His sons, but by having the birth of His life
derived into us : the new paradisaical man must be
brought forth in the same manner in every individual
person.   That which brought forth this holy birth in
the first Adam at his creation, and in the second Adam
in the Virgin Mary, that alone can bring it forth in
anyone of their offspring.' " [1]

Law then quotes Dr. Trapp's reply to this boldly
mystical passage, proceeding thus :—

" ' Whether,' says the Doctor, ' you consider the
divinity or the sense of this, could George Fox himself have
outdone it ? '   This reply, considered in itself, might have
its place amongst those algebraic quantities that are some
degrees less than nothing ; but with regard to the Doctor's
purpose it has something in it, for it is an appeal to that which
is very powerful, which has suppressed many a good truth ;
it is an appeal to vulgar prejudice, and shows that the
Doctor is not without his expectations from that quarter.
And thus it is that the Catholic artist in his country plays a
Martin Luther when he wants to reproach that which he
knows not how to confute.   What degree of sense or
divinity George Fox was possessed of, I cannot pretend to
say, having never read any of his writings ; but if he has
said any good and divine truths, I should be as well pleased
in seeing them in his books as in any of the Fathers of the
primitive Church.   For as the Gospel requires me to be
as glad to see piety, equity, strict sobriety, and extensive

[1] *Animadversions*, pp. 179–180.

charity in a Jew or a Gentile as in a Christian ; as it obliges me to look with pleasure upon their virtues and be thankful to God that such persons have so much of true and sound Christianity in them ; so it cannot be an unchristian spirit to be as glad to see truths in one party of Christians as in another, and to look with pleasure upon any good doctrines that are held by any sect of Christian people, and be thankful to God that they have so much of the genuine saving truths of the Gospel amongst them.   For if we have no anger or complaint against those that are divided from us but what proceeds from a Christian fear that what they hold and practise will not be so beneficial to them as our religion will be to us, must we not have the utmost readiness and willingness to find, own, and rejoice in those good doctrines and practices which they still retain and profess ?   If a poor pilgrim, under a necessity of travelling a dangerous and difficult road by himself, had through his own perverseness lost the use of a leg and the sight of one eye, could we be said to have any charitable concern for his perverseness and misfortune, unless we were glad to see that he had one good leg and one good eye still left, and unless we hoped and desired they would bring him at last to his journey's end ? Now let every part of the Church which takes itself to be sound and good, and is only angry at every other part because they have lessened the means of their own salvation ; let her have thus much charity in her anger, and then she will be glad to see in every perverse division something like the one good leg and the one good eye of the pilgrim, and which she will hope and wish may do them the same good.

" Selfishness and partiality are very inhuman and base qualities, even in the things of this world, but in the doctrines of religion they are of a baser nature.   Now this is the greatest evil that the division of the Church has brought forth ; it raises in every communion a selfish, partial orthodoxy, which consists in courageously defending all that it has, and condemning all that it has not.   And thus every champion is trained up in defence of their own truth, their own learning, and their own Church, and he has the most merit, the most honour, who likes everything, defends everything amongst themselves, and leaves nothing un-censured in those that are of a different communion. Now how can truth and goodness and union and religion be more struck at than by such defenders of it ? If you ask why the great Bishop of Meaux [1] wrote so many learned books against all parts of the Reformation, it is because he was born in France and bred up in the bosom of Mother Church. Had he been born in England, had Oxford or Cambridge been his *Alma Mater*, he might have rivalled our great Bishop Stillingfleet,[2] and would have wrote as many learned folios against the Church of Rome as he has done. And yet I will venture to say that if each Church could produce but one man apiece that had the piety of an apostle and the impartial love of the first Christians in the first Church at Jerusalem, that a Protestant and a Papist of this stamp would not want half a sheet of paper to hold their Articles of Union, nor be half an hour before they were of one religion. If therefore it should be said that Churches are divided, estranged, and made unfriendly to one another by a learning, a logic, a history, a criticism in the hands of partiality, it would be saying that which every particular Church too much proves to be true. Ask why even the best amongst the Catholics are very shy of owning the validity of the orders of our Church, it is because they are afraid of removing any odium from the Reformation. Ask why no Protestants anywhere touch upon the benefit or necessity of celibacy in those who are separated from worldly business to preach the Gospel, it is because that would be seeming to lessen the Romish error of not suffering

---

[1] Jacques Bossuet (1627–1704), the adversary of Madame Guyon and Fénelon.

[2] Edward Stillingfleet (1635–1699), Bishop of Worcester, author of *The Doctrines and Practices of the Church of Rome truly represented* and other controversial works.

marriage in her clergy.[1]   Ask why even the most worthy
and pious amongst the clergy of the Established Church are
afraid to assert the sufficiency of the Divine Light, the
necessity of seeking only to the guidance and inspiration of
the Holy Spirit, 'tis because the Quakers, who have broken
off from the Church, have made this doctrine their corner
stone.

" If we loved truth as such ; if we sought it for its own
sake ; if we loved our neighbour as ourselves ; if we
desired nothing by our religion but to be acceptable to God ;
if we equally desired the salvation of all men ; if we were
afraid of error only because of its hurtful nature to us and
our fellow-Churches, then nothing of this spirit could have
any place in us.

" There is therefore a catholic spirit, a communion of
saints in the love of God and all goodness, which no one
can learn from that which is called orthodoxy in particular
Churches, but is only to be had by a total dying to all
worldly views, by a pure love of God, and by such an
unction from above as delivers the mind from all selfishness
and makes it love truth and goodness with an equality of
affection in every man, whether he be Christian, Jew, or
Gentile.   He that would obtain this divine and catholic spirit
in this disordered, divided state of things and live in a
divided part of the Church without partaking of its division,
must have these three truths deeply fixed in his mind :—

" First, that universal love, which gives the whole
strength of the heart to God, and makes us love every man as
we love ourselves, is the noblest, the most divine, the God-
like state of the soul, and is the utmost perfection to which
the most perfect religion can raise us ; and that no religion
does any man any good but so far as it brings this perfection of love into him.   This truth will show us that true
orthodoxy can nowhere be found but in a pure disinterested
love of God and our neighbour.

[1] Law himself more than once pleads eloquently for " the benefit or
necessity of celibacy " for the clergy.

" Secondly, that in the present divided state of the Church truth itself is torn and divided asunder ; and that therefore he can be the only true Catholic who has more of truth and less of error than is hedged in by any divided part. This truth will enable us to live in a divided part unhurt by its division, and keep us in a true liberty and fitness to be edified and assisted by all the good that we hear or see in any other part of the Church.   And thus uniting in heart and spirit with all that is holy and good in all Churches, we enter into the true communion of saints and become real members of the holy Catholic Church, though we are confined to the outward worship of only one particular part of it.   It is thus that the angels, as ministering spirits, assist, join, unite, and co-operate with everything that is holy and good in every division of mankind.

" Thirdly, he must always have in mind this great truth, that it is the glory of the divine justice to have no respect of parties or persons, but to stand equally disposed to that which is right and wrong as well in the Jew as in the Gentile. He therefore, that would like as God likes and condemn as God condemns, must have neither the eyes of the Papist nor the Protestant ; he must like no truth the less because Ignatius Loyola or John Bunyan [1] were very zealous for it ; nor have the less aversion to any error because Dr. Trapp or George Fox had brought it forth.   Now if this universal love and impartial justice is the spirit which will judge the world at the Last Day, how can this spirit be too soon or too much in us, or what can do us more hurt than that which is an hindrance of it ? " [2]

At this point Law takes the opportunity of censuring the bitter prejudice against Roman Catholicism, characteristic of almost the whole Anglican Church of his day, while he acknowledges that the spirit of persecution is rampant in the Roman Church—persecution,

---

[1] We know that in William Law's original lending library there was a copy of *Pilgrim's Progress* and of at least four other works of Bunyan.

[2] *Animadversions*, pp. 181-185.

which is the Beast, " the frightful monster of the Church." [1]
" When it shall please God ", he continues, " to dispose the hearts of all princes in the Christian world entirely
to destroy this anti-christian Beast, and leave all their
subjects in that religious freedom which they have from
God, then the light of the Gospel, the benefit of its faith,
the power of its ministers, the usefulness of its rites, the
benediction of its sacraments will have proper time and
place to show themselves ; and that religion which has the
most of a divine power in it, whose offices and services do
most good to the heart, whose ministers are most devoted to
God and have the most proof of the power and presence of
Christ with them, will become, as it ought to be, the most
universal ; and by this destruction of the Beast, nothing
but the errors, delusions, corruptions, and fictions of every
religion will be left in a helpless state.   All that I have said
on this matter has been occasioned by the Doctor's appeal
to vulgar prejudice ; and all that I have said is only to
intimate this much, that the greatest evil which the division
of the Church brings forth is a sectarian, selfish spirit, that
with the orthodoxy of the old Jews would have God to be
only their God and themselves only His chosen people.   If
therefore we would be true Christians of the Catholic
Church, we must put off this selfishness and partiality of
the carnal Jew, we must enter into a Catholic affection for
all men, love the spirit of the Gospel wherever we see it, not
work ourselves up into an abhorrence of a George Fox, or
an Ignatius Loyola, but be equally glad of the light of the
Gospel, wherever it shines or from what quarter it comes ;
and give the same thanks and praise to God for an eminent
example of piety, wherever it appears, either in Papist or
Protestant." [2]

---

[1] It is greatly to Law's credit that at an earlier date he had admitted
the folly of persecuting freethinkers, even in the comparatively mild way
practised in England during the eighteenth century. (See *Case of Reason*,
p. 115.)

[2] *Animadversions*, pp. 187–8.

When it is remembered that the passages just quoted were published and probably composed by William Law in the same year as *The Appeal*, it will be seen that the high sacramental doctrine of that work was combined with a conception of the Holy Catholic Church and its branches, which is very far removed from the strict Anglo-Catholic position of the *Three Letters to the Bishop of Bangor*.

CHAPTER VIII

THE LAST STAGE OF LAW'S THOUGHT

THE years 1739 and 1740 were, as we have seen, a most fruitful period in Law's literary career. Thereafter there comes a break, a long silence, the importance of which has been realized by no writer on William Law except Christopher Walton.[1] Between the last words of the *Appeal* volume and the first words of the *Spirit of Prayer* (published in 1749) Law produced no printed work, nor have we any letter dating from this period of over eight years' quiescence. It is true that in the earlier half of it Law's time and energies must have been a good deal occupied with his move from London to his native Kingscliffe, with settling down into the joint household arrangements with his two women disciples, with the organization of the various village charities —schools, almshouses, tramps' soup-kitchen, and the like. But such considerations do not adequately account for his literary silence. It was probably quite deliberate. He was a man who had to master his subject ; and could any subject be more exacting than the marvellous but chaotic profundities of Jacob Behmen ? He was presumably learning German at this time—his beautiful German edition of Behmen is still in the Kingscliffe library, carefully underlined in red ink. And besides Behmen he was studying the manuscripts of at least two of Behmen's greatest disciples, Andreas Freher and Dr. Francis Lee. Many pages of transcripts from their works in Law's flowing handwriting still exist. All Boehme's ideas were as it were sifted in Law's intensely logical and morally sensitive mind, and emerged in a more intelligible and more truly Christian form.

By the year 1749, as it seems to me, Law's theological

---

[1] *Notes and Materials,* pp. 524 and 532-3.

and ecclesiastical outlook had become finally settled, no doubt as the result of this long interval of quiet meditation freed from the heats and excitements of controversy. I can trace no signs of development during the remaining twelve years of his life. So far as there are apparent differences of treatment in one or other of the nine publications which he wrote during these years, it is because certain topics, and particularly the more abstruse parts of Boehme's mystical system, were best put on one side in the work in question. Indeed the five most important of his books, the group comprising the *Spirit of Prayer*, the *Way to Divine Knowledge*, and the *Spirit of Love*, published at intervals during a period of five years, form closely connected numbers of a single series, in which the deepest truths of Divine and human nature are gradually unfolded. In them and in the *Collection* of his edited *Letters*, we have, it seems to me, one harmonious system of thought—Law's final and considered views on creeds and sacraments, on the Incarnation and the Atonement, on the universe and God.

In the very latest of Law's works there is a certain diffuseness and prolixity from which he had before been free : we are also justified in criticizing him for his exaggerated depreciation of book-learning and for his adhesion to some of Boehme's fantastic assertions as to the life of Adam in paradise. But, unless it be in these particulars, there is no trace in Law of any weakening of his intellectual power, his ready wit, his command of profound imagery. He died almost with his pen in his hand at the age of seventy-five, and all accounts agree that he was free to the last from the infirmities of age, with " the strength and vivacity, both in body and mind, of a man in the prime of life ". Moreover his soul had by dint of the constant practice of devotion become more and more completely filled with the spirit of love and the spirit of prayer which he preached.

So much has been said, in order to stress the special significance of Law's teachings in this last group of his writings. I must now return to our study of the place of

sacraments and church observances in his conception of
the good Christian's life.

In the *Serious Call* the emphasis was, as we have seen,
on the common duties of man and the specific virtues to be
sought in our daily prayers. Here in these last writings of
Law, while these duties are assumed, it is the inward states
of the soul, and the manner of God's revelations to the
soul, which are all-important. During the four years inter-
vening between the *Henshaw Letters* and the concluding
words of the *Appeal* the supreme mystical significance of
the two great sacraments of the Church had been much
present in Law's thoughts. Now these sacraments recede
once more into the background, they are indeed assumed
as " ministerial helps ", but are very seldom mentioned,
except as being of no avail, if the true " spirit of prayer "
and " spirit of love " is absent from the heart. The whole
emphasis is on the need of " continual, immediate inspiration " of the Holy Spirit and on the possibility of possessing
this gift in field or shop, as much as at a service in church.

As regards the sacrament of baptism there is a very distinct approximation in these later writings to the position
taken up by Barclay, against which Law was arguing in the
drafts printed in Chapter I above. Only twice, briefly and
incidentally, does he refer to baptism as a profitable ordinance. Indeed he twice suggests that the sprinkling of infants
is unscriptural. It is significant that he uses the term
" water-baptism " somewhat in disparagement, and that it
is the baptism of fire and the Holy Spirit which he stresses.
Several times he quotes the " proof-text " in John iii. 5,
but in doing so he either omits the reference to water altogether, or else interprets " born of water " as referring
mystically to the " heavenly materiality " of which angelic
bodies were supposed to be made—the " glassy sea " of
the Book of Revelation. Wesley noticed this point and
charges Law with heresy in regard to it.

Turning to the other great sacrament of the Church,
it is impossible at this later stage to find any unambiguous

passages in praise or honour of it, such as I have quoted from the pages of the *Demonstration* and the *Appeal*. The image of feeding on Christ of course occurs, but not nearly as frequently as we would expect it in mystical writings of this type : more often we meet with the idea of supping *with* Christ, the thought of the marriage feast of the Lamb and of Revelation iii. 20. Where either of these expressions is used (Law rightly insists that they are real truths, not mere figures) it is, I think, assumed that " the bread from heaven, of which I may always eat ", is to be found on the altar of the heart, which is always with us wherever we go. The outward ceremony has only a value, in so far as it can stir up within us the spirit of prayer and of love. Thus, Law says, you will be taught " the true difference between the means and end of religion ; and the regard thou showest to the shell will be only so far as the kernel is to be found in it." [1]

As for controversies respecting the right method of celebrating the sacraments or the exact relationship of Christ to the bread and wine, Law will have nothing of them. " Bad syllogisms ", he writes, " for transubstantiation and better syllogisms against it signify no more towards the casting Satan out of our souls, than a bad or better taste for painting." [2]

In the same way there is scarcely any indication in this last decade of his life that Law regards the English Church as having more right to represent the Church of Christ than have other bodies of worshipping believers. This will appear particularly when I come to the *Letter on Church Membership*. True, he assumes that he is addressing many readers who like himself belong to the Established Church : thus once we find one of his characters expressing the hope that the other will conform to the Church service " as a true

---

[1] *Spirit of Prayer*, Part I, p. 37. See also the reference to the altar of the heart in *Address to the Clergy*, p. 70 ; and to the body of Christ *continually* forming itself in the soul in *Collection of Letters*, p. 148.

[2] *Address to the Clergy*, p. 32.

son of your Mother the Church ". And in his dialogue on
Justification (although at that date [1757] the Calvinistic
Methodists, whose doctrines he was assailing, regarded
themselves emphatically for the most part as members of the
Established Church) he puts his own opinions exclusively
into the mouth of the " Churchman ". But as a rule he
includes under the term " sect " his own Church as well as
all other denominations. He classes the Anglican Thirty-
Nine Articles with the decrees of the Council of Trent, the
Augsburg Confession, and the Assembly's Catechism, as
all equally unlikely to bring a man to Christ, the Light
within.[1]

The following quotation is typical of this super-denom-
inational attitude. It is at the end of the little book, which
was to prepare the reader to understand the works of Jacob
Boehme. Speaking of " the great mystery " which, by the
goodness of God, had been opened in those works, he
writes :

" It disturbs no one, who is in possession of the
Truth, because it points at nothing, drives to nothing,
but to the opening the heavenly life in the soul. It calls
no man from any outward form of religion, as such, but
only shows that no outward form can have any good in
it, but so far as it only means and seeks and helps the
renewed life of heaven in the soul. ' A Christian,' says
he [*i.e.* Boehme], ' is of no sect, and yet in every sect ' :
a truth which all sects as such will dislike : and therefore a truth equally wanted to be known and equally
beneficial to all sects. For the chief hurt of a sect lies
in this, that it takes itself to be necessary to the Truth:
whereas the Truth is only then found, when it is known
to be of no sect, but as free and universal as the goodness of God, and as common to all names and nations
as the air and light of this world." [2]

---

[1] *A Collection of Letters*, VI, p. 160. Compare also the passage beginning " Creeds, canons, articles of religion ", in *Address to the Clergy*, p. 95.
[2] *Way to Divine Knowledge*, pp. 261–2.

In complete harmony with this position is a striking unpublished fragment in Law's handwriting preserved in Dr. Williams' Library. It was almost certainly, I think, intended by Law as the beginning of a preface to his last work, *An Humble, Earnest, and Affectionate Address to the Clergy*. If so, it has a peculiarly sacred interest, for it is very possibly the last piece of writing to which he put his hand before he left this earth. The central theme of the *Address to the Clergy* is the all-important necessity of living under the continual inspiration of the spirit of Christ within : and, with some revision, the following fragment would therefore find a very suitable place in a preface to that work.[1]

" The many janglings about religion, and the variety of sects and forms of religious worship set up to find and practise the true way of serving God, is the reason of the following Preface. It is addressed to the Clergy, not because the things spoke of relate only to them, but because, if that which is most fundamental in religion is either neglected or unknown by them, it is of the saddest consequence both to them and the churches in which they minister. Now it is certainly true, that where dispute and contrariety in religion prevail, however learned the disputing dividers may be, that religious ignorance and darkness is prevalent in the same degree. For Christ cannot be known, His salvation is not known, where different opinions and forms are set up in order to find and know them. He that sees and enjoys the light cannot dispute about ways of seeing the light. He that is in Christ a new creature has a religion that gives him all that he wants from religion, and they that are of this religion cannot [more] dispute with or divide from another, in order to be in Christ new creatures, than those

<hr/>

[1] The suggestion as to the purpose of the manuscript was made by Christopher Walton (in his usual casual manner in the form of a note on the document itself). Law, as we are informed in a foreword to the *Address*, did not live to correct the proofs of its last pages, and it is quite natural that this sheet should have been overlooked by his literary executors, Messrs. Langcake and Ward, when they were putting the *Address* through the press.

who see and enjoy the light can quarel about ways to see and enjoy it.

" This comparison relates to the truth of the matter. For religious truth is as experimental, and only experimentally to be known, as seeing and experiencing and enjoying the light is the only knowledge we can have of it. *Christ*, or, which is the same thing, *Truth*, calls Himself the *light of the world*, but how can they see in this *light*, enjoy this light, be possessed of this truth, who are in the darkness of dispute and the enmity of division about the *what* and the *where* it is ?   This ought deeply to affect the authors or abettors of every division, that has broke forth in Christendom.   They can begin no sooner, last no longer, than the darkness ruleth over them.   As soon as they have but so much of light, as to see and know that *Christ cannot be divided*, they will see and know that every Church division is caused by something and for the sake of something that is not Christ, nor can be Christ *formed and revealed in them*. (Every division, possible or Protestant, justifyes itself, as being all that it is and doing all that it does, for the sake of Christ and His truth.)   And if we would know, what that something else is, we have seen and heard it, as often as we have these words of the Apostle, ' whilst one saith, I am of Paul, another I am of Appollos, and another of Cephas, are ye not carnal and act as men ? ' " [1]

[1] 1 Cor. iii. 3, 4, quoted from memory—" act " for " walk."

CHAPTER IX

THE SPIRIT AND THE FORMS OF PRAYER

At the beginning of the last chapter the titles were given of the most important writings published by William Law during the last and maturest stage of his life. Of these writings three, namely, the *Way to Divine Knowledge* and the two Parts of the *Spirit of Love* may be set aside almost entirely for the purposes of our present enquiry : for the first two of these books serve as a kind of introduction to the nature mysticism of Jacob Boehme, while the *Second Part* of the *Spirit of Love*, perhaps Law's literary and theological masterpiece, is devoted to the great theme of punishment and consequence in relation to the love of God—a subject deeply rooted in Boehme's philosophy. It is therefore to the *Spirit of Prayer* and the *Collection of Letters* (these last all written within twelve years of Law's death) that one turns for illustrations and confirmations of the general statements made in the last chapter as to the character of Law's churchmanship. Long passages of a similar tenor might be quoted also from the valedictory *Address to the Clergy* (to which I have recently referred), but that work suffers for the most part through a certain diffuseness and lack of finish which weakens its appeal.

This is perhaps a suitable place to add an assurance that, having read all the later writings of Law more than once with considerable care, I have not noticed any passages or sentences more high-church or " Catholic " in their significance than those I have quoted in Chapters VIII, IX, and X of this book.[1]

The central theme of the various discourses and dia-

---

[1] There is, as far as I know, no printed index in existence to William Law's nine volumes. I have used my summarized notes as a kind of rough index of my own.

logues which are grouped together under the title of *The Spirit of Prayer* (1749 and 1750) is the need for a worshipping heart at all times and in all places, quite independently of the external forms and rites of religion. The following series of extracts has been chosen in order to illustrate, in particular, Law's later opinions on the use of books and other forms of prayer, in the course of which much of his religious outlook generally will emerge. The discussion is here cast in the form of a kind of Platonic dialogue between *Theophilus*, the inspired teacher, and his disciple *Academicus*.

" Therefore, *Academicus*, the way to be a man of prayer, and be governed by its spirit, is not to get a book full of prayers ; but the best help you can have from a book is to read one full of such truths, instructions, and awakening information as force you to see and know who and what and where you are ; that God is your all, and that all is misery but a heart and life devoted to Him. This is the best outward prayer-book you can have, as it will turn you to an inward book and spirit of prayer in your heart, which is a continual longing desire of the heart after God, His Divine life and Holy Spirit. When for the sake of this inward prayer you retire at any time of the day, never begin till you know and feel why and wherefore you are going to pray, and let this why and wherefore form and direct everything that comes from you, whether it be in thought or word. As you cannot but know your own state, so it must be the easiest thing in the world to look up to God with such desires as suit the state you are in ; and praying in this manner, whether it be in one or more or no words, your prayer will be always sincere and good and highly beneficial to you. Thus praying, you can never pray in vain ; but one month in the practice of it will do you more good, make a greater change in your soul, than twenty years of prayer only by books and forms of other people's making.

" No vice can harbour in you, no infirmity take any root, no good desire can languish, when once your heart is in this method of prayer, never beginning to pray till you first see how matters stand with you, asking your heart what it wants, and having nothing in your prayers but what the known state of your heart puts you upon demanding, saying, or offering unto God. A quarter of an hour of this prayer brings you out of your closet a new man ; your heart feels the good of it ; and every return of such a prayer gives new life and growth to all your virtues with more certainty than the dew refreshes the herbs of the field. Whereas, overlooking this true prayer of your own heart and only at certain times taking a prayer that you find in a book, you have nothing to wonder at, if you are every day praying and yet every day sinking further and further under all your infirmities. For your heart is your life, and your life can only be altered by that which is the real working of your heart. And if prayer is only a form of words made by the skill of other people, such a prayer can no more change you into a good man, than an actor upon the stage who speaks kingly language is thereby made to be a king. Whereas one thought or word or look towards God, proceeding from your own heart, can never be without its proper fruit or fail of doing a real good to your soul." . . .

To this *Academicus* replies, " O *Theophilus*, you have shown me that it is almost as easy and natural a thing to pray as to breathe ; and that the best prayer in the world is that which the heart can thus easily send forth from itself, untaught by anything but its own sense of God and itself. And yet I am almost afraid of loving this kind of prayer too much. I am not free from suspicions about it ; I apprehend it to be that very praying by the Spirit or as moved by the Spirit or from a light within, which is condemned as Quakerism."

" There is ", continues *Theophilus*, " but one good prayer that you can possibly make, and that is a prayer in and from the Spirit, or as the Spirit of God moves you in it or to it. This, this alone is a divine prayer ; no other prayer has or can possibly have any communion with God. . . . Therefore to ridicule praying by the Spirit or as moved by the Spirit, is ridiculing the one only prayer that is divine or can do us any divine good ; and to reject and oppose it, as a vain conceit, is to quench and suppress all that is holy, heavenly, and divine within us. For if this Holy Spirit does not live and move in us, and bring forth all the praying affections of our souls, we may as well think of reaching heaven with our hands as with our prayers." [1]

Standing by itself, this passage might appear to encourage the entire disuse of a prayer-book, except as a temporary stage in the devout life. That this is not Law's intention is shown, not only by his own personal practice of regular attendance at church, but by the following passages (occurring somewhat earlier in the same dialogue).

Theophilus has been saying that " all Scripture brings us to this conclusion, that all religion is but a dead work, unless it be the work of the Spirit of God ; and that sacraments, prayers, singing, preaching, hearing, are only so many ways of being fervent in spirit and of giving up ourselves more and more to the inward working, enlightening, quickening, sanctifying Spirit of God within us ". He has been lamenting, on the other hand, that " there is so much praying, and yet so little of true piety amongst us ", and that " the bells are daily calling us to church, our closets abound with manuals of devotion, yet how little fruit ! " For the singing of David's psalms without David's spirit can in no way profit us.

This and much else causes *Academicus* to remark that, in spite of the reasonableness of what he has heard, he is afraid of following it, for the speaker seems to " condemn forms of prayer in public and manuals of devotion in private. What will become of religion ", he asks, " if these are set aside or disregarded ? " *Theophilus* then beautifully explains how forms may be used to increase devotion.

" Dear *Academicus* ", he says, " abate your fright.   Can

[1] *Spirit of Prayer*, Part II, pp. 136-8.

you think that I am against your praying in the words of
David or breathing his spirit in your prayers, or that I
would censure your singing his Psalms seven times a day ?
Remember how very lately I put into your hands the book
called *A Serious Call to a Devout Life, etc.*, and then think
how unlikely it is that I should be against times and methods
of devotion.   At three several times we are told our Lord
prayed repeating the same form of words ; [1] and therefore
a set form of words was not only consistent with, but may
be highly suitable to the most divine spirit of prayer.   If
your own heart for days and weeks was unable to alter or
break off from inwardly thinking and saying, ' Hallowed be
Thy name, Thy Kingdom come, Thy Will be done ' ; if
at other times, for weeks and months, it stood always
inwardly in another form of prayer, unable to vary or
depart from saying, ' Come, Lord Jesus, come quickly,
with all Thy holy nature, spirit and tempers, into my soul,
that I may be born again of Thee, a new creature ' ; I
should be so far from censuring such a formality of prayer,
that I should say, ' Blessed and happy are they whose hearts
are tied to such a form of words.'   It is not therefore, Sir,
a set form of words that is spoken against, but an *heartless*
form, a form that has no relation to, or correspondence
with, the state of the heart that uses it.   All that I have said
is only to teach you the true nature of prayer, that it is only
the work of the heart, and that the heart only prays in
reality (whatever its words are) for that which it habitually
wills, likes, loves and longs to have.   It is not therefore the
using the words of David or any other saint in your prayers
that is censured, but the using them without that state of
heart which first spoke them forth, and the trusting to them
because they are a good form though in our hearts we have
nothing that is like them.   It would be good to say inces-
santly with holy David, ' My heart is athirst for God.   As
the hart desireth the water-brooks, so longeth my soul
after Thee, O God.'   But there is no goodness in saying

[1] Matt. xxvi. 36–46.

these words if no such thirst is felt or desired in the heart. And, my friend, you may easily know that dead forms of religion and numbers of repeated prayers keep men content with their state of devotion because they make use of such holy prayers, though their hearts from morning to night are in a state quite contrary to them, and join no further in them than in liking to use them at certain times." [1]

In this *Academicus* acquiesces, but still objects that he remains " almost afraid of going to church ", lest the repetition of the liturgy-prayers should " become only a lip-labour or . . . an hypocrisy before God ". In his answer to this point Law here assumes (as he hardly does at a later date) that the Anglican liturgy is generally speaking calculated to draw the heart up higher than itself. Still his advice is, I think, more adapted to encourage the enquirer to find God in everything than in the church services in particular.

" Go to the church ", he says, " as the publican went into the temple . . . stand unchangeably (at least in your desire) in this form and state of heart [*i.e.* that of humility] ; it will sanctify every petition that comes out of your mouth . . . you will then be helped and highly blessed by those prayers and praises which seem only to fit and belong to a better heart than yours." . . . " Shut up yourself therefore in this *form* of humility, all good is enclosed in it ; it is a water of Heaven, that turns the fire of the fallen soul into the meekness of the divine life, and creates that oil, out of which the love to God and man gets its flame. Be inclosed therefore always in it ; let it be as a garment wherewith you are always covered, and the girdle with which you are girt ; breathe nothing but in and from its spirit ; see nothing but with its eyes ; hear nothing but with its ears ; and then, whether you are in the church or out of the church, hearing the praises of God or receiving wrongs from men and the world, all will be edification, and every thing will help forward your growth in the life of God."

Somewhat later on in the dialogue the speaker refers to

[1] *Spirit of Prayer*, Part II, pp. 113 and 119–20.

manuals of prayer as rather inferior kinds of crutches for the spiritual life, " they are not necessary, nor the most natural and excellent way of praying. If they happen to be necessary to any person, or to be his most excellent way, it is because the natural, real prayer of his heart is already engaged, loving, wishing, and longing after the things of this life ; which makes him so insensible of his spiritual wants, so blind and dead as to the things of God, that he cannot pray for them, but so far as the words of other people are put into his mouth." . . . " So if the soul is in this state with regard to its spiritual wants, a manual may be of good use to it, not so much by helping it to pray, as by showing it at what a miserable distance it is from those tempers which belong to prayer."

Very beautifully Law shows, with examples taken from the Gospels, that the " most simple, short [extempore] petitions, when truly spoken by the heart, have all the perfection that prayer can have." . . . " It is not therefore silence or a simple petition or a great variety of outward expressions, that alters the nature of prayer or makes it to be good or better, but only and solely the reality, steadiness, and continuity of the desire." [1]

All the preceding extracts are taken from the last dialogue of the Second Part of the *Spirit of Prayer*. The most essentially Quaker and at the same time splendidly eloquent passage on true worship is to be found in the First Part of the same work. (This Part forms a little self-contained treatise, which has in the past gained great favour with members of the Society of Friends.[2]) It is a passage which has found its way into at least one sacred anthology, and it was by true instinct, I think, seized upon by John

---

[1] *Spirit of Prayer*, Part II, pp. 120–133. To some extent Law had already anticipated in *The Serious Call* this estimate of the comparative value of formal and extempore prayer. See page 56 above, especially the footnote.

[2] Quaker reprints of the whole or portions of this book were published in the years 1815, 1822 (in French), 1836, 1875 and 1876, and 1886 at the least.

Wesley as a proof of the discouraging influence exerted by Law's writings upon reliance on the services and sacraments of the Church.

Law has been bidding the slumbering Christian awake, and search and dig in his own field for " the pearl of eternity " hidden within himself. This pearl is the hitherto despised Light and Wisdom and Love of God in his soul, which can, when heeded, " bring forth the birth of Christ, with all His holy nature, spirit, and tempers within thee ".

" Again ", he says, " this pearl of eternity is the church or temple of God within thee, the consecrated place of divine worship, where alone thou canst worship God ' in spirit and in truth.' [1]   In spirit, because thy spirit is that alone in thee, which can unite and cleave unto God and receive the workings of His divine Spirit upon thee.   In truth, because this adoration in spirit is that truth and reality, of which all outward forms and rites, though instituted by God, are only the figure for a time ; but this worship is eternal.   Accustom thyself to the holy service of this inward temple ; in the midst of it is the fountain of living water, of which thou mayest drink and live for ever. There the mysteries of thy redemption are celebrated, or rather opened in life and power.   There the supper of the Lamb is kept ; the ' bread that came down from heaven, that giveth life to the world,' is thy true nourishment : all is done and known in real experience, in a living sensibility of the work of God on the soul.   There the birth, the life, the sufferings, the death, the resurrection, and ascension of Christ, are not merely remembered, but inwardly found and enjoyed as the real states of thy soul, which has followed Christ in the regeneration.   When once thou art well grounded in this inward worship, thou wilt have learnt to live unto God above time and place ; for every day will be Sunday to thee, and wherever thou goest, thou wilt have a priest, a church, and an altar along with thee.   For when

[1] Compare with this Law's first manuscript fragment, where he says that this principle is " the foundation of Quakerism."

God has all that He should have of thy heart, when, renouncing the will, judgment, tempers, and inclinations of
thy old man, thou art wholly given up to the obedience
of the light and Spirit of God within thee, to will only in
His will, to love only in His love, to be wise only in His
wisdom ; then it is that every thing thou doest is as a song
of praise, and the common business of thy life is a con-
forming to God's will on earth, as angels do in heaven."

CHAPTER X

THE LETTER ON CHURCH MEMBERSHIP

THE fullest statement of William Law's final position as regards the orders, sacraments, and membership of the Church is to be found in the Letter " To Mr. J. L.", which stands first in his published *Collection of Letters*. I think too that for the following reasons the views therein expressed may be regarded as authoritative. Firstly, it was written to a friend who had " difficulty to join in any Church communion ", and it therefore had a practical and not merely an academic object. Secondly, it was written originally in February, 1756, *i.e.* not long after the publication of the maturest of Law's masterpieces, the Second Part of the *Spirit of Love* ; and when, four years later, Law's friends Langcake and Ward issued the volume of selected Letters (all, they say, " having been experimentally found of great private benefit "), Law, if he did not actually suggest, at any rate acquiesced in the selection of this particular letter (though by no means the first in order of time) to stand at the very head of the *Collection*.[1]

We are also informed that he approved of a certain amount of editing of the *Letters*, to adapt them to the needs of the general reader. For these reasons this Letter deserves our special attention, and all its eleven pages are well worth reading. The following somewhat condensed

---

[1] In the second edition of Law's *Letters*, published after his death in 1769, the editors have removed this letter to the second place, putting a letter to Bishop Sherlock in the first place.

Overton says that the " Mr. J. L." to whom the letter was addressed was probably John Lindsay. This seems to me a most unlikely guess of Law's biographer, to whose interpretation of Law this letter is moreover most disconcerting. John Lindsay was priest of a Nonjurors' chapel in London, and the difficulties discussed here would not, as far as I can discover, be at all relevant to his position and opinions.

form will be found to contain the important points for our present purpose.[1]

Law begins this letter by describing at length the inward and outward marks of Church membership.

"Religion or Church communion is in its true nature both external and internal, which are thus united and thus distinguished ; the one is the outward sign, the other is the inward truth signified by it. . . . The inward truth gives forth its outward proper manifestations of itself, and these manifestations bring forth the true outward Church and make it to be visible and outwardly known. . . .

" Inwardly, nothing lived in Christ, but the sole will of God, a perpetual regard to His glory, and one continual desire of the salvation of all mankind. When this spirit is in us, then are we inwardly one with Christ and united to God through Him.

" Outwardly, Christ exercised every kind of love, kindness, and compassion to the souls and bodies of men ; nothing was visible in the outward form of His life, but humility and lowliness of state in every shape ; a contented want or rather total disregard of all worldly riches, power, ease or pleasure, a continual meekness, gentleness, patience, and resignation, not only to the will of God, but to the haughty powers of the world, to the perverseness and contradiction of all the evil and malice of men, and all the hardships and troubles of human life. Now this and such like outward behaviour of Christ, thus separate from and contrary to the spirit, wisdom, and way of this world, was that very outward Church of which He willed all mankind to become visible and living members. And whoever in the spirit of Christ lives in the outward exercise of these virtues, lives as to himself in the highest perfection of Church unity and is the true inward and outward Christian.

[1] For the full text see *op. cit.*, pp. 109–119. It is interesting to find that the whole Letter was reprinted as a pamphlet in 1911, the anonymous publisher being apparently a high-churchman, who wished to make his protest against the exclusiveness of some of his fellow Anglo-Catholics.

He is all that can be, he hath all that he can have, he doth all that he can do and enjoyeth all that he can enjoy, as a member of Christ's body or Church in this world.

"For as Christ was God and man, come down from heaven, for no other end but fully to restore the union that was lost betwixt God and man, so Church unity is and can be nothing else, but the unity of this or that man or number of men with God, through the power and nature of Christ. And therefore it must be the truth, that nothing more is required, nor will anything less be able, to make anyone a true member of the one Church of Christ, out of which there is no salvation and in which there is no condemnation, but only and solely his conformity to and union with the inward Spirit and outward form of Christ's life and behaviour in this world. This is *the one fold under one Shepherd*; though the sheep are scattered, or on mountains ever so distant, or separate from one another.

"On the other hand, not only every unreasonable unjust action, be it done to whom it will, not only every unkind, proud, wrathful, scornful, disdainful inward thought or outward behaviour to any person, but every unreadiness to do good of all kinds to all that we can ; every unwillingness to rejoice with them that rejoice and to weep with them that weep and love our neighbour as ourselves ; every aversion to be inwardly all love, and outwardly all meekness, gentleness, courtesy, and condescension in words and actions towards every creature for whom Christ died, makes us schismatics, though we be ever so daily gathered together into one and the same place, joining in one and the same form of creeds, prayers, and praises offered to God, and is truly a leaving or breaking that Church unity which makes us one with Christ as our Head, and unites us with men as the members of His body." [1]

"That the true Church unity", Law continues, "consists in our walking as Christ walked, fully appears from such plain words of our Lord, as . . . ' This is my com-

[1] A similar definition of Schism appears in the *Address to the Clergy*, p. 32.

mandment, that ye love one another as I have loved you, and by this shall all men know that ye are my disciples.'

"Therefore the true and sufficient mark of our outward Church membership is there only and fully outwardly known and found in every man where the outward form of Christ's loving behaviour to all men is outwardly seen and known to be in Him. These and the like passages of Christ and His apostles (though quite overlooked by most modern defenders of the one Church) are the only places that speak home to the truth and reality of Church unity."

Law then enquires, "What is the divine service or worship in this Church?" The answer is, that all depends upon the words of St. John iv. 24, that right worship is "worship in spirit and in truth", and that under the new dispensation of Christ, which is "freed from veils, shadows, and figures of good things absent or to come, God Himself is manifested" as indwelling Light, Word, and Spirit.[1]

"If it should here be asked, 'How are we to become and continue worshippers of the Father in spirit and truth?', it is answered: all consists in turning inwards, in attention to that which is daily and hourly stirring, living, and working in our hearts. Now, though the Scripture nowhere gives this direction in these very words, yet, since it is said in Scripture, that God dwelleth not in temples made with hands, but in the temple of our hearts; since the Kingdom of God is said to be within us and not to come with outward observation, but to be in us as a secret, living seed of the incorruptible word; since our hearts is our whole life, and we are said to live and move and have our being in God, it is directly telling us that we are to turn inwards, if we would turn to and find God."

True worship, Law says, "is living to God, in and through the power of Christ, as He lived; it is praying with Him and by His spirit, that continual prayer, which He always had, whether speaking to the multitude, or

[1] This is the teaching which Law (in 1737) rightly called "the foundation of Quakerism".

healing their diseases, or alone by Himself in the stillness of nights and loneliness of mountains. For this inward prayer, in which the whole heart and soul and spirit loves, worships, and applies to a God, not absent or distant, but to a Trinity of goodness and mercy, of light and love, of glory and majesty, dwelling and working within us, willing and desiring to do all that in the temple of hearts, which is done and always doing in His own temple in heaven, is a prayer that only needs outward words for the sake of others ; and of which it may be said, as Christ said : ' Father, I knew that thou always hearest me, but because of the people which stand by, I said it.' "

Law then goes on to disclaim any intention of ever " entering into the merits of divided Churches ", (which are one and all in a " fallen state "), but to insist that in the case " where the Church and State are incorporated and under one and the same power ", peculiarly gross corruptions are bound to enter into the external Church.

It is significant that, up to this point, while dwelling on the all-importance of the spiritual bonds of the Church, he has not referred once, even implicitly, to the sacraments of baptism and the Lord's supper, to the Church liturgy or to the apostolical priesthood. He deals with these questions in the following most interesting paragraphs.

" But suppose errors of the following kind got into the Church, viz., 1. The Scripture baptism of the whole body under water, only as it were mimicked by scattering a few drops of water on a new-born child's face. 2. The supper of the Lord in one Church held to be bread and wine changed into the real flesh and blood of Christ : in another as bread and wine not changed into, but substantially united with the real flesh and blood of Christ : in another, mere bread and wine, only made memorials of the body and blood of Christ. In one Church this, in another that form and manner of consecration held to be essential ; in another, all priestly consecration rejected as rank superstition. 3. Suppose the original apostolic constitution of Church assemblies, where all meet together, that all in their turns might prophesy one by one, that all might learn and all be comforted, should in some Churches be so changed that all praying, speaking, or prophesying as from the power and presence of Christ amongst them was quite prohibited ; where one and the same long, tedious, humanly-contrived form of worship is daily, from year's end to year's end, to be read by one, who is become their only speaker and instructor, not because he alone is daily full of faith and of the Holy Ghost, but because he is either hired to that office or because, by some means or other, the church and church-yard are become his freehold.   Is not such a state of Church assemblies in full contrariety to the first assemblies and to the Apostle's injunction, ' quench not the Spirit, despise not prophesyings ? '   4. Suppose again that in the settled service of the Church certain prayers and petitions, not according to truth and righteousness or suitable to the goodness of the evangelical spirit, are read, as prayers for success in unchristian wars, prayers for the destruction of our Christian brethren called our enemies, for the violent slaughter and successful killing of mankind.   When these are made parts of the Church service, are we, in obedience to the providence of God suffering things in Church assemblies to come to this pass, to unite and bear a part in such Church service ?

" My answer to this shall be only personal ; that is, what I would do myself in these supposed cases.

" First, as to any defects, mutilation, or variations in the outward form and performance of baptism and the supper of the Lord in the Church, I am under little or no concern about them ; and that for this very good reason— because all that is inwardly meant, taught or intended by them as the life, spirit, and full benefit of them, is subject to no human power, is wholly transacted between God and myself and cannot be taken from me by any alteration made by man in the outward celebration of them.

" If the Church in my baptism should sprinkle a little

milk or wine, instead of water, upon my face, it would be no defective baptism to me if I had all that inward disposition of repentance, of faith in Christ to be born again of Him, which was meant, figured, and implied by such immersion into water as was the first baptism.

" The same may be said of the supper of our Lord, however altered or varied in its outward manner from what it was at first ; if the inward truth pointed at by it is in me, is loved and adhered to by me, I have all the benefit that was meant or could be had by it when it was kept to a tittle in the same outward form in which the first Church used it.

" And therefore the outward celebration of these sacraments is reverenced by me, wherever they are observed, as standing in the same place and significant of the same inward blessing as in their first institution.

" As to the fore-mentioned supposed prayers, though I am present when they are read in the Church, I neither make, nor need I make them any more my own prayers than I make, or need to make, all the curses in the Psalms to be my own curses, when I hear both priest and people reading them in the church as a part of divine service. Nor is there any more hypocrisy or insincerity in one case than in the other.

" I join therefore in the public assemblies, not because of the purity or perfection of that which is done or to be found there, but because of that which is meant and intended by them. They mean the holy, public worship of God ; they mean the edification of Christians ; they are of great use to many people ; they keep the world from a total forgetfulness of God ; they help the ignorant and letterless to such a knowledge of God and the Scriptures as they would not have without them.

" And therefore, fallen as these Church assemblies are from their first spiritual state, I reverence them as the venerable remains of all that which once was and will, I hope, be again the glory of Church assemblies, viz., the ministration of the Spirit and not of the dead letter."

After these remarkable confessions Law refers, as being significant of a revival of religion, first to the restless search for new forms and opinions and outward Church distinctions, a search bound to end in disappointment and so indirectly to draw men to inward religion as the only true substitute. (He is doubtless here thinking primarily of the Methodists and the Moravians,[1] with whom he had far less sympathy than he should have had.)

The other encouraging sign, Law says, is to be found in " a much awakened people, in most parts of these kingdoms, who in the midst of the noise and multiplicity of all Church strife, having heard the still and secret voice of the true Shepherd, are turned inwards and wholly attentive to the inward truth, spirit, and life of religion, searching after the mystical, spiritual instruction, which leads them from the outward cry of a *Lo here or there is Christ* to seek to Him and His redeeming spirit within them, as the only safe guide from inward darkness to inward light, and from outward shadows into the substantial everlasting Truth ; which Truth is nothing else but the everlasting union of the soul with God as its only good, through the spirit and nature of Christ truly formed and fully revealed in it ".

It might even be thought here, so closely similar is the above to Quaker language, that Law is referring to the Friends. Doubtless he would not exclude many of these, but it is more probable that he is judging from the number of earnest seekers, isolated in their own churches, who sought his advice and sympathy by correspondence.

The letter ends as follows :—

" Under this light I am neither Protestant nor Papist, according to the common acceptation of the words. I cannot consider myself as belonging only to one society of Christians, in separation and distinction from all others. It would be as hurtful to me, if not more so, than any worldly partiality. And therefore, as the defects, corruptions, and imperfections, which some way or other are to be found in

[1] Specifically mentioned in the *Address to the Clergy*, p. 28.

all Churches, hinder not my communion with that under which my lot is fallen, so neither do they hinder my being in full union and hearty fellowship with all that is Christian, holy, and good in every other Church division.

"And as I know that God and Christ and holy angels stand thus disposed towards all that is good in all men and in all Churches, notwithstanding the mixture in them is like that of tares growing up with the wheat, so I am not afraid but humbly desirous of living and dying in this disposition towards them."[1]

A very similar view of the significance of the sacraments is to be found in the letter ("To the Reverend Mr. S.", also dated 1756) which is placed second in the first edition of the published *Collection*. It is further dealt with in a brief but unambiguous manner in the following extract from an unpublished letter to the most intimate friend of Law's later years.[2]

My dear Langcake, . . . As to external ordinances, be no more concerned about who are right or wrong in their opinions and practices of them, than about the right or wrong of the *external pale* of the Church. You are content with that in which you are enclosed, though others call it an exclusion from the Church. It is not needful for you to determine anything about those that use or disuse the sacrament of the Lord's supper ; it

[1] Law to a large extent anticipated the views of these last two paragraphs in his *Animadversions on Dr. Trapp* (1740, p. 185)—in the form of a death-bed prayer, which Byrom afterwards put into verse. I have seen it stated that, " according to mystical doctrine, everyone should remain in the Church in which he was born, unless driven out by urgent necessity ". However this may be, it was, I think, the view at which Law arrived.

[2] I have taken a copy of the original manuscript. Walton prints the letter (not quite accurately) in two instalments, on pages 162 and 598-9 of *Notes and Materials*. The first half of the letter contains the reference to Dr. Henry More which is quoted in Overton's *Life of Law*, page 416. This second half Overton either judiciously ignores, or he perhaps overlooked it in Walton's ill-arranged medley.

is possible for both to be in the right. It is enough for you that you love the *sign* and the *figure*, till you find them to be an hindrance to that which is higher ; and, if that time never comes, your time of leaving them off will never come.

If it was not for the tradition and practice of the Church, the *washing of feet* would appear from Scripture to be a perpetual Gospel ordinance ; it has every mark of it.

In the primitive Church the supper of the Lord had always the *feast of love* along with it. After a few ages it was laid aside, because of the abuses arising from it.[1]

The Quakers have no other objections to the sacraments, but the *bad use* that is made of them, and the *carnal trust* that is put in them.[2] And when this is the case with Gospel signs and figures, they have not the nature of those that were first instituted in the Gospel ; they cannot answer the same end or be justly

---

[1] To this Law has appended a marginal note : " Hence, I suppose, came the Corinthian drunkenness, etc., 1 Cor. c. xi."

Barclay discusses the feet-washing at length in his chapter on the Lord's supper, and asks " seriously ", " whether this ceremony, if we respect either the time it was appointed in or the circumstances wherewith it was performed or the command enjoining the use of it, hath not as much to recommend it for a standing ordinance of the Gospel, as either water-baptism or bread and wine, or any other of that kind ? " (*Apology*, Prop. XIII, Sect. VI.)

[2] Isaac Penington wrote in regard to the " ordinances " with a tolerance that was rare among the early Quakers : " We deny nothing that the Apostles and [first] Christians formerly practised ; nor do we deny anything that any now practise in the light and in the faith ; but the setting up such things in the will, that we deny ; or the imitating these without the command of the Spirit, that we deny also. And this we testify, that Antichrist crept in here and that they are his great cover to keep men from the life ; and therefore warn men to mind the life and to take heed that they be not kept from the substance by the shadows, where Antichrist lies lurking, to bewitch from the substance." (From *The Jew Outward*: *Works*, vol. i, p. 165 (1761).)

Law, who had recently purchased Penington's Works, may have had this passage in mind.

called the same things, but in such a sense as a dead man may be said to be [the] same that was alive.   For this reason J. B.[1] calls the two sacraments *hidden seals*.

But more than enough of this. . . .

Yours for life,—W. Law.

Sept. 29, 1759.

I do not propose to comment on the two last letters from which I have quoted.   If the reader will compare the sentiments therein expressed with the position taken up by Law in his Letters to Fanny Henshaw or in his drafts against Quakerism, he will be able to judge just how far Law has moved in the direction of the Quaker view of worship and Church membership.   It is of course apparent that he is by no means in agreement with the absolute Quaker rejection of rites and ordinances :   but he has surely made a very long pilgrimage indeed from the ecclesi-astical position which we met with forty years earlier in the pages of his *Letters to the Bishop of Bangor*, or even from the state of mind which led him twenty years before to make such stern strictures upon the forms of worship to which Fanny Henshaw was inclining.

I have avoided in the preceding pages any references to current interpretations of Law's Anglican position.   But here, towards the close of my study, I feel that I must allude to the idea that has grown up, as it seems to me quite erroneously, that Law remained a consistent high-churchman throughout his life.   For this opinion Overton's otherwise quite admirable biography is chiefly responsible.   It is impossible for any critic to be entirely " objective " in the interpretation of his hero, especially where apparently

---

[1] *i.e.* Jacob Boehme.   In the Preface to his *Treatise of Christ's Testa-ments* we read : " Christ's Testaments [*i.e.* of Baptism and the Supper] are to reason without divine light a closed book, but to the true children of Christ they are an opened book.   Christ's Testaments are a seal of the sure, everlasting Covenant of God."

inconsistent statements can be quoted from different portions of his writings ; but I have done my best to avoid the kind of bias to which I think Canon Overton has unwittingly fallen a victim. In this respect the greatest churchman among Law's contemporaries appears to me to be a more trustworthy authority, and I propose to say something in the next chapter about John Wesley's estimate of William Law.

NOTE ON J. H. OVERTON'S *LIFE OF WILLIAM LAW*

As Canon Overton's *Life and Opinions of William Law* is the standard book on the subject and the only book to be found in many libraries, a note is here added giving in more detail my reasons for thinking it in some important respects misleading. Overton's fundamental errors are firstly, that he has formed an exaggerated opinion of William Law's consistency and conscientiousness as clergyman and writer from one end of his career to the other ; and secondly, that he has omitted to notice that all the passages he quotes from Law's later writings, to show that he remained a high-churchman after becoming a mystic, are taken from the period 1737–1740. I have given my reasons for believing that his views on the sacraments during these four years are by no means characteristic of his life as a whole.

Moreover as regards the two most important works published during this period—the *Regeneration* and the *Appeal*—the reader of Overton's *Life* might suppose that the sacraments of baptism and the Lord's supper respectively were the principal subjects under discussion. This, as anyone examining these books will discover for himself, is not at all the case. Overton further almost entirely ignores passages, such as those which have been quoted in the last few chapters, wherein the essence of church membership is placed by Law in the spirit of prayer and the spirit of love, rather than in obedience to any church order. This is broad-church or Quaker, rather than high church doctrine. Overton's short section on Law and the Quakers is on the whole fair to the Quakers, but not, I think, to Law. In his treatment of the mystics and Law's mysticism, one feels that he is upon unfamiliar ground, but has made a valiant attempt to do justice to this aspect of his subject. With these reservations, the biography is a masterly and quite fascinating work, to which I owe a great debt.

CHAPTER XI

JOHN WESLEY'S TESTIMONY

JOHN WESLEY was undoubtedly the greatest religious leader produced by the British Isles during the eighteenth century. Many would call him the greatest in Christendom since the era of the Protestant Reformation at least. It is therefore of much interest to find that we have in him an emphatic contemporary witness to the essential Quakerism of Law's later writings.

To William Law the indebtedness of Wesley and of the Methodists in general was, as we have already mentioned, very large. We even find two of the best known among Anglican divines asserting that Law was the parent of Methodism ; and Wesley himself agreed that there was " some truth in this account ".[1] This opinion was almost entirely due to the fact that Law was the author of the *Christian Perfection* and the *Serious Call*. Moreover for a time Law became " a kind of oracle " to John Wesley, who consulted him in matters of difficulty. So also did Charles Wesley. In the retrospect of his career, which John Wesley wrote out at a turning-point in his life, he says that " meeting now [*i.e.* while at Oxford in 1726–1730] with Mr. Law's *Christian Perfection* and *Serious Call*, although I was much offended at many parts of both, yet they convinced me more than ever of the exceeding height and breadth and depth of the law of God ".[2] In spite of the severe criticism contained in this remark, in spite too of his specific objection to Law's guarded statement that " there is not one command in all the Gospel for public worship ",[3] Wesley frequently used these two books, both

[1] Sermon 107 (2nd Series) referring to Dr. Trapp and Bishop Warburton, who were equally opposed to Law and Wesley.

[2] Wesley's *Journal*, May, 1738.

[3] See page 262 above, and Byrom's *Remains*, vol. II, 2, p. 182.

on his voyage to Georgia and afterwards, to read aloud to members of his flock. He published reprints of them, and they became the text-books of the Methodist classes. For two years he even (as he wrote to Law in 1738) made them " the model " of most of his preaching.

Then in May, 1738, came the breach with Law, and the unhappy exchange of letters, which accompanied it.[1] As the result of his conversion under Moravian influences to the overwhelming importance of justification by faith in the atonement of Christ, Wesley thought that he had discovered an immense void in Law's great practical treatises, which seemed to him at that time to come dangerously near teaching a Pharisaic gospel of works ; and he charged Law with never having in his personal intercourse with him sought to remedy this void by helping him " to seek first a living faith in the blood of Christ ".

The breach was never remedied ; it became tenfold widened in the years immediately following, when Law began to publish his first mystical works. As far as we know, the two men never again had any private correspondence or personal intercourse with each other. On Wesley's part this must have been deliberate, for he could easily in the course of his incessant travels have visited the mystic of Kingscliffe.[2]

[1] It is unfortunate that Law's second and final letter is not included in the copy of the correspondence appended to the Standard (1909) edition of Wesley's *Journal*. But I understand this omission may be remedied in a further volume to be published by the editors.

[2] I have recently entertained myself by reading through (in the admirable résumé published by the Wesley Historical Society) the itinerary of Wesley's amazing 250,000 miles of preaching tours in the United Kingdom between 1738 and his death in 1791, with the object of discovering how far and how often Wesley came into the near neighbourhood of Law's home at Kingscliffe. Law was residing there without intermission from 1740 till his death in 1761. I find that during those years Wesley (though he travelled to the North from London at least once almost every year of his life) probably passed only three times within ten miles of Kingscliffe, viz., in the years 1747, 1749, and 1758. In the first and last of those years he passed through in some haste the market town of Stamford, only about six miles from Kingscliffe ; he did not preach there on either occasion. It

Law's first distinctively mystical work was the *Christian Regeneration* published in 1739. Wesley naturally bought and read it, and he records his distress at its contents in vigorous language : " philosophical, speculative, precarious, Behmenish, void, and vain ". The *Appeal* he seems to have ignored, and we find only a comparatively mild comment in his Journal on the *Spirit of Prayer*, which appeared after Law's eight years of silence. It was not till 1755, after the second part of the *Spirit of Love* was published, that Wesley determined to take action. He had evidently been re-reading with considerable attention the various essays and dialogues comprehended under the two last-named titles, and had gained a profound sense of disquiet at the amount of error and falsehood which these books appeared to him to contain. He thought it his duty to devote a long pamphlet, in the form of a *Letter to the Rev. Mr. Law*, to exposing these errors—for the sake of the unwary, who might easily be led astray by their admiration for the writer of the *Serious Call*, and become seduced (to use his own words) " from the Bible way of salvation ".[1]

Wesley's Letter to Law covers a very wide field, from the Behmenist views of Adam before the Fall to the conception of hell as merely a state of the soul.[2]   The longest

would appear that he never spent the night at any place within say twenty miles of Law's village. At first sight this would suggest that he consciously avoided the near neighbourhood of William Law, so as not to appear discourteous in withholding a visit. But I find in the thirty years of his wanderings which intervened between Law's death and his own no single record of his stopping at any place so near to Kingscliffe as even Stamford. The truth seems to be that none of Wesley's usual lines of travel naturally came through this district ; and that he thought that to go out of his way to visit his former friend would only cause friction.

[1] *Journal*, September 17, 1760.   In May, 1757, he wrote to a correspondent, " You are more liable to receive hurt from Mr. Law's late writings than from any others that I know ".   (Letter 162, to Miss Furly.)

[2] The original *Letter* is a pamphlet of 102 pages, published at one shilling in 1756.   It is, I should think, now very rare ; but a reprint of it in a slightly abbreviated form may be found included in Wesley's *Works* (vol. ix of the 1830 edition, pp. 466–509).   On the title-page of the pamphlet Wesley has placed a quotation from Law's *Spirit of Prayer* : " Unwearied

sections of it are naturally those which expose Law's errors in regard to the all-important doctrines of the atonement, of faith and justification, of God's justice and His mercy. But some seven pages deal with what Wesley might readily have described, like John Newton afterwards, as Law's Quakerism. First he quotes a number of pages illustrative of Law's teaching on the Inner Light : " every man has Christ in his spirit, lying there as in a state of insensibility or death ",[1] and many other striking assertions of Divine immanence, which could easily be paralleled from Quaker descriptions of the " hidden seed ".

Wesley maintains with some force that such teaching is both unscriptural and calculated to keep men asleep in unbelief and sin. He then ironically congratulates Law on having " made ample amends for this, by providing so short and easy a way to heaven ", the way, that is to say, of inward prayer, without an equal reliance on public worship or Bible reading : " stop all self-activity, be retired, silent, passive, and humbly attentive to the inward light ".[2] He indicates the dangers of subjective illusion to which the practice of solitary introversion exposes the Christian. Then after rather unfairly accusing Law of " setting Christ and the Bible in flat opposition to each other ", he proceeds to quote the central sentences of the fine passage of the *Spirit of Prayer*, which is printed at the end of Chapter IX above. " The plain inference is ", Wesley comments, " ' thou wilt not need to make any difference between Sunday and other days. Thou wilt need no other Church than that which thou hast always along with thee ; no supper, worship, priest, or altar. Be well grounded in this inward worship, and it supersedes the rest.' " In fact he accuses Law of encouraging the " total neglect of the ordinances ". Elsewhere he refers

patience, unalterable meekness, are the only proofs that God is in me of a truth "—apparently as a rebuke to Law, for what he conceived as his dogmatic arrogance.

[1] *Spirit of Love*, Part II, p. 48.   [2] *Spirit of Prayer*, Part I, p. 39.

to the depreciation of the sacrament of baptism, implied in his mystical interpretation of John iii. 5.[1]

There can be little doubt that the pernicious influence which Wesley attributed to Law's later writings was closely associated in his mind with the tendency to " stillness ", which he was often, as we know from his *Journal*, encountering among the members of the Methodist societies. This phenomenon was primarily the result of teaching which was dominant for a considerable time among the London Moravians.[2]   Their leaders taught that, until anyone had attained a perfect faith and assurance of salvation, it was well to live a life of silent devotion, avoiding attendance at church and at the Lord's supper, and even the reading of the Scriptures. Wesley regarded such a course as direct disobedience to the expressed will of Jesus Christ and as calculated to lead to serious moral and spiritual degeneration. In this particular phase of the Moravian Church the quietist practices do in fact appear to have been bound up with an outbreak of temporary fanaticism, not unlike what George Fox had to deal with in the case of some of his followers.

It seems quite likely that among those thus led astray, as he thought, John Wesley had come across individuals who had been reading Law's mystical writings with admiration.[3]   At a later date there is good evidence for this, since John Byrom records how, when Wesley visited him at Manchester in April, 1761 (only a week, as it happened, before Law's sudden death), he brought up before Wesley

[1] See page 284.

[2] It is curious that the only Moravian, whom we know of as an active disciple of Law, Francis Okely, was a trusted fellow-labourer of Wesley, even while his admiration of Law was at its height. Law himself had no more sympathy with the Moravians as a body than he had with the Methodists.

[3] Possibly Benjamin Ingham was one of these. (See page 242 above and footnote.)   Among the Moravians, at any rate in the year 1760, we are informed that " many have had a sincere veneration for Mr. Law " (Walton, *op. cit.*, p. 615) ; and the Moravians and Methodists were at first very closely associated.

the case of six men, who had been " read out of his society for reading Jacob Behmen and Mr. Law ". (Byrom was actually bold enough, apparently without any breach of friendly intercourse, to suggest that Wesley's autocratic methods might justify his nickname " Pope John ".) Wesley, so Byrom says, merely replied that the expulsion was for *preaching* the doctrines of Law and Behmen, and otherwise seems to have approved of the measures taken.

Incidentally this was the second or third occasion when Byrom vigorously tackled Wesley on his published letter against Law, " but to no other effect than two years ago ". On the first occasion Wesley was prevailed upon to agree that if he lived to print a second edition, he would soften some of the expressions in it. Another edition Wesley did not publish, but he made generous amends to Law in a different way. In the year 1768 he brought out, as a part of his " Christian Library ", two substantial volumes of *Extracts from the Rev. Mr. Law's later Works* (*i.e.* those published *after* the *Serious Call*, and including the non-mystical *Case of Reason*). He has of course omitted, as was his wont in similar cases of editing, much of the most distinctively mystical teaching, but he has also left much that *is* mystical, with no protests other than a few footnotes of gentle correction. In the *Animadversions on Dr. Trapp* he has reproduced in full the splendid passage on the tolerance of religious differences, which I have printed in Chapter VII above. From both parts of the *Spirit of Prayer* he has given long extracts, among them being most of the passages which I have quoted above about forms of prayer and even a part of the very passage in Part I which he had in 1756 singled out as supremely obnoxious. He has printed, too, a large part of Law's last work, the *Address to the Clergy*, with its constant emphasis on the need of the continuous inspiration of the Holy Spirit, including even a considerable portion of the passage about the wrongfulness of oaths and practically all of Law's magnificent outburst against war. Indeed, when we consider the

character of these volumes of extracts as a whole and the
amount of mystic and Quaker teaching that has been left
in them, we can only regard it as an amazing concession
on Wesley's part, considering that the books were intended
to be spread broadcast among his societies. Who knows
what seeds they may have sown ? Nevertheless I am inclined to consider this publication rather as a spontaneous
act of generosity on Wesley's part—perhaps some com-
punction for his *Letter* made him a little reckless—than
as an indication of any marked change of view as regards
the tendency of Law's writings. He may have been
influenced by the fact that the danger from Moravian
fanaticism was now passed.

Wesley's hostility to William Law is only part of his
rooted distrust of the mystical writers in general. Already
in 1739 Law had been much distressed by reading in the
Preface to one of Wesley's hymn books a strong expression
of regret for having " greatly erred " in accepting some of
the unscriptural notions of the mystics. At a later date
Wesley well summed up his general objections to the
mystical writers in an entry in his *Journal* (February 5,
1764) made at a time when he was reading the *Defence of
the Mystics* by Thomas Hartley (1709–1784), an admirer
of Law, who afterwards became a leading Swedenborgian.
He objects firstly, because they " have no conception of
Church communion. They slight not only works of piety,
the ordinances of God, but even works of mercy." Yet
they mostly hold justification by works. Secondly, in their
spirit they are shy and unsociable, despising other Christians. (This was a charge he somewhat unfairly brought
against Law. An intellectual intolerance Law certainly
had ; but then so had Wesley.) In their writings, he
continues, they are both unscriptural and obscure.[1] Ob-

---

[1] Compare with this Charles Wesley's definition of the mystics (in a
conversation with Byrom in 1737) as " those who neglected the use of
reason and the means of grace " (Byrom's *Remains*, II, I, p. 181). He
meant by the first term that mystics tend to rely on the intuition of experience, instead of using their reason to interpret a Scripture that is infallible.

scurity, combined with what Wesley could only regard as sheer unmitigated nonsense, was the primary charge he brought against Jacob Behmen, whom Law set out to interpret. To spend valuable time in puzzling over mystic obscurities seemed to Wesley sinning against the Lord, who had placed him to labour in His vineyard, and to whom he would have to render an account of how he had spent every hour of his stewardship.

To the above objections Wesley might have added that mystics tend to regard the Incarnation rather than the Cross as the central fact of Christianity, and so to neglect the truth that we are saved by faith in the blood of Christ. This William Law would to some extent have admitted ; he insists that we are saved by the " whole process " of Christ, not merely by His death.

A study of Wesley's Journal, letters, and various treatises reveals the interesting fact that the mystical influences, with which Wesley felt he had in actual practice to reckon for the sake of his flock, sprang from four different sources, from the Moravians, from William Law and his master Jacob Behmen, from Madame Guyon, and from Quakerism.[1]

To the Moravians I have already briefly referred ; their general influence on Wesley is known to every student of his life. In many respects he retained his admiration for them. His attitude to the French quietist saint was also a mixed one. Thus in the year 1742 (just after a disgusted perusal of Boehme's redoubtable *Magnum Mysterium*) he was reading Guyon's *Method of Prayer* and *Spiritual Torrents*, and he records how he recognized in these books the very words that some of his misguided brethren had used. He wishes they might " drop quietists and mystics ". And yet twenty-five years later he made

---

[1] It is curious that he never shows any mistrust of Antoinette Bourignon (for some time John Byrom's favourite mystic), though she was well known in Britain. He reprinted some of her writings, without apparently realizing her great deviations from Christianity.

compensation to her, as he had done already to Law, by editing for his *Christian Library* an expurgated edition of her life. In the Preface to this he goes so far as to say that it would be very difficult " to find another woman who was such a pattern of true holiness ", and this in spite of the fact that she was so often deceived. The grand source of all her mistakes is that " she did not take the Scripture for her rule of action ". Her errors, he adds, are also the errors of most mystics.

It remains to say a few words about Wesley's feeling towards Quakerism. Though he modestly says that he had read but little Quaker literature, he was acquainted with Fox's *Journal* and Barclay's *Apology*, together with at least two or three other works. In Wesley's *Journal* we come across numerous encounters with members of the sect. He talked with them at times on the road, and they came to hear him preach. Occasionally some were converted to Methodism by his preaching. He disputed to little purpose with others, and was disposed to curse them (on paper at least), if he thought they were hindering the saving of souls. In spite of the strong words he uses as to their lack of Christianity in matters of belief and the worldliness of some among them, he often bears testimony to the good fruits of their faith. The expression "an honest Quaker" recurs a number of times in the *Journal*, and when, as he records somewhere, he feels a sense of the love of God in their hearts, he will not allow the doctrinal chasm between them and himself to stand in the way.[1]

On two occasions Wesley was drawn into a literary

---

[1] For the noble words he spoke about William Edmundson, see Rufus Jones' *Later Periods*, vol. i, pp. 269–70, which contain a brief estimate of Wesley's position. It has scarcely, I think, been noted that Wesley was not above extracting truth from Robert Barclay's works for the benefit of his people, in a similar way to that in which he used William Law and Madame Guyon. In 1741 he reprinted some extracts from Barclay in the form of a tract entitled *Serious Considerations on Absolute Predestination*, and distributed several thousand copies of it in London.

discussion of Quakerism.[1] Herein he asserts that the vital differences between Quakerism and Christianity are in regard to baptism and the Lord's supper, the primacy of Scripture above inward illumination, and the all-important doctrine of justification by faith only. He could further see no good at all in meetings based on silent worship. It is however significant that in his two dealings with Quakerism he does not develop these differences, but emphasizes the true and worthy tenets of Quaker belief and practice, reserving his chief reproofs of the Society for their not living up to these professions, especially in the matter of excessive love of the things of this world, of expensive dress and ways of living. Evidently Wesley came across many lax and worldly Quakers (though we must remember that his standard as regards *e.g.* recreations was almost as puritanic as was Law's).

The earlier of the two criticisms referred to might have been reprinted with but few omissions as a Quaker tract. It concludes with a powerful passage wherein he queries whether contemporary Quakers do not " lean too much on the spirit and power of their forefathers, having lost the substance of religion for the shadow ". " Moreover if ye find not some effectual means to prevent it, your rising generation will utterly cast off the shadow as well as the substance." Such thoughts were on the hearts, if not on the lips, of not a few of the ministering Friends of the time, who were striving to keep alive the great traditions of their Society.

I must ask the reader's pardon, if I have digressed somewhat from my subject. But, having set out to indicate the kind of association which existed in Wesley's mind between William Law on the one hand and Quakers and other mystics on the other, it seemed worth while collecting here some results, not, I think,

[1] See (1) *A farther Appeal to Men of Reason and Religion* (1745) and (2) *A Letter to a Person lately joined with the Quakers* (1747–8).

elsewhere accessible, of an examination of John Wesley's writings.[1]

Other leading Methodists and evangelicals might be called as witnesses for Law's kinship with Quakerism, that is, for his primary emphasis on the inspiration of the Spirit, rather than on the rule of Scripture or the ordinances of the Church. George Whitefield, it is true, refused to condemn him. He expressed himself as sorry for Wesley's attack on Law in 1756.[2] And after reading one of the most offending treatises—Part II of the *Spirit of Prayer*—the worst he could say was that, though Law wrote many chimerical things, " he says many things truly noble " ; " the sun hath its spots, and so have the best of men ". But Whitefield is an exception to the general chorus of disappointment and disapproval, voiced by such earnest Christians as Hervey, Venn, Madan, and Alexander Knox.

For our present purpose the most relevant of Law's critics is John Newton, inspired hymn-writer and friend of Cowper. Newton objected especially to Law's doctrine of the Inner Light. In the course of a series of letters addressed (about the year 1778) to a learned Oxford doctor who was fascinated by Law's mystical works, he refers explicitly to " the scheme of the Quakers, as set forth with some supposed improvements by Mr. Law " ; and, with a not unnatural want of understanding, he contrasts the salvation that comes through " the cherishing an inward something within me " with that which God brings from without " with a high hand and in defiance of myself ".[3]

One of John Byrom's poems is in the form of a long paraphrase of and commentary on Law's *Letter on Church*

---

[1] Since writing this chapter I have read the first volume of *A New History of Methodism* (Townsend, Workman and Eayrs), which contains an interesting discussion of the relations of Wesley's Methodism with mysticism (pp. 53 ff. and 185 ff.), without, however, covering the ground traversed here.

[2] Whitefield's *Letters*, vol. iii, p. 184.

[3] John Newton's *Works*, vol. vi, (1816), pp. 205 and 240.

Membership, from which I gave extracts in the last chapter. It is for the most part a rather dull piece of rhyming, vastly inferior to the Letter in literary effect. And Byrom shows himself in it a more orthodox churchman than Law, *e.g.* in emphasizing " correspondent rites ordained " as a mark of the true outward Church. In the following stanza he cleverly sums up the gist of one common line of attack on Law, in words which were an anticipation of what we have just quoted from Newton, and doubtless represent what he had himself already heard and read.

> The Church of Christ, as thus you represent,
> And all the world is of the same extent :
> Jews, Turks, and Pagans may be members too ;
> This some may call a dreadful mystic clue,[1]
> A combination of the Quaker schemes
> With latitudinarian extremes.[2]

If it were possible to recover all the numerous sermons and pamphlets that appear to have been produced in the middle years of the eighteenth century against the mystical errors of the author of the *Serious Call*, I think we should find the specific attribution of Quakerism to him a frequent point of attack. The reader has now had the opportunity of judging how far the charge was justified in the sphere of churchmanship and sacraments, to which I have found it necessary to confine the scope of this book. In the concluding chapter I can only briefly touch on other distinctively Quaker elements which appear in William Law's thought and writings.

[1] *i.e.* a tangled mystery.
[2] From Part 4 of *On Church Communion*, Byrom's *Poems*, Vol. II, Part II.

CHAPTER XII

OTHER QUAKER FUNDAMENTALS

THE most obvious point of contact between William Law's teaching and Quakerism was in the doctrine of the Inner Light, which he himself puts in the forefront of his creed. In an unpublished letter, in which he is reprobating the " severity against the Light within " of the Cambridge Platonist, Henry More, he adds immediately " which is, in other words, a God within ".[1] But like the Quakers, he insists in a most emphatic and reverent way that this Light is the same as was revealed supremely in the person of the historic Jesus.   " All that is said of an inward Christ, inwardly formed and generated in the root of the soul, is only so much said of an inward life, brought forth by the power and efficacy of that Blessed Christ that was born of the Virgin Mary." [2]

It has already been shown in earlier portions of this volume that Law recognized his kinship with Quakerism in this doctrine of the Inner Light.[3]   And there are many other points of agreement, some of which are of course common ground with the more orthodox theology of the time, whether Calvinist or Arminian.

Thus Law's theology began from the great truth that man was originally made in the image of God, but by the Fall he has become entirely sinful and corrupt : consequently the supreme task of religion and of life is, in George Fox's language, to come up into that state of innocency in which Adam was before he fell.   For Christ is in a very real sense the second Adam.

This recovery can only be won, Law held, by emptying

[1] This is in the same letter to Langcake from which I have quoted on page 306 above.
[2] *Spirit of Prayer*, Part I, p. 24.   [3] See pages 209, 278, and 291.

the heart of self, and opening it by the will, which remains perfectly free, to the influence of the Spirit of Christ, which has hitherto lain dormant therein, like a seed. This gift of the indwelling Christ was in virtue of the promise as regards the seed of the woman given to Adam by God immediately after the fall.[1]

Such a conversion of the heart, a new birth of God within us, is entirely distinct from the adopting of a set of beliefs.[2] Human reason avails us nothing, until after conversion, when it receives enlightenment from the indwelling Spirit. By nature it has shared in the general corruption of the Fall, and therefore all mere book-learning and theological discussion should be distrusted and avoided.[3]

Self is the great enemy, emptying of self the great means of preparation for a new inflowing of the Spirit, the prayer of passivity and silence the best way of accomplishing this end.

Again Law held in abhorrence the doctrines of election and reprobation, and of a divine righteousness that was " imputed " to the believer, apart from actual holiness of life. We are saved, he taught, by works as well as by faith. The test of the new birth is whether we conform to the precepts of the Sermon on the Mount, and practise the love of our neighbour as well as the love of God. Our hearts must be set on the Kingdom of God and not at all on the pursuit of pleasure or of wealth. Simplicity and

---

[1] So George Fox says, referring to Genesis iii. 15 : " And therefore in the seed of life live, which bruiseth the seed of death ", and again, " Through this power of God, ye come . . . to a higher state [than Adam], to the Seed Christ, the second Adam ". (*Journal*, vol. ii, pp. 344 and 345, 1656.)

[2] Compare Isaac Penington (*Works*, vol. i, p. 63), " Redemption is not by believing of a thing done without man . . . but by receiving Him into the heart ".

[3] Compare Barclay : " Man . . . in this [fallen] state can know nothing aright : yea his thoughts and conceptions concerning God and things spiritual, until he be . . . united to the Divine Light, are unprofitable both to himself and others ". (*Apology*, Prop. IV, *ad init.*) Compare also Roger Shackleton's remarks on page 239 above.

plainness of dress and the proper use of money must be made matters of conscience. Stage-plays, dancing, and novels are inventions of the devil, and most other forms of diversion are at best an undesirable waste of time. And at least at the end of his life Law had reached a pretty clear conviction, that oaths, and lawsuits, and war are forms of human activity forbidden to the true disciple of Christ.

In all these respects William Law is in thorough agreement with the most representative Quakerism of his day. In some most important respects he rose to greater heights than any Quaker writer had reached, in his insistence on the joys of the spiritual life and in his conviction of the immutability of God's love.

It is impracticable to illustrate here at all fully the features of Law's thought that I have been attempting to summarize. A few more quotations must suffice, and I hope they will incite some of my readers to turn to the original volumes.[1]

It is a constantly repeated doctrine of William Law, that Jesus Christ, the " Seed of the Woman " promised in Genesis iii. 15, is the source and substance of all goodness in every man since the Creation.

> " It is therefore a great truth that all that is said in the Gospel of the power of Christ and the availing efficacy of His whole process, from His divine birth to His ascension into heaven, is in truth and reality so much said of the *why* and the *how* the Seed of the Woman has worked from the beginning and been the one power of salvation through every age of the world.
>
> " Not the smallest spark of goodness ever sprung up in fallen man, no kind of faith, hope, or trust in God, no patience in adversity, no self-denial, no love of God, or desire of doing His will, no truth of humility,

---

[1] A few typical passages are also collected by Rufus Jones in *Later Periods*, vol. i, pp. 259–266. Alexander Whyte's *Characters and Characteristics of William Law* is a volume of selections, which form an admirable introduction to the study of his works.

meekness, and compassion ever did or could work in the heart and spirit of any son of Adam, but solely for this reason, because all these tempers were the spirit of Christ's process,[1] which spirit was inspoken or ingrafted into fallen man, as soon as God looked with pity, compassion, love, and relief towards Adam and Eve." [2]

The relationship of this natural religion, which only knows an inward Christ, to the full knowledge of the Christian is beautifully described in the following simile :—

" If you only stood for some time in the first break of day, sensible of the misery of darkness and only feeling some hope and expectation of the light, yet knowing nothing of that globe of fire that afterwards was to appear and bless you with so many unknown and unhoped-for joys and comforts of the noonday light, you would then resemble one standing for some time in the daybreak of natural religion, sensible of the weight of his sins and only hoping in God for some kind of mercy towards him ; yet knowing nothing of that globe of fire, that mystery of divine love, that was by degrees to discover itself and bless him with so many unknown, unhoped-for joys and comforts of the divine mercy towards him.

" The original instinct of goodness in the soul, which I have shown to be the only religion of nature, is the light of daybreak in the soul, and is that Light

---

[1] *i.e.* the whole course of His love and labour for mankind, the unity of which was an important conception with Law.

[2] *Confutation of Warburton*, pp. 166–7. With this compare Isaac Penington : " Ever since the fall of man, man hath been secretly or more manifestly directed by a Light or the principle within to direct or guide his ways. To Adam the holy Seed was promised, which was not only to appear outwardly in a body of flesh, but also within, in man's heart, to bruise the serpent's head there. And the holy patriarchs had not the letter outwardly, but God's Spirit inwardly. . . . The Jews also were directed to the Word, nigh in the mouth and heart ; and this Word shewed also to the Gentiles what was good." . . . (Penington, *Considerations concerning Church Government*, p. 591.)

which lighteth every man that cometh into the world. The light of the Gospel is that noonday light which discovers such joys and comforts as no one could have thought of, that had only stood in the break of day." [1]

It is not however the written Gospel, Law insists, which saves us, which is the true Word of God.

"The letter of the New Testament", he says, like the law and the prophets, "is but our schoolmaster unto Christ, a light like that of prophecy, to which we are to take great heed, until Christ, as the dawning of the day or the day-star, arises in our hearts. Nor can the thing possibly be otherwise ; no instruction that comes under the form of words can do more for us than sounds and words can do ; they can only direct us to something that is better than ourselves, that can be the true Light, Life, Spirit, and power of holiness in us. . . .

"Would you then have me to say, that *the written word* of God is that Word of God which liveth and abideth for ever, that Word which is the wisdom and power of God, . . . that Word which lighteth every man that cometh into the world, that Word which in Christ Jesus is become wisdom and righteousness and sanctification in us, would you have me say that all this is to be understood of *the written word* of God ? But if this cannot possibly be, then all that I have said is granted, namely that Jesus is alone that Word of God, that can be the Light, Life, and Salvation of fallen man. Or how is it possible more to exalt the letter of Scripture than by owning it to be a true outward, verbal

---

[1] *Demonstration,* p. 99. With this compare the following from one of the best living interpreters of Quakerism. "The early Friends spoke not only of the 'Light' in men, but of the 'Seed'. They knew the difference between the diffused light of dawn and the clear shining of the risen sun : between the seed with its hidden possibilities and the rich beauty of the opened flower." (Edward Grubb, *What is Quakerism ?* 1917, p. 44.)

direction to the one, only true Light and Salvation of man ? " [1]

The truth of the inward Christ was taught in another form as the necessity of continual immediate inspiration by the Holy Spirit, a doctrine which orthodox eighteenth-century Christians stigmatized as deceitful "enthusiasm". Much of Law's writing has to do with defending this need of continual inspiration, and in several places he specifically links it up with the spiritual feeding on or with Christ. Thus :—

" 'Lo, I am with you always,' says the holy Jesus, 'even to the end of the world.' How is He with us ? Not outwardly, every illiterate man knows ; not inwardly, says many a learned doctor, because a Christ within us is as gross enthusiasm or Quakerism, as the Light within us." Then, after quoting the verse of Revelation iii. 20, containing the promise that whoever opens the door to Christ will sup with Him, he goes on,

" Behold the last finishing work of a redeeming Jesus entered into the heart that opens to Him, bringing forth the joy, the blessing and perfection of that first life of God in the soul which was lost by the Fall, set forth as a supper or feast of the heavenly Jesus with the soul, and the soul with Him. Can anyone justly call it enthusiasm to say that this supping of the soul with this glorified Christ within it must mean something more heavenly transacted in the soul than that last

---

[1] *Spirit of Love*, p. 105. Similarly Isaac Penington writes : " Who esteems and honours the Scriptures aright ? He that believes their testimony, comes to Christ, and makes His spirit, light, and life all ? or he that sets the Scriptures in the stead of that Word of life which they came from, testify of, and point men to, as the fountain and foundation of life and salvation to all mankind ? " (*Naked Truth*, Sect. vi.) And again : " The Scriptures are not that living Word, which is appointed by God to be the rule of a Christian ; but they contain words spoken by the Spirit of God, testifying of that Word, and pointing to that Word, which is to be the rule." (*The Way of Life and Death*, Sect. II.) The parallel is remarkable, but Law did not apparently become acquainted with the Quaker mystic's works till about four years after he had written the passage given above.

supper which He celebrated with His disciples, whilst He was with them in the flesh ? For that supper of bread and wine was such as a Judas could partake of, and could only be an outward type or signification of that inward and blessed nourishment, with which the believing soul should be feasted, when the glorified Son of God should as a creating spirit enter into us, quickening and raising up His own heavenly nature and life within us. . . . Now let anyone tell me . . . how any heathenish, profane person can do more despite to this presence and power of Christ in his own soul, or more effectually lead others into it, than that ecclesiastic who makes a mock at the Light within, a Christ within, and openly blasphemes that faith and hope and trust which solely relies upon being moved by the Spirit, as its only power of doing that which is right and good and pious, either towards God or man." [1]

At the end of Part I of this book a description has been given of the quietist beliefs and practices which dominated the more spiritual Quakerism of the time. The same distinctive ideas may be found in Law's later works—in such a passage, for instance, as the following. It is also implied in much that has been quoted from Law in the previous chapters.

"The kingdom of self is the fall of man, or the great apostasy from the life of God in the soul : and every one, wherever he be, that lives unto self, is still under the fall and great apostasy from God. The kingdom of Christ is the Spirit and power of God dwelling and manifesting itself in the birth of a new inward man : and no one is a member of this kingdom, but so far as a true birth of the Spirit is brought forth in him. These two kingdoms take in all mankind, he that is not of one is certainly in the other : dying to one is living to the other.

"Hence we may gather these following truths :

[1] *Address to the Clergy*, pp. 25–6.

first, here is shown the true ground and reason of what was said above, namely, that when the call of God to repentance first arises in thy soul, thou art to be *retired, silent, passive, and humbly attentive to this new risen Light within thee*, by wholly stopping or disregarding the workings of thy own will, reason, and judgement. It is because all these are false counsellors, the sworn servants, bribed slaves of thy fallen nature, they are all born and bred in the kingdom of self : and therefore, if a new kingdom is to be set up in thee, if the operation of God is to have its effect in thee, all these natural powers of self are to be silenced and suppressed, till they have learned obedience and subjection to the Spirit of God. Now this is not requiring thee to become a fool or to give up thy claim to sense and reason, but is the shortest way to have thy sense and reason delivered from folly, and thy whole rational nature strengthened, enlightened, and guided by that Light, which is wisdom itself." [1]

As to the indispensable fruits of the Spirit of God, William Law, who lays great stress on good works, has many beautiful passages which I must leave the reader to discover. Perhaps the most needed and most distinctively Quaker of them all is his magnificent sermon against the wickedness of war—of those very wars that were at the time (1761) securing territory for the British Empire in India, Canada, and elsewhere. There are in all literature few condemnations of war that rise to the height of the

---

[1] *Spirit of Prayer*, Part I, p. 39. The words in italics are underlined boldly in black in the edition of this work published in 1876 by a Manchester Quaker. With the passage compare the *Letter on Church Membership* on page 301 above, and the following from Barclay's *Apology* (Prop. XI, Sect. X). " This great duty then of waiting upon God must needs be exercised in man's denying self both inwardly and outwardly in a still and mere dependence upon God, in abstracting from all the workings, imaginations, and speculations of his own mind, that being emptied, as it were, of himself, and so thoroughly crucified to the natural products thereof, he may be fit to receive the Lord, who will have no co-partner nor co-rival of His glory and power."

eleven pages devoted to this subject in the *Address to the Clergy*.[1]   Moreover Law had made a discovery in this field, to which no Quaker writer had so far attained.   He links up the unlawfulness of war with the Divine Love, and proclaims to an unbelieving Christendom a God, who is indeed constantly warning His children against the terrible and inevitable consequences of sin, but who is without a spark of wrath against them, and who never punishes in the ordinary human sense of that word.   It is just here, I believe, that future generations will come to realize the greatness of their debt to William Law, as an interpreter of the revelation of God's love in Christ Jesus.

[1] William Law's convictions on war are more appropriately considered, as indicated above, in connection with his teaching in regard to punishment and consequences and the " wrath " of God.   If circumstances are favourable, I am hoping to make this the subject of a separate study.   But for the convenience of the reader of this book, a portion of the passage referred to here is printed in an Appendix to this chapter.

WILLIAM LAW ON WAR AND MILITARY ESTABLISHMENTS

Note.—The following pages are extracted from the latter part of *An Address to the Clergy* (pages 82 ff.), composed in 1760–61. I have omitted two passages which are somewhat obscure without an understanding of Law's convictions on the attitude of God to wrong-doers. It should be explained that he is in the course of giving " two or three particular instances " to show the extent of the " power of Antichrist in and through every part of governing Christendom", with special reference to the current Protestant belief that Satan or the " fiery Dragon " had his seat in the hierarchy of the Roman Church. The first of these instances is the widespread worship of Mammon, especially among the English clergy. The second is the prevalence of " swearing and forswearing " in connection with trans-actions and appointments of every kind. The third instance is as follows :—

In the darkest ages of Romish superstition a martial spirit of zeal and glory for the Gospel broke forth in kings, Cardinals, Bishops, monks, and friars, to lead the sheep of Christ, saints, pilgrims, penitents, and sinners of all kinds, to proceed in battle array, to kill, devour, and drive the Turks from the land of Palestine and the old earthly Jerusalem. These bloodthirsty expeditions were called an holy war, because it was a fighting for the holy land ; they were called also a *Croisade*, because crosses and crucifixes made the greatest glitter among the sharpened instruments of human murder. Thus under the banner of the Cross went forth an army of Church wolves, to destroy the lives of those, whom the Lamb of God died on the Cross to save.

The light which broke out at the Reformation abhorred the bloody superstitious zeal of these Catholic heroes.—But (N.B.) what followed from this new-risen, reforming light ? What came forth instead of these holy *Croisades* ? Why, wars, if possible, still more diabolical—Christian kingdoms with bloodthirsty piety destroying, devouring, and burning one another, for the sake of that which was called Popery and that which was called Protestantism.

Now who can help seeing, that Satan, the prince of the powers of darkness, had here a much greater triumph over Christendom than in all the holy wars and *Croisades* that went before ? For all that was then done by such high-spirited fighters for old Jerusalem's earth could not be said to be so much done against Gospel-light, because not one in a thousand of those holy warriors were allowed to see what was in the Gospel. But now, with the Gospel opened in everyone's hands, Papists and Protestants make open war against every divine virtue that belonged to Christ, or that can unite them with that Lamb of God, that taketh away the sins of the world :—I say against every divine, redeeming virtue of the Lamb of God, for these are the enemies which Christian war conquers. For there is not a virtue of Gospel-goodness, but has its deathblow from it. For no virtue has any Gospel-goodness in it any further, than as it has its birth and growth in and from the Spirit of Christ ; where His nature and Spirit is not, there is nothing but the heathen to be found, which is but saying the same truth, as when the Apostle said, that he, who hath not or is not led by the Spirit of Christ, is none of His.

Now fancy to yourself Christ, the Lamb of God, after His divine Sermon on the Mount putting Himself at the head of a bloodthirsty army, or St. Paul going forth with a squadron of fire and brimstone, to make more havoc in human lives than a devouring earthquake.

But if this be too blasphemous an absurdity to be

supposed, what follows, but that the Christian, who acts in the destroying fury of war, acts in full contrariety to the whole nature and Spirit of Christ and can no more be said to be led by His Spirit, or be one with Him, than those His enemies who " came forth with swords and staves to take Him " ?

Blinded Protestants think they have the glory of slaughtering blind Papists ; and the victorious Papist claims the merit of having conquered troops of heretics : but alas ! the conquest is equally great on both sides, both are entitled to the same victory ; and the glorious victory on both sides is only that of having Gospel-goodness equally under their feet.

When a *Most Christian* Majesty with his Catholic Church sings a *Te Deum* at the high altar, for rivers of Protestant blood poured out ; or an Evangelic Church sings praise and glory to the Lamb of God, for helping them from His holy throne in heaven, to make Popish towns like to Sodom and Gomorrah, they blaspheme God as much as Cain would have done, had he offered a sacrifice of praise to God for helping him to murder his brother. Let such worshippers of God be told this, that the field of blood gives all its glory to Satan, who was a murderer from the beginning and will to the end of his reign be the only receiver of all the glory, that can come from it.

A glorious Alexander in the heathen world is a shame and reproach to the human nature, and does more mischief to mankind in a few years, than all the wild beasts in every wilderness upon earth have ever done from the beginning of the world to this day. But the same hero, making the same ravage from country to country with Christian soldiers, has more thanks from the devil than twenty pagan Alexanders would ever have had. To make men kill men, is meat and drink to that roaring adversary of mankind, who goeth about seeking whom he may devour. But to make Christians kill Christians for the sake of Christ's Church, is his highest triumph over the highest mark, which Christ has set upon those whom He has purchased by His blood. "This commandment," says He, "I give unto you, that ye love one another.—By this shall all men know that ye are my disciples, if ye love one another as I have loved you."

Can the duelist, who had rather sheathe his sword in the bowels of his brother than stifle that which he calls an affront, can he be said to have this mark of his belonging to Christ? And may not he, that is called his *second*, more justly be said to be second to none in the love of human murder? Now what is the difference between the haughty duelist with his provided second, meeting his adversary with sword and pistol behind a hedge or a house, and two kingdoms with their high-spirited regiments slaughtering one another in the field of battle? It is the difference that is between the murder of one man and the murder of an hundred thousand.

Now imagine the duelist fasting and confessing his sins to God to-day, because he is engaged to fight his brother to-morrow; fancy again the conqueror got into his closet, on his bended knees lifting up hands and heart to God for blessing his weapons with the death of his brother; and then you have a picture in little of the great piety, that begins and ends the wars all over heavenly Christendom.

What blindness can well be greater, than to think that a Christian kingdom as such can have any other goodness or union with Christ, but that very goodness, which makes the private Christian to be one with Him and a partaker of the divine nature? Or that pride, wrath, ambition, envy, covetousness, rapine, resentment, revenge, hatred, mischief, and murder, are only the works of the devil, whilst they are committed by private or single men; but when carried on by all the strength and authority, all the hearts, hands, and voices of a whole nation, that the devil is then quite driven out of them, loses all his right and power in them, and they become holy matter of Church thanksgiving and the sacred oratory of pulpits?

Look at that which the private Christian is to do to his

neighbour or his enemy, and you see that very thing which one Christian kingdom is to do to another.   Look at that which proves a man to be not led and governed by the Spirit of Christ, and you see that, which proves a kingdom to be under the dominion and power of Satan.   Wherever pride is, there the devil is riding in his first fiery chariot ; and wherever wrath is, there he has his first murdering sword at work.   What is it, that fallen man wants to be redeemed from, but pride and wrath, envy and covetousness ? He can have no higher separation or apostasy from God, no fuller union with Satan and his angels, than he has of the spirit of these tempers : they constitute that, which whether you call it *Self* or *Satan* in him, the meaning is the same.   Now suppose man not fallen into this *Self* or *Satan*, and then there could be no more war or fighting in him, than there was in the Word made man in our flesh. Or suppose him redeemed from his fallen nature by a new birth of the Lamb of God born in his soul, and then he can no more be hired to kill men gloriously in the field, than to carry a dark lanthorn by night to a powder-plot.

*   *   *   *   *

The temporal miseries and wrongs which war carries along with it, wherever it goes, are neither to be numbered or expressed.   What thievery bears any proportion to that which with the boldness of drum and trumpet plunders the innocent of all that they have ?   And if themselves are left alive with all their limbs or their daughters unravished, they have many times only the ashes of their consumed houses to lie down upon.   What honour has war not gotten from its tens and tens of hundreds of thousands of men slaughtered on heaps, with as little regret or concern, as at loads of rubbish thrown into a pit ?   Who but the fiery Dragon would put wreaths of laurel on such heroes' heads ?   Who but he could say unto them, " Well done, good and faithful servants " ?

But there is still an evil of war much greater, though

less regarded. Who reflects how many hundreds of thousands, nay millions of *young men*, born into this world for no other end, but that they may be born again of Christ and from sons of Adam's misery become sons of God and fellow heirs with Christ in everlasting glory ; who reflects, I say, what nameless numbers of these are robbed of God's precious gift of life to them, before they have known the one sole benefit of living ; who are not suffered to stay in this world, till age and experience have done their best for them, have helped them to know the inward voice and operation of God's Spirit, helped them to find and feel that evil, curse, and sting of sin and death, which must be taken from within them, before they can die the death of the righteous ; but instead of all this, have been either violently forced, or tempted in the fire of youth and full strength of sinful lusts, to forget God, eternity, and their own souls, and rush into a kill or be killed, with as much furious haste and goodness of spirit, as tiger kills tiger for the sake of his prey ?

That God's Providence over His fallen creatures is nothing else but a Providence of love and salvation, turning through ways of infinite wisdom sooner or later all kinds of evil into a new good, making that which was lost to be found, that which was dead to be alive again, not willing that one single sinner should want that which can save him from eternal death, is a truth as certain, as that God's Name is, I AM that I AM.

*   *   *   *   *

Sing, O ye heavens, and shout, all ye lower parts of the earth, This is our God that varies not, whose first creating love knows no change, but into a redeeming pity towards all His fallen creatures.

Look now at warring Christendom, what smallest drop of pity towards sinners is to be found in it ?   Or how could a spirit all hellish more fully contrive and hasten their destruction ?   It stirs up and kindles every passion of fallen nature that is contrary to the all-humble, all-meek, all-loving, all-forgiving, all-saving Spirit of Christ. It unites, it drives and compels nameless numbers of unconverted sinners to fall, murdering and murdered among flashes of fire with the wrath and swiftness of lightning, into a fire infinitely worse than that in which they died. O sad subject for thanksgiving days, whether in Popish or Protestant churches ! For if there is a joy of all the angels in heaven for one sinner that repents, what a joy must there be in hell over such multitudes of sinners, not suffered to repent ? And if they who have converted many to righteousness, shall " shine as the stars in the firmament for ever," what Chorazin's woe may they not justly fear, whose proud wrath and vain glory have robbed such numberless troops of poor wretches of all time and place of knowing what righteousness they wanted for the salvation of their immortal souls ?

Here my pen trembles in my hand. But when, O when, will one single Christian Church, people, or language, tremble at the share they have in this death of sinners ?

For the glory of His Majesty's arms, said once a *Most Christian* King. Now if at that time his Catholic Church had called a solemn assembly to unite hearts and voices in this pious prayer, " O blessed Jesus, dear redeeming Lamb of God, who camest down from Heaven to save men's lives and not destroy them, go along, we humbly pray Thee, with our bomb-vessels and fire-ships, suffer not our thundering cannon to roar in vain, but let Thy tender hand of love and mercy direct their balls to more heads and hearts of Thine own redeemed creatures than the poor skill of man is able of itself to do,"—had not such prayers had more of the man of the earth, more of the son of perdition in them, than the *Most Christian* King's glorying in his arms ?

Again, would you further see the fall of the universal Church, from being led by the Spirit of Christ to be guided by the inspiration of the great fiery Dragon, look at all

European Christendom sailing round the globe with fire and sword and every murdering art of war, to seize the possessions and kill the inhabitants of both the Indies. What natural right of man, what supernatural virtue which Christ brought down from heaven was not here trodden under foot ? All that you ever read or heard of heathen barbarity was here outdone by Christian conquerors. And to this day what wars of Christians against Christians, blended with scalping heathens, still keep staining the earth and the seas with human blood, for a miserable share in the spoils of a plundered heathen world !—a world, which should have heard or seen or felt nothing from the followers of Christ, but a divine love, that had forced them from distant lands and through the perils of long seas to visit strangers with those glad tidings of peace and salvation to all the world, which angels from heaven and shepherds on earth proclaimed at the birth of Christ.

THE PUBLISHED WORKS OF WILLIAM LAW
(1686–1761)

Short Title	Date of Publication	No. of Volume in Moreton's 1893 Edition
Three Letters to the Bishop of Bangor	1717	I
Remarks upon *The Fable of the Bees*	1723	II
The Unlawfulness of Stage Entertainment	1726	II
A Treatise upon Christian Perfection	1726	III
A Serious Call	1729	IV
The Case of Reason	1731	II
Letters to a Lady on the Church of Rome	1779 (written in 1731–2)	IX
[Letters to Fanny Henshaw]	[1736]	
A Demonstration of the Errors of *A Plain Account*, etc.	1737	V
The Grounds and Reasons of Christian Regeneration	1739	V
An Answer to Dr. Trapp's Discourse	1740	VI
An Appeal to all that Doubt the Truths of the Gospel	1740	VI
Some Animadversions on Dr. Trapp's Reply	1740	VI
The Spirit of Prayer	1749	VII
The Second Part of The Spirit of Prayer	1750	VII

Note.—All of the above works (except the Letters to the two Ladies) reached *at least* their third edition during the eighteenth century ; several went considerably beyond the third.   Thus we can trace during the century (apart from extracts or abridgements) eleven editions of the *Bangorian Letters* and twelve of the *Serious Call* ; and of his mystical works, seven editions of the *Christian Regeneration* and of the first part of *The Spirit of Prayer*, and five editions of the *Second Part* of the same.

The page references in the footnotes of this book are to the volume of Moreton's edition containing the work in question.